CELEBRATING
75
YEARS
1938 – 2013
JACKSON EMC
PEOPLE. POWER. PROGRESS.

PEOPLE·POWER·PROGRESS
The Story of Jackson EMC

CELEBRATING
75
YEARS
1938 – 2013
JACKSON EMC
PEOPLE. POWER. PROGRESS.

PEOPLE·POWER·PROGRESS
The Story of Jackson EMC

By

Jackie Kennedy

THE
DONNING COMPANY
PUBLISHERS

This book is dedicated to all the men and women, past and present, who have labored

to bring electricity to the farms, homes, and businesses of northeast Georgia

and unselfishly served the members of Jackson Electric Membership Corporation.

The Donning Company Publishers
184 Business Park Drive, Suite 206
Virginia Beach, VA 23462

Steve Mull, General Manager
Barbara Buchanan, Office Manager
Anne Burns, Editor
Chad Harper Casey, Graphic Designer
Kathy Adams, Imaging Artist
Lori Kennedy Project Research Coordinator
Tonya Washam, Research and Marketing Supervisor
Pamela Engelhard, Marketing Advisor

Lynn Walton, Project Director

Library of Congress Cataloging-in-Publication Data

Kennedy, Jackie, 1962-
  People, power, progress : the story of Jackson EMC / by Jackie Kennedy.
    pages cm
  Includes bibliographical references and index.
  ISBN 978-1-57864-852-8
1. Jackson Electric Membership Corporation (Jefferson, Ga.) 2.
Electric utilities--Georgia--History. 3. Electric
cooperatives--Georgia--History. I. Title.
  HD9688.U54J33245 2013
  334'.6813337932097581--dc23
                        2013024575

Printed in the United States of America at Walsworth Publishing Company

Table of Contents

Acknowledgments

"I've found out so much about electricity that I've reached the point where I understand nothing and can explain nothing."

Dutch scientist Pieter van Musschenbroek wrote those words in 1746 when describing work with his invention, the Leyden jar, which was central to the early study of electricity as a precursor to the capacitor.

To paraphrase the Dutchman, I have found out so much about Jackson EMC that I've reached the point where I understand nothing and can explain nothing. It is difficult to explain what defies the imagination, how a once-rural electric cooperative grew beyond its limitations and won competition for customers against a mammoth private power company to become the second largest electric cooperative in the nation. With assistance and inspiration from numerous people connected in various ways to Jackson EMC, I have tried.

My deepest gratitude goes to the Jackson EMC Board of Directors and President/CEO Randall Pugh for assigning me the task of writing the history of this dynamic electric membership corporation in celebration of its seventy-fifth anniversary. Their deliberate effort to preserve the history of Jackson EMC is to be commended.

Likewise, appreciation goes to the marketing and member relations department whose members are so well versed on this co-op's history they could have written this book, if only they had the time. But as has been the case for decades at this progressive, fast-paced, rural/urban mash-up of an EMC, the marketing staff's days are filled and the privilege of writing the co-op's history was passed on to me. Staff members never hesitated though, no matter how busy they were, to point me in the right direction, to answer questions without exasperation, and to lend support in multiple ways. Thank you especially to Roy Stowe, vice president of marketing/member relations, who led this endeavor with professionalism and integrity; Bonnie Jones, director of PR/communications, who masterfully coordinated this project with equal professionalism and integrity along with a heart for historical accuracy and an exemplary eye for detail; Crystal Baldwin, marketing secretary, for scheduling interviews and identifying employees in historic photographs; Mark Owen, PR/marketing representative, for technical expertise in tracking recorded interviews and imagery; and Bill Zook, coordinator of GIS, for creating a map of the cooperative's substations for inclusion in this book.

Over a five-month period in 2012, numerous interviews were conducted in an effort to obtain the information assembled in this history. Without the insights of those who shared their time and memories, either by meeting me at co-op offices or welcoming me into their homes, this book would not have been possible. Sincere gratitude goes to each of those retirees, employees, and friends of the cooperative.

Interviews conducted by the co-op marketing department in 2004 and preserved on videotape also proved helpful in piecing together this history. Those individuals' recollections helped paint a complete portrait of Jackson EMC.

Others who have lent support, and to whom sincere thanks goes, include Jill Severn of the Richard B. Russell Library for Political Research and Studies, University of Georgia Libraries, in Athens; Scott Hodges of The Adsmith in Athens; Scott Mozley and Greg Jones of Oglethorpe Power Corporation in Tucker; Magen Howard of the National Rural Electric Cooperative Association; and Robb Maag and Larry Griffeth, owners of Light Sources, Inc., in Gainesville. For the past thirty years, Light Sources has captured the history of Jackson EMC in photographs, many of which are featured throughout these pages. Their contributions in creating this book have been immeasurable.

Finally, I must express sincere gratitude to Bill Carpenter, current board member and former manager of member services, who, with the unique perspective of having worked with all four of Jackson EMC's managers, added invaluable insight. Equal gratitude goes to Charles Dawson, Jackson EMC's retired director of public relations, who set the stage for this book in the early 1980s when he compiled and wrote a thorough history of the cooperative's first few years. His investigation into the origins of Jackson EMC and his meticulous attention to detail in chronicling those formative years proved to be the foundation on which this historic account is built.

While working on this project, I encountered numerous consumer-members who, upon learning I was writing the history of their co-op, immediately lit up with recognition and offered their own recollections of and praise for Jackson EMC. Discovering, firsthand and unsolicited, the level of respect these hotel clerks, restaurant servers, and retail salespeople have for the company that supplies them electricity was confirmation of what I was hearing from co-op employees and retirees—Jackson EMC is more than a business selling a product; it is a valued and deeply respected community partner that cares for its own and has for seventy-five years. If the cooperative's past is indicative of its future, it will for years to come.

—Jackie Kennedy

Introduction

For seventy-five years, Jackson Electric Membership Corporation has been a not-for-profit electric cooperative owned by the members to whom it provides electricity. Headquartered in the northeast Georgia city of Jefferson, Jackson EMC in 2013 has more than 210,000 meters and almost 197,000 accounts served by 408 employees.

Jackson EMC is one of 3,190 electric utilities in the United States. Of these, 242 are investor-owned utilities (IOUs), like Georgia Power Company; 2,013 are publicly owned municipal electrics, including the northeast Georgia cities of Lawrenceville and Commerce; and 935 are electric cooperatives, like Jackson EMC, which is the largest electric cooperative in the state and the second largest in the nation. Only Pedernales Electric Cooperative in southwest Texas is larger.

Jackson EMC is markedly different from most of its peers. In the decade prior to the global recession that began in 2007, Jackson EMC routinely added an average of 8,500 members to its lines annually, in effect growing the size of a small cooperative each year in terms of membership. While most electric co-ops conduct business from one office building, Jackson EMC maintains a corporate headquarters along with four full-service district offices. The majority of the nation's electric co-ops serve mainly rural environs; Jackson EMC delivers electric power to rural residents on northeast Georgia farms and urban citizens in gated communities just outside Atlanta.

The history of the American farmer's struggle to acquire electricity has been well documented. Those who grew up in the rural United States in the middle of the twentieth century are well acquainted with the slow but steady shift from existence on the farm without electricity, and the drudgery of innumerable manual chores demanded by its absence, to a more manageable life and livelihood made possible with electric power, the silent helping hand. Our parents and their parents knew the story because they lived it. They hauled water from streams or lugged it up in buckets from backyard wells. Our grandmothers labored over cauldrons filled with boiling water, struggling to stir the muck out of work clothes dirtied by their husbands and sons who plowed red clay fields or slopped muddy hogs to eke out a living. Those of our lineage whose backs were bent due to the manual labor demanded in the country remember how their city neighbors gained the same results minus the strenuous labor because they had electric appliances that minimized the work.

Our grandparents well recall and often pronounce their praise for Franklin D. Roosevelt, the Depression-era president who witnessed the hardships faced by farm families while living in the west Georgia village of Warm Springs, only one hundred miles or so south from what would become Jackson EMC territory. Their president, the old-timers will say, brought the REA. This Rural Electrification Administration, they will exclaim, did more than supply electric light: It changed lives.

Most of America's rural electric cooperatives reach their seventy-fifth anniversary during this decade. Many of them have and others will continue to commemorate the milestone with publications and special events, each cooperative sharing its story of origin and endurance. Jackson EMC, through this book, tells its story and in so doing tells, in microcosm, the history of rural electricity in this country. Yet even as its history shares a common thread with each of its sister electric cooperatives, Jackson EMC's story is unique in pertinent ways, most obviously by its size and demographics. In terms of membership, its numbers loom over those of other electric cooperatives, and while territory served by most EMCs remains predominantly rural, that served by Jackson EMC is a hodgepodge of rural, suburban, and urban. How the cooperative grew to this size with these demographics is its story. The "how it got there" depends on who's telling the story, but common explanations surface, namely: leadership, legislation, and, as the real estate adage goes, location, location, location.

In seventy-five years, only four men have helmed the president/CEO (general manager) position at Jackson EMC. Each had his own managerial style and brought a different set of strengths and priorities. The leadership they provided has been crucial to the development of the cooperative, but they did not lead alone. Boards of directors since 1938 have been filled with conscientious citizens, first farmers and then business leaders, who originally sought electricity for themselves and their neighbors and ultimately pursued economic health and prosperity for their communities. Employees, from upper management to line workers, toiled through the decades to build the electric system and, as a consequence, helped build a powerful reputation for the cooperative.

Born out of legislation in 1935, the rural electric movement brought electric power into every hidden pocket of this land, creating a seismic shift from only 10 percent of American farms being served with electricity in the mid-1930s to 90 percent of farm families obtaining electricity by 1953. While formation of the REA remains the most critical piece of legislation in the history of any electric cooperative, legislation passed into law in the early 1970s is an extremely close second in importance relative to Jackson EMC's evolution. The Georgia Territorial Electric Service Act of 1973 changed the game by leveling the playing field, enabling electric cooperatives to compete with private, investor-owned utilities and municipalities for customers. During this same time period, two other historic game-changing events occurred: the nation's electric cooperatives formed their own bank, the National Rural Utilities Cooperative Finance Corporation, to supplement their capital needs which, until then, had been fully funded through the REA; and Georgia's electric cooperatives formed their own generation and transmission cooperative, Oglethorpe Power Corporation, which provided additional avenues from which to obtain power. These three milestones combined to provide unique opportunities for Jackson EMC which, more than most electric cooperatives, was able to use the territorial act to great advantage.

And that is due to location. Jackson EMC's territory, because of its proximity to Atlanta, was obliged to grow. Through the last half of the twentieth century, Atlanta bulged beyond its city limits, ever creeping in all directions but, primarily, northward. As interstate highways stretched through and beyond the state capital, residential and commercial growth along those routes followed, and once-tiny towns became small cities that transformed rural communities into suburbia. Whereas Jackson EMC originated as a cooperative serving farm families and rural dwellers, the scope of its service territory through the decades evolved dramatically, especially in the area just northeast of Atlanta, where no dam could have blocked the flow of humanity.

Today Jackson EMC provides electricity to members in ten northeast Georgia counties, including Banks, Barrow, Clarke, Franklin, Gwinnett, Hall, Jackson, Lumpkin, Madison, and Oglethorpe. Its rates remain competitive and its attention to customer service, impeccable. Along with providing electricity to its members, the cooperative has produced leadership within its communities and is known for its faithful support of charitable organizations and initiatives.

The story of Jackson EMC is one of people, of power, and of progress: the people who dreamed, then put muscle and machismo behind their dream to bring a before-unknown commodity to northeast Georgia; the electric power that transformed this place, and the manpower it took to build the electric system; and progress, the unbridled growth of a region that resulted from the unique combination of a particular location in America and its people—the men and women who started, sustained, and continue to serve Jackson EMC.

"Electricity," said the comedian George Carlin, "is really just organized lightning."

Jackson EMC, for seventy-five years, has organized that lightning with great finesse.

Book One: People

Chapter One
Discovery and Invention

"We will make electricity so cheap that only the rich will burn candles."

—Thomas Edison
At the first public demonstration of his incandescent bulb on December 31, 1879
Quoted in *Chronology of Americans and the Environment* by Chris Magoc

On March 30, 1842, the tiny town of Jefferson, Georgia, became central to the world of medicine when Dr. Crawford W. Long— in order to ease the pain and suffering of his patient—was the first to use ether as an anesthetic.

Almost one hundred years later, this same town became central to the prosperity of a region when the charter to incorporate Jackson EMC was granted on June 27, 1938. Residents had banded together—in order to ease the burden and limitations of manual labor—as a cooperative to bring electricity pulsating through rural northeast Georgia.

The county seat of Jackson County, Jefferson has a population of about 9,500 while the county's total population is close to 61,000. An hour's drive northeast of Atlanta, the area is graced with rolling pastureland, family farms, and small town charm. The community exudes confidence and credibility, attributable in part to the gritty toil and persistence of the town's forebears who concentrated their efforts to make life better for themselves and their neighbors.

Dr. Long was such a man. Perhaps the most celebrated individual to hail from this region, Long was born in 1815 in Danielsville, Madison County, adjacent to Jackson County. The son of a wealthy planter and merchant, he earned his associate's degree from the University of Georgia in Athens in 1835 before moving to Lexington, Kentucky, to study medicine at Transylvania College; there, he observed patients writhing in agonizing pain as they endured surgery without sedation. The following year, he transferred to the University of Pennsylvania where he witnessed the effects of nitrous oxide (laughing gas) on people who inhaled it for entertainment at "laughing gas parties" and "ether frolics." English chemist Humphry Davy in 1800 had described the physiological effects of nitrous oxide and suggested it be used as an anesthetic during minor surgeries; Davy's idea for using the gas for medicinal purposes was ignored, but breathing nitrous oxide became trendy at these social gatherings. Attending such events, Long watched as those who used laughing gas fell or bumped into things without experiencing pain. His desire to harness ether as an anesthetic was born.

After earning his medical degree in 1839 and completing an internship in New York City, Long returned to Georgia in 1841 to head a rural medical practice in Jefferson. In 1842, his first surgery using ether as an anesthetic was successful when he removed a tumor from the neck of James Venable. Soon, he was using ether anesthesia when delivering babies and performing amputations. Long practiced medicine in Jefferson for ten years before moving his practice to Athens where, as the Civil War raged from 1861 to 1865, he performed surgeries on wounded soldiers from both armies.

Opposite page: Thomas Alva Edison invented the first bulb capable of producing safe, practical, and affordable electric light. (Photo courtesy of National Archives and Records)

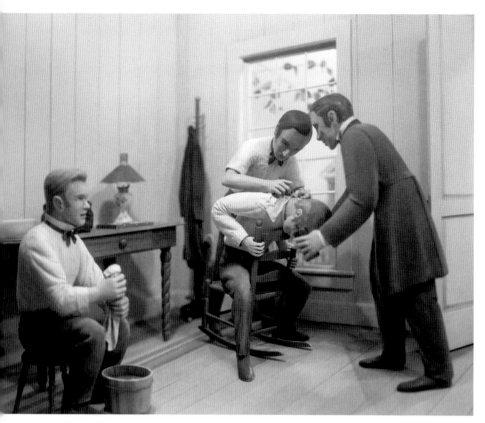

Dr. Crawford Long first used ether as an anesthetic on March 30, 1842, at his practice in downtown Jefferson when he administered it to James Venable to relieve the patient's pain while performing surgery to remove a tumor. A recreation of the event is on display at the Crawford W. Long Museum in Jefferson.

The Crawford W. Long Museum in downtown Jefferson pays tribute to the doctor who first successfully used ether as an anesthetic and to the history of Jefferson and Jackson County, Georgia.

Dr. Long has been memorialized throughout the world for his contribution to medicine. A US postage stamp featured his picture. Emory University Hospital Midtown in Atlanta originally was named in his honor. A statue of Long stands in the National Statuary Hall Collection at the US Capitol in Washington, DC. In 1957, at the site of his first medical practice in downtown Jefferson, the Crawford W. Long Museum opened to hail his achievements.

The same spirit of discovery that propelled Long to invent a painless approach to surgery had long been evident throughout the United States, itself an experiment in freedom and democracy. From railroads and steamships to the telephone and typewriter, American inventions and discoveries punctuated the nineteenth century. It can be reasoned that none, however, were as far-reaching and as life-changing as those involving electricity, the fascinating, naked-to-the-eye wonder that would eventually power man-made marvels affecting every facet of American life, from farm to factory, education to healthcare, and all in between.

Benjamin Franklin was the first to realize lightning as a manifestation of electricity, a feat he achieved while flying a kite in Philadelphia on a stormy night in June 1752. With an iron key tied to the string, he lifted his kite into a thunderstorm and, just as he imagined it would, the key attracted lightning. The incredible discovery by America's founding father spawned more intense study of electricity by history's most renowned chemists, physicists, and inventors. In England, Humphry Davy invented the world's first electric light in 1809 when he connected a pair of wires to a battery with a charcoal strip in the middle, producing the first arc lamp. Also in England, chemist Michael Faraday discovered electromagnetic induction and in 1832 created the induction ring, acknowledged as the first electric transformer. His experiments led to the development of devices that would lead to creation of the electric motor and generator.

Building on Davy's work with electric light, Henricg Globel in Germany crafted the first light bulb in 1854. Twenty-four years later, English physicist Sir Joseph Wilson Swan invented a better bulb, one capable of producing light for thirteen-and-a-half hours. That same year, in 1878, Ohio engineer Charles Brush invented the first practical arc lighting device and managed to make several lamps light from one dynamo to provide street lighting.

While Brush worked on his system in Ohio, Thomas Alva Edison continued work he'd begun in 1876 in Menlo Park, New Jersey, to produce an electric lamp for indoor use. In October 1879, Edison crafted a carbon filament from a cotton thread and sealed it inside a globe without oxygen to create light for forty hours. "If it will burn forty hours now," said Edison, "I know I can make it burn a hundred."

And he did. Within a year, he produced an improved filament from carbonized strips of bamboo to fashion a light bulb that burned for more than 1,200 hours. As the first safe, practical, and affordable means to produce electric light, Edison's light bulb would ensure his place in history.

He did not stop his work with electricity at the incandescent light bulb, however; with a goal to make electric light available at home and in the workplace, he formed Edison Electric Illuminating Company in New York City in 1881. The following year, Edison developed the world's first central electric generating system, the Pearl Street Power Station in lower Manhattan. The station utilized one generator to produce enough power to light five thousand lamps and distribute electricity to eighty-five customers within a one-square-mile area. By producing reliable central generation, efficient distribution, affordable rates, and meters to calculate the electricity consumed, this central station electric system, the world's first power plant, gave birth to the modern electric utility industry. Lamps and generators were produced at fever pitch and, within relatively few years, city homes and offices glowed with electric light.

Thomas Edison held 1,093 patents, a world record, for inventions that greatly influenced quality of life. Among the most influential were the long-burning incandescent light bulb and the first electric power plant. (Photo courtesy of the Library of Congress)

Beyond Edison, other inventors improved upon the systems in place. William Stanley crafted the induction coil, a transformer that created alternating current. George Westinghouse, the founder of Westinghouse Electric Company in 1886, helped develop the electric transformer that enabled electricity to be transmitted over long distances. Nikola Tesla invented an arc lighting system in 1886, the alternating current motor and alternating current transmission system in 1888, and high-frequency current generators in 1890. His creations enabled electricity to power industrial machines and made electric lighting a common feature in homes.

With electricity harnessed, man's imagination was unleashed. As the United States approached the twentieth century, the only thing that outshone electric light was the American citizen's determination to build, to create, to improve, and to prosper.

In 1893, President Grover Cleveland pushed a button at the White House to open the World Columbian Exposition in Chicago, more than a thousand miles away. Electricity was the expo theme, and the world's first Ferris wheel was the star attraction. Throughout the decade, numerous inventions that operated off electricity were introduced, from the electric stove to the electric chair. By the turn of the century, businesses and homes in American cities buzzed with lighting, machines, and appliances powered by electricity. Since Edison opened the first electric generation plant in 1882, the nation, it seemed, had zoomed from darkness into illumination. So much had changed, thanks to the delivery of electricity. So much was fresh and new and exciting in the city.

On the farm, though, nothing was different. Throughout rural America, families continued to live off the land and the efforts of their labor. Nights in the country were as dark as ever, save for the glow from a kerosene lamp inside and the twinkling of a million stars outdoors.

In Jefferson, where Dr. Long's miraculous introduction of anesthesia first produced painless surgery, electricity brightened downtown offices and homes within the city limits. But mere miles away, in rural Jackson and neighboring counties, the miracle of electricity was nowhere evident.

Chapter Two
Pushing for Rural Electrification

"I do remember how it was to be poor. I do remember that in my early years, we had to grow and raise all of our food, even our animals. And I remember in my early life, we didn't even have electricity. So it was very, very hard times then."

—Dolly Parton
Singer and songwriter

Retired dairy farmer Tom Nelson Stovall resides in Madison County's Pocataligo community where he has lived all his eighty-six years. His father, George Stovall, was a founding director of Jackson EMC and its board of directors' first chairman. Tom eventually served on the board as well.

As he ages, Tom Stovall admits, it's sometimes less difficult to remember yesteryear than yesterday. His memories of life on the farm before electricity come easy. "We had a wood stove over in one of the corners of the kitchen," he recalled. "When you had a cook-stove, you had heat in the kitchen."

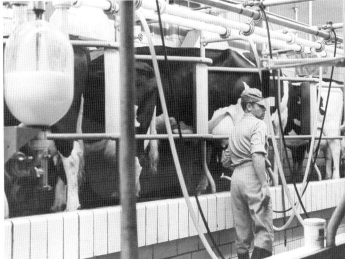

Farmer, member, and former EMC director Tom Nelson Stovall used electricity to great advantage at his dairy in Madison County. His father, George Stovall, was a founding director of Jackson EMC and its board's first president.

Before rural electricity, farmers and families in northeast Georgia depended on water carried from the creek or drawn from the well.

Opposite page: When dedicating Lamar Electric Membership Corporation, now Southern Rivers Energy, in Barnesville on August 11, 1938, President Franklin D. Roosevelt called his Little White House at Warm Springs "the birthplace of the Rural Electrification Administration."

Washing clothes in washtubs was a backbreaking chore, as demonstrated here at a 1950s annual meeting of the cooperative.

As a child, he brought wood in for the stove, "and then after I got big enough, I had to draw the water," said Tom. "We had a well on the back porch. The bucket would be full of water and you had a place wide enough on top of your well box to set it. I remember we had an ice box. You kept a block of ice in that box, the total block, so you'd chip off what you might need. You were stingy with that ice." Stingy, he said, because it may be a week before the ice truck came by the farm to deliver another block.

The most cumbersome pre-electric chore belonged to his mother, Fannie, who, like farm women throughout America, toiled one day each week washing the family's clothes. First, water had to be drawn from the well to fill the No. 3 zinc washtubs used on washday. Next, a fire was built for boiling water used to clean clothes. Finally, the washing commenced. "You had three tubs," Tom recalled. "One was the scrub tub, and then you'd put the wash in the rinse tub, and then it would go into the third tub. Then you'd hang clothes on the line to dry. It was a hard job." That concluded not washing for the day, but washing for one load; the number of loads depended on a family's size and could run into double digits, extending washday into early evening.

George and Fannie Stovall, like their neighbors throughout rural Madison County, still did house and farm chores in much the same way the pilgrims had toiled after landing at Plymouth Rock. By the mid-1930s, only one out of ten rural households in America had electricity. The remaining 90 percent relied on manual labor to complete common tasks. Cows were milked by hand before sunup by the light from a kerosene lantern. Water for the livestock was hauled from the creek or pulled up in buckets from the well. Farm families raised their own food in the garden or at the pen. Hogs were killed in autumn with the meat packed in salt to cure and then

Wood-burning stoves kept country kitchens warm in winter but unbearably hot in summer. A young homemaker puts in more wood for cooking, while Mr. and Mrs. L. B. Parks of Commerce prepare to enjoy a cup of coffee warmed on their wood stove. The Parks were the twenty-fifth family to sign up for electric service from Jackson EMC.

placed in sacks to hang in the smokehouse. Without refrigeration, families could not store leftovers, but nothing went to waste; whatever the family didn't eat for supper went to feed the livestock and family pets, typically hogs and dogs.

One of the most despised pre-electric tasks involved a heavy triangular wedge of iron heated on the wood stove then used to press clothes. Betty Hutchins, born in Jackson County in 1909, recalled her childhood chores included cleaning the kerosene lamp chimneys and refilling the base with kerosene and at night, by the dim light of the lamp, reading the newspaper to her father who couldn't read. Washing clothes was manual labor, but "the biggest problem was ironing," said Hutchins. "The temperature would be eighty-five degrees outside and that got very hot, but you had to build a fire to get the iron going, and the home wouldn't cool off by bedtime."

Not all was work and drudgery, though. Hutchins recalled playing cards for fun, attending summer revivals at church, and traveling with her family to Athens in horse-drawn buggies. The eighteen-mile trip from her home in rural Jackson County took two-and-a-half hours "and we'd know everybody on the highway," said Hutchins. Everyone had a Sears Roebuck Catalog, she added: "It was entertainment; even if you couldn't buy the things in there, you could look at them."

By the time she married, the United States had spiraled into the Great Depression. "The boll weevil ate up the cotton and times got so hard," she said. "The first year we farmed, we raised cotton and corn and peas, and in the fall when we settled up, we made $32 for the year's work." The consolation most families felt laid in the fact that everyone's experience was similar. "We were all in the same fix," said Hutchins. "Nobody had anything to spend."

John Wiley "J. W." Cato, an early director of Jackson EMC, plowed his Hall County farm with mules and did farm chores solely with manual labor before electricity was run to rural communities.

Farm families picked cotton, drew water from a well, chopped firewood, bundled up in the winter, and burned up in the summer. If the farmer wished for more income than his land and hands could provide, he moved his family to the nearest small town. That's where the jobs were, because that's where the factories and businesses were, because that's where electricity was. The disparity between rural communities and city neighborhoods, between those who didn't have electricity and those with electric power and the tools it energized, grew increasingly evident as the new century unfolded.

Even as farms remained dark, wheels were set in motion that eventually would turn to enable electric progress in the farthest reaches.

Assessing the Situation

While Franklin D. Roosevelt's name is more often associated with the rural electric movement, it was his cousin and predecessor, President Theodore Roosevelt, who in the first decade of the twentieth century pushed for federal multi-use development of the nation's river systems for water supply, flood control, irrigation and, yes, electricity. At the suggestion of Gifford Pinchot, his chief forester, the first President Roosevelt commissioned a fact-finding board to study the disparities between rural and city dwellers. The Country Life Commission produced its findings in February 1909, after which Theodore Roosevelt said, "It is the obvious duty of the Government to call the attention of farmers to the growing monopolization of water power. The farmers above all should have that power, on reasonable terms, for cheap transportation, for lighting their homes, and for innumerable uses in the daily tasks on the farm."

Two years later, the National Electric Light Association reported on rural electrification at its annual convention in 1911, noting that few farms outside irrigation districts were equipped with electricity. The private electric industry was warned that unless farms obtained electricity at the same rates applied in adjacent towns, farmers would turn to other means for electric power. The utility executives who heard the report were impressed, but they didn't think line extensions to farmers would pay off. During World War I and the boom that followed, private utilities were under great pressure to supply more electricity to city users and to manufacturers in particular. Rural families—whose homes were scattered with only one, two, or three to a mile—took a back seat.

A decade passed. The First World War ended in 1918, and through the Roaring Twenties, more city residents obtained electric light. Farmers and rural leaders wanted, needed, and finally insisted on electric power like that delivered to their urban neighbors. Responding to the increased demand for rural service, the National Electric Light Association, along with the American Farm Bureau Federation and state agricultural colleges, in 1923 formed the Committee on the Relation of Electricity to Agriculture (CREA) to study how power could be provided in rural areas. The CREA study focused on a small Minnesota town where six miles of power line were built to serve twenty farm homes. Lines were extended into barns, chicken houses, and work sheds; electric motors cut wood and dried hay. The experiment raised the standard of living for everyone involved, but the committee dissolved in the early 1930s, concluding that, due to the excessive amount of money it would take to run electric lines into rural areas, American farmers would have to seek electricity from suppliers other than private power companies.

In the first half of the 1930s, the United States fell sorely behind Europe in terms of electricity provision in rural communities. Almost 90 percent of farms in France and Germany enjoyed electricity and the tools it powered, while only 10 percent of US farmers had electric power. The investor-owned utilities estimated that line construction to farms cost, on average, $2,000 per mile and deemed it unprofitable to extend lines. If farmers wanted electric service, the private companies argued, they would have to pay for their own lines. Most farmers couldn't afford that, but even if they could, the rural rates they would have to pay for electricity could be four times as high as that of their city neighbors. The farmers sulked. The private utilities stalled. Advocates for rural electricity stepped up.

Chief among them was Morris Cooke, a Philadelphia engineer and longtime champion of rural electricity. Then governor of New York, Franklin D. Roosevelt tapped Cooke to serve on the Power Authority of the State of New York, which FDR created in 1931 to study power development along the St. Lawrence River. As a consultant, Cooke was to come up with a distribution plan for marketing power to farmers; in short time, his study revealed that round-the-clock operations of power plants decreased the costs associated with building power lines from the $2,000 per mile figure the private companies had estimated to actual cost of $500 to $1,700 per mile. "Widespread rural electrification is socially and economically desirable and, financially, both sound and feasible," Cooke proclaimed.

The numbers were right, but the timing was wrong. In 1931, the country was two years deep into the Great Depression. Although costs associated with line extension were not as much as anticipated, individuals and businesses had far less cash in hand, including the private power companies. As even their more advantaged city kin felt the strain of the Depression, the country cousins who had done without electricity for so long could hardly hope for it now.

FDR and the Stroke of His Pen

The need for electricity in northeast Georgia paralleled that of any rural area in the nation. In a 1932 presidential campaign speech, FDR addressed the issue when he said: "Electricity is no longer a luxury. It is a definite necessity… It can relieve the drudgery of the housewife and lift the great burden off the shoulders of the hardworking farmer."

The second President Roosevelt had witnessed the hardships of country life during his 1920s visits to Warm Springs for polio treatments and feared the lack of electricity would stunt development of the rural South. Upon his inauguration as president in March 1933, FDR began what would be known as his "First 100 Days" in office, a dynamic time period he devoted to social, economic, and job creation initiatives in hopes of delivering the country out of the choking Great Depression. In these three months, the president pushed fifteen major items of legislation through Congress, including two that would hasten rural electricity: the Tennessee Valley Act, which authorized construction of transmission lines to supply electricity to farms at reasonable rates, and the Federal Emergency Relief Administration, under which the Rural Electrification Administration would be established two years later.

On May 11, 1935, FDR signed Executive Order No. 7037 to create the REA, a New Deal project geared, per the document itself, "to initiate, formulate, administer, and supervise a program of approved projects with respect to the generation, transmission, and distribution of electric energy in rural areas." Roosevelt named Cooke the first administrator and work got underway, with the hope that inexpensive REA loans would motivate the private power companies to build lines into rural communities. Cooke asked power company leaders to propose how they would utilize REA loans to carry out a national plan for rural electrification. Their answer dismayed the REA administrator: the power companies sought all of the $100 million allotted to REA to serve only 351,000 rural customers, essentially the large farms and businesses easiest to connect, while leaving five million farms in the dark. As they had from the start, the private utility companies feared the average farmer would never use enough electricity to pay for service into the sparsely populated countryside; if the farmers failed to pay, the private companies' ability to provide electricity to their city customers could be jeopardized. They would, however, agree to extend service to the larger farms.

Cooke said thanks, but no thanks, and began weighing the merits of cooperatives. The farmers, after all, were those most eager for electric power and farm groups were among those who sent in the first loan applications after the REA was announced. As the private power companies and municipalities pondered how they might recoup any investment, independent cooperatives sprang up throughout the country. In November 1935, the REA approved its first loans for eleven proposed cooperatives.

The march was on to light the land, but there were missteps. Formed under the Federal Emergency Relief Administration, the REA suffered from its status as a relief agency. A longtime legislative peer and friend of Morris Cooke, US Senator George Norris of Nebraska was convinced that rural electrification would never be realized in America unless the REA received full status as a government agency capable of granting loans. Norris had been the primary author of the legislation that created the Tennessee Valley Authority and worked four decades pursuing a progressive agenda that included relief for the American farm family. "I had seen first-hand the grim drudgery and grind which had been the common lot of eight generations of American farm women," Norris said. "Why shouldn't I have been interested in the emancipation of hundreds of thousands of farm women?"

In January 1936, Norris and Representative Sam Rayburn of Texas introduced similar bills, Norris in the Senate and Rayburn in the House of Representatives. Both called for setting up the REA as an independent agency and authorizing it to make loans for rural electrification. On May 21, 1936, FDR signed the Rural Electrification Act, authorizing $410 million for a ten-year loan program to take electricity to America's farms. Norris has been called the "father" of the Rural Electrification Act.

Electric cooperatives started forming throughout the country with farmers and their rural neighbors racing to secure REA loans. To assist the budding co-ops in their home states, the REA in 1937 presented a

In his book about the advent of electricity in rural America, Marquis Childs summarized that electric power on the nation's farms was responsible for transforming the country from Tobacco Road to the twentieth century.

model law, the Electric Cooperative Corporation Act, which gave rural residents authority to organize cooperatives and build electric systems. In Georgia, the act became law later that year. Electric cooperatives were granted exemption from regulation by state commissions due to the fact that, as member-owned nonprofit organizations, they were self-directed. Eventually, electric cooperatives banded together to purchase supplies in bulk, bringing the average cost of line construction down to less than $1,000 per mile.

In Georgia, rural electric proponents and pioneers worked as hard as their counterparts in Washington, DC. In his 1952 book, *The Farmer Takes a Hand: The Electric Power Revolution in Rural America*,

Jackson EMC charter director and, later, general manager, William Booth, left, took rural electric leadership cues from Walter Harrison, center, the longtime manager of Georgia EMC, editor of *Rural Georgia* magazine, and state and national rural electric leader. The men are shown here with James B. Polhill Jr., another of the state's rural electric pioneers.

Marquis Childs applauded the state's rural electrification leaders for their unrelenting efforts in the rural electric movement. When considering James B. Polhill Jr., Valene Bennett, Walter Harrison, T. H. Mason, and other state rural electric pioneers, Childs wrote, "…you get a sense of what REA has meant in Georgia and throughout the South. These men—and they are hardworking, organizing, intensely practical Americans—believe that power on the farms has supplied the margin to work the transformation from Tobacco Road to modern Twentieth Century farming."

The part-time Georgian who had established his second home at his Little White House in Warm Springs, President Roosevelt credited Georgia as integral to the hard-won race for rural electricity when he dedicated Lamar EMC, now Southern Rivers Energy, in Barnesville on August 11, 1938. There he spoke of the only "discordant note" in his early days as a west Georgia resident, fourteen years earlier: "When the first-of-the-month bill came in for electric light for my little cottage, I found that the charge was 18 cents a kilowatt-hour—about four times as much as I paid in Hyde Park, New York. That started my long study of proper public utility charges for electric current and the whole subject of getting electricity into farm homes. So, it can be said that a little cottage at Warm Springs, Georgia, was the birthplace of the Rural Electrification Administration."

That birth brought light upon the land of rural America where farmers and their friends rallied to form electric cooperatives. Farm communities had been deprived of the one vital tool that supplied social and economic vitality to city residents.

That tool was coming, about to buzz breathlessly on power lines through northeast Georgia.

Chapter Three
Farmers and Friends

"Wisdom is like electricity. There is no permanently wise man, but men capable of wisdom, who, being put into certain company, or other favorable conditions, become wise for a short time, as glasses rubbed acquire electric power for a while."

—Ralph Waldo Emerson
Nineteenth-century author

The story of rural electric pioneers in northeast Georgia is similar to that of almost a thousand electric cooperatives that sprang up throughout the nation in the two decades following establishment of the Rural Electrification Administration.

Operating within the US Department of Agriculture (USDA), the REA promoted itself with the motto: "If you put a light on every farm, you put a light in every heart." In an early issue of the REA publication, *Rural Lines*, the story was told of a Georgia farmer who, seeking to light his farm, tried to join his local electric cooperative but was turned away because his house was too far from the nearest line; he would have to pay $165 to extend the line if he wanted electricity. A week later, the man returned to the co-op office with a $5 bill, the amount necessary to sign up for membership. "I moved my house," he exclaimed. He had spent $50 to build a new foundation, rolled his house across the field, and set it up a few feet from the electric line.

The story is indicative of the lengths rural folks would go to acquire electricity and illustrates the ingenuity of the farmer who, while he may not have had electric lighting, was brilliant in terms of creativity and a make-it-happen work ethic. Put people like that together and, capable of wisdom, they will work wonders.

The methodology of forming electric cooperatives was basically the same, state to state. Cooperative Extension Service agents with the USDA visited farms and explained to farmers how they could set up electric cooperatives to utilize REA loans. The Extension Service and REA were sister agencies, both under the umbrella of the USDA, whose sole mission was to help farmers increase productivity; helping them acquire electricity became a top priority. To facilitate their own and REA's goals, Extension Service agents surveyed rural residents to determine their level of desire for electric service and submitted to the REA information about their county's population, need for electricity, and estimated cost to build lines. Typically, the REA approved loans for new cooperatives if at least three members per mile paid the $5 membership fee and when right of way was obtained from property owners granting permission to run lines across their fields.

Opposite page: As in much of the rural South, cotton was king in northeast Georgia until the Great Depression and soil erosion dethroned the cash crop. Farmers like W. G. Legg worked the land during daylight hours and dreamed of electricity in the dark nights.

J. W. Cato and his son, Otis, baled kudzu in Hall County in the first half of the twentieth century. Here, they work the field with helpers who lived on the farm, from left, Fletch Williams, Red Sailors, James Williams, and J. W. and Otis Cato. Like other farmers of the era, the Catos were concerned that soil depletion left them with little choice for money-making crops; kudzu was considered useful in controlling erosion and improving fertility of soil and also provided grazing and hay for cattle. Both Catos served on the Jackson EMC Board of Directors, and the younger was recognized throughout the region for his efforts in soil conservation. His grandson, Lee Chapman, serves as director of commercial/industrial marketing at Jackson EMC in 2013.

Farmers in favor of gaining electricity had to convince their neighbors that only by organizing cooperatives, by handling the need for electric power themselves, could rural electricity be achieved. They took the lead in spreading information about the REA. Throughout rural America, meetings to secure electricity were held and visits were made to those not at the meetings. After working in the fields all day, farmers called on their neighbors in the evening to talk up what country folks called "the current" or "the electric." Dairymen visited their neighbors in between morning and afternoon milkings to sign up members and collect membership fees. Realizing the emotional tug the prospect of electricity presented to farm wives, sign-up teams asked to meet not just with men, but with their wives, emphasizing to the farm matriarch the benefits of electric refrigerators and stoves and how electric lights could help children study their lessons at night. Farm wives pointed out to each other the appliances they could utilize if only they had electricity, how the electric washing machine could free up a whole day's time, precious hours they could devote to chores less laborious and more rewarding, like stitching up a new dress on an electric Singer sewing machine.

In the mid-thirties, farmers in and around Jackson County began talking about how they could, how they *would*, get electricity into their homes and onto their farms. While just more than 10 percent of the nation's farms had electricity when the REA was established in 1935, the percentage was far less in northeast Georgia where one published account estimated that 5 percent of Jackson County farms had electricity. Another estimated that only 3.5 percent of Jackson County farm families received electricity, while yet another put the estimate at a mere 3 percent. Rural residents longed for electric power.

A County Agent Leads the Way

The man most closely associated with spearheading the local effort was J. W. Jackson, Cooperative Extension Service agent for Jackson County from 1935 to 1939. Prior to moving to northeast Georgia, Jackson had established county extension offices all over the state, according to his daughter Lois Jackson Brooks, who as a child moved with her family almost a dozen times before settling in Jackson County. "He was helping farmers learn how to improve farming methods so they wouldn't deplete the soil but enrich it and increase their income through proper farming techniques," Brooks said of her father.

Jackson, like Extension Service agents throughout the country in the mid-1930s, was charged with teaching area farmers and families about the new rural electric program. Throughout the spring and summer of 1936, he led meetings in local school districts, informing residents how they could obtain an REA loan to build electric lines. Farm families in Jackson County experienced electric power when they came into towns like Jefferson or Commerce and were awestruck at the idea of having it in their own homes. In his regular column in the local newspaper, *The Jackson Herald*, Agent Jackson wrote in 1936: "We are having a wonderful response to this program. We are anxious to see every home in Jackson County have electricity. This will mean more for the farm women of our county than anything else we could do for them."

As one who had lived in town and on the farm, with electricity and without, Brooks was aware of the social implications electricity carried with it. "People with power sort of looked down on us without it," she said. Country folks without it, she added, were handicapped as compared to city dwellers whose homes glowed with electric light. On the farm, said Brooks, "if you had to work outside all day then do homework at night, you had to do it by lamplight or not do it at all. I knew people who had to repeat school, not because they were not smart but because they did not have light to do lessons at night."

To get an idea of how many households wanted and were willing to pay for electricity, the county agent surveyed farm families. He sent his findings to REA offices in Washington, DC, but this first loan application to build an electric distribution system was rejected by REA officials who considered the average income per Jackson County farm family too low to merit a project. Simultaneously, communities in Jackson, Madison, and Banks Counties attempted, individually and to no avail, to obtain electric service from Georgia Power Company.

In spring 1937, Georgia Power representatives met with County Agent Jackson to assess his work to secure REA lines. Soon after, the Commerce Kiwanis Club sponsored a meeting of farmers from Jackson, Banks, and Madison Counties to discuss the merits of organizing a cooperative to serve all three counties; attendees decided to develop a three-county project in hopes of attracting the REA's attention. Residents

Extension agents with the University of Georgia Extension Service were charged with going into rural communities to teach farmers improved methods of farming that would enrich, rather than deplete, the soil. Banks County Extension Agent Emmett Lyons assisted farmers through the 1950s and 60s.

forked over the sign-up fee of $5, an equivalent of $82 today and a substantial amount in the midst of the Great Depression, especially for cash-strapped dirt farmers who counted on cotton to make a living off the land. Exhibiting great faith, the farmers agreed to become members of a cooperative that did not yet exist in order to obtain an unfamiliar commodity.

Reports in local newspapers on the proposal to build power lines in the rural areas prompted more residents to inquire about electric service. Meetings were held at country stores, churches, schoolhouses, and in private residences where groups gathered to explore how they might obtain electricity.

To facilitate organization of the cooperative, County Agent Jackson formed relationships with a host of people throughout northeast Georgia. "He cultivated friendships with people who were politically powerful and those who had resources to help," said his daughter. "He visited the counties and also made trips to Washington D.C. on behalf of this program."

Among those assisting Jackson were his fellow county agents, Goss Thomas from Madison County and J. F. McMullan and W. L. Garner from Banks County. Others who helped recruit members included, from Jackson County, G. Hubert Martin, Hoke Hardy, J. M. Davenport, J. A. Bell, Fred Baird, J. C. Head, William Booth, Rupert Talmadge Farmer, and D. P. Bolton; from Madison County, George Stovall and Lonie Seagraves; and from Banks County, W. A. Chambers, Judge and Mrs. W. M. Thomas, and William C. Alexander.

Rupert Talmadge Farmer of Nicholson was among the early advocates for rural electricity in northeast Georgia and represented Jackson EMC as a charter member of the Jackson EMC Board of Directors.

William C. Alexander of Banks County was one of seven founding directors of Jackson Electric Membership Corporation.

As they worked to organize the cooperative, the men who would become its first directors met personally with potential members to garner interest in rural electrification. Lonie Seagraves's twenty-two-year service to the cooperative began when he traveled northeast Georgia without pay to tell farmers about the rural electrification program. William "Will" C. Alexander and his wife, Jessie, worked together to help form the cooperative, volunteering alongside Banks County Agent Garner to persuade their neighbors to pay membership fees and give access to their property for stringing wires. Jessie recalled one occasion when she reached her boiling point over a neighbor's reluctance to apply for power. "One night we pleaded and pleaded for a fellow to sign up," she said. "He turned to Will and said, 'What you gonna pay me?' That infuriated me. I whispered to Will, 'Slap his face and let's go home!'"

She knew her husband would pull the $5 from his own pocket to pay for his neighbor's membership. He did on that occasion, and more. To gain one family as members, he wired their house free of charge.

Tom Nelson Stovall was about ten years old when his father, George Stovall, went house to house telling his Madison County neighbors about the REA. An adamant volunteer who put in countless hours to form the cooperative, George Stovall often met with success when encouraging his neighbors to sign up for electricity. The Stovalls lived near Ila on farmland worked by sharecroppers; in the 1930s, George Stovall ran a store and operated both a corn mill and blacksmith shop. Add the long hours it took to help form the cooperative, and he essentially worked four jobs. It was important to him, and to the whole community, his son recalled, noting that "it had to be important because the federal government was putting a pile of money into it."

George Westmoreland was another rural electric pioneer instrumental in the local effort. A Jefferson lawyer, he accompanied County Agent Jackson to Lafayette, Alabama, and Newton, Georgia, in the fall of 1937 to visit REA projects in progress. In October 1937, Jackson sent a revised plan to the REA, this time presenting a strategy for electricity in Jackson, Madison, and Banks Counties. The plan included the required surveys, statistics, documentation, and blueprints for building a 210-mile distribution system. The hopeful farmers and friends waited to hear back from the REA. Weeks passed.

Campaigning for a Cooperative

In December, an Atlanta engineering firm, J. B. McCrary Company, apparently scouting for new business, wrote a letter to Jackson, Thomas, and McMullan, the county agents of Jackson, Madison, and Banks Counties. The letter stated that REA Administrator John M. Carmody planned to redistribute REA funds previously earmarked for other states, noting, "…it would be a good idea for you gentlemen as county agents and some of your leading men to make efforts to contact Senators Richard B. Russell and Walter F. George and Congressmen Frank Whelchel and Paul Brown during the holidays before they return to Washington for the next session of Congress."

Heeding the advice, Jackson, Westmoreland, and other local leaders mailed letters almost every week to the senators, congressmen, and REA officials, requesting something be done about the project. In late February

1938, the REA updated organizers on the loan application, reporting the proposed project had been labeled "Georgia 83 Jackson." The project had been reviewed but, before further action could take place, an REA field representative would visit the site. The REA letter noted that loan applications from Georgia alone totaled $4 million. "Our funds this year are completely exhausted," the REA officials wrote. "You may be sure that your project will receive every consideration when funds become available from next year's appropriation."

The local letter-writing campaign resumed, this time with the county agents and attorney urging Senators Russell and George and Representatives Whelchel and Brown to allot sufficient funds from relief appropriations "at the present time so they may approve projects such as ours… This would give hundreds of people employment and, at the same time, give rural people a service to which they are entitled."

County Agent Jackson was informed via a letter from the REA on April 13, 1938, that before their loan could be approved, the three-county contingency would have to provide the REA with customer contracts, membership fees, right-of-way easements, and a detailed map of the proposed project; those hoping to form the cooperative would have to conduct a formal meeting and elect a board of directors. For the past year, self-appointed committees from each of the three counties—Jackson, Madison, and Banks—had been meeting on their own turf. To proceed, the committees would have to come together, just as they'd done the prior April in Commerce.

On April 27, the REA wrote Jackson another letter, advising him it would be awhile before they could send a field representative to review the site project and encouraging him to begin "pre-allotment work" immediately, noting that "expenses may be advanced from membership fees and reimbursed if and when an allotment is made." The REA urged the organizers to downsize their proposed plan from 210 to 150 miles of line, noting it would not be possible for the federal agency to budget the full project that year. The REA advised local leaders to encourage potential members to sign up for amounts in excess of the minimum; those able to afford using large amounts of electricity were asked to indicate so when signing their application.

One week later, on May 4, 1938, a meeting of rural electric proponents from Jackson, Madison, and Banks Counties was held in Commerce and, from the group, seven directors were elected and eventually became Jackson EMC's first board of directors. The board consisted of three representatives from Jackson County: William H. Booth, Rupert Talmadge Farmer, and J. C. Head; two from Banks County: William C. Alexander and Mrs. W. M. Thomas; and two from Madison County: Lonie Seagraves and George Stovall, who was elected board chairman. Head was chosen as vice chairman and Booth was elected secretary-treasurer.

Later that day, County Agent Jackson wrote the REA to inform them of the meeting and election of directors. Jackson advised the agency that the directors had agreed to select 150 miles to develop as an electric distribution system and work would begin simultaneously in each county as soon as the REA approved Westmoreland as attorney for the group. "He has quite a bit of experience in obtaining loans from the WPA to build city halls," Jackson wrote, "and is attorney for several consolidated school districts that voted bonds and obtained large WPA loans. It is his opinion that within forty days from the time he is affirmed, the project can be incorporated."

A follow-up meeting was held May 8, 1938, at a school in Commerce where representatives from the three counties agreed to divvy up the 150-mile electric system with fifty miles each in Jackson and Madison Counties, forty in Banks, and ten miles left open for emergency needs. Directors met at Westmoreland's office in Jefferson on May 20 to discuss funding to incorporate the not-for-profit cooperative. Minutes from that meeting indicate the directors agreed to advance $65 to pay for incorporation costs, with $25 each coming from Jackson and Madison Counties and the remaining $15 from Banks County. On May 28, Westmoreland filed a petition for charter to incorporate, and in the following weeks meetings were held and farmers visited their neighbors to collect more application fees. On June 22, Jackson informed the REA that the project revisions were complete and more than seven hundred signed contracts for service were mailed to Washington, DC, along with a map of the proposed service area.

Success, Finally

After two years of convincing farmers to sign up for electricity, drawing and then redrawing plans for a distribution system, and working ceaselessly with REA representatives, the farmers were finally granted a charter for Jackson Electric Membership Corporation on June 27. The name "Jackson" was chosen to signify the new cooperative was incorporated in Jackson County. The remainder of the name was in accordance with Georgia General Assembly requirements that "Electric Membership Corporation" be included in the name of each cooperative formed under the Rural Electrification Act.

On July 1, 1938, the board of directors held its first official meeting and officers were elected. Named chairman at the May meeting, Stovall's title turned to president when he was again elected to the top spot. Previously elected vice chairman, Head was named vice president, and Booth remained secretary-treasurer. Bylaws were adopted with the first paragraph spelling out what would become the organization's original mission statement: "The aim of Jackson Electric Membership Corporation is to make electric energy available to its members at the lowest cost consistent with sound economy and good management."

Other matters of business included setting the day for the REA-required annual meeting of members as the first Friday following the first Monday in February and establishing 10 percent of the cooperative membership

L. C. "Lonie" Seagraves, shown here with his family, represented Madison County as a founding director of Jackson EMC.

as the quorum necessary for voting at annual meetings. Rather than receive a salary, the board voted for compensation of $3 per director, per meeting, with mileage at .05 cents per mile. The board chose J. B. McCrary Company of Atlanta as engineer for its first line construction project and named Westmoreland attorney. A stenographer-bookkeeper in Westmoreland's law firm, John Edward Lord, who had helped the organization during its formative stages, was hired at a salary not to exceed $50 per month.

At the board's second official meeting on August 9, directors reviewed applications of two men, W. L. Williamson and Robert J. "Rob" Kelly, seeking to lead Jackson EMC as superintendent, a title that evolved to general manager. The board hired Kelly, a civil and electrical engineer who had graduated from the Georgia School (later, Institute) of Technology, and set his salary at $100 per month, plus expenses up to $50.

On October 11, 1938, Jackson EMC entered into its first contract to purchase wholesale power from Georgia Power Company. Construction would begin on the first lines on January 2, 1939, and on January 5, *The Jackson Herald* would carry an article entitled "Rural Electrification Almost in Sight," chronicling the cooperative's formative months and lauding County Agent Jackson as the leading force behind the push for rural electricity in northeast Georgia: "The one man who has been patient, but persistent, who has worked not too rapidly, but surely, is the county agent, J.W. Jackson. Never has he faltered or wearied in his efforts to secure rural electrification for Jackson County. In recognition of his service to the county, he was recently chosen president of the Commerce Kiwanis Club."

Robert Judson "Rob" Kelly was hired as Jackson EMC's first superintendent (a title later changed to general manager and now president/CEO) in August 1938 and led the cooperative with distinction for twenty-seven years.

The imagination of Benjamin Franklin, the ingenuity of Humphry Davy and Thomas Edison, the concern for farm women voiced by George Norris, the dedication to rural prosperity advanced by Morris Cooke, the power of a signature penned by Franklin D. Roosevelt, the tenacity of County Agent J. W. Jackson, the legal expertise of George Westmoreland, the dedication to helping their neighbors exhibited by Jackson EMC's original directors, and the cotton and cattle farmer's dream of rural electricity as a reality—all combined, over the course of two centuries—brought light to the dark nights of northeast Georgia. All involved, it can be said, were electric pioneers, and rural electric heroes.

Together, the farmers and community leaders of northeast Georgia achieved what none could have accomplished as individuals. They pooled their resources to obtain a service that would benefit, and be owned by, all who participated. Similar group efforts defined by neighbors helping neighbors brought electricity to rural communities across America.

At his home in rural Madison County, the first electric tool George Stovall purchased after lines came to the Pocataligo community was a well pump. His son, Tom, some seven decades later could not recall the day the lights came on, or the moment his father's new well pump put an end to drawing water from the well. But he could remember the difference of "before electricity" and "after electricity." When asked to sum up, in a phrase, what electricity means to him, the octogenarian's answer was thoughtful: "It just changes life, wouldn't you say?"

Electricity not only changed life but what one could do with a life, according to Lois Jackson Brooks who credited rural electricity with empowering country people. "They could become anything they wanted to be," she said. "They didn't have to stay on the farm. They could study at night; they could listen to the radio

Farm homes along the dirt roads of northeast Georgia were introduced to a new way of living after electric lines were strung through the rural communities.

and learn of opportunities out there in the world they'd never heard of. It changed everyone's outlook on what was possible."

After Jackson EMC was formed, her father farmed, taught school, and eventually moved with his wife to Braselton. What would J. W. Jackson think if, decades later, he could see the cooperative he helped form? "I think he'd be popping his buttons if he knew what he'd started had grown to be such a viable force for the economy in this part of north Georgia," said Brooks. "He'd be so proud of what's been accomplished. And I could hear him saying, 'See Mama, I told you this was a good thing.'"

Book Two: Power

Chapter Four
First Loans, First Lines

"And so, we watched the REA arrive. Poles began being hoisted and packed and guy-wired. Great rolls of shining wire, like spun thread, pulled and stretched and attached by strong-faced linemen, perched godlike on limbless creosoted black pine poles."

—Terry Kay
Author of *The Year the Lights Came On*

Even in its earliest stages, Jackson EMC proved itself a company devoted not only to supplying its customers with electricity, but as a community partner providing electric power at the lowest cost possible with the highest quality of service. At times, the local cooperative had to buck the national agency to which it owed its very existence.

While it had taken two years to drum up enough support to launch, once Jackson EMC gained its charter, all pieces seemed to fall in place. In late July 1938, REA Administrator John Carmody notified the new cooperative that $157,000 was allocated for its first system project, set to string 171 miles of single phase line serving 664 farms in Jackson, Banks, and Madison Counties. This first loan was executed on August 10 for twenty-five years at a 2.73 percent interest rate. Building lines, however, would not begin for five months due to a difference of opinion between the cooperative and the REA over construction materials.

The disagreement stemmed from the co-op's desire to accept a bid from a company using copper conductor and General Electric transformers and meters, even though the bid was higher than that from a competing contractor using aluminum conductor and transformers from a company in Wisconsin. The local board preferred copper to aluminum conductor and wanted to utilize companies with warehouses in Georgia to ensure twenty-four-hour delivery of supplies. From August to December, the new cooperative flexed its infant muscles in an attempt to persuade the REA to allow it to select its own materials. In an October 1, 1938, letter to the REA, Jackson EMC Board President George Stovall wrote: "If, in the event we don't have the right (to select material), then we bow to those who have, and we agree to cooperate as best we can, even though our wishes have been thwarted and our enthusiasm dampened."

On October 5, Directors Stovall and Booth, Manager Kelly, and County Agent Jackson traveled to Washington, DC, to discuss the matter with REA officials. Not convinced that copper would save the co-op money, the REA refused to alter its position. In late October, the low bidder withdrew its bid and the second low bidder, W.A. Mathis Construction of Athens, offered to substitute, at no extra cost, General Electric transformers. The board accepted the bid, and the REA approved the contract in December.

Opposite page: Any time new power lines went up in Jackson EMC service territory, like this construction on Highway 60 at Candler United Methodist Church, it was considered a good day for rural residents who lived without electricity a quarter-century longer than their neighbors in the city.

A groundbreaking to commemorate beginning construction of the first Jackson EMC substation was held January 2, 1939, in Jefferson. Taking part in the ceremony were those among the most integral in bringing rural electricity to the area, including, from left, George W. Westmoreland, co-op attorney; Rob Kelly, manager; J. W. Jackson, county agent; and J. C. Head, vice president of the board of directors.

On January 2, 1939, a groundbreaking ceremony was held with Attorney Westmoreland, Manager Kelly, County Agent Jackson, and Board of Directors Vice President J. C. Head each shoveling a ceremonial pile of dirt from where the first power poles would be set; ironically, some forty years later, Jackson EMC would build its headquarters within a mile of this historic location. According to the January 5, 1939, edition of *The Jackson Herald*, line construction "began on the Jefferson and Commerce road on the farm of Mrs. Ora Smith only a short distance from the Mauldin Filling Station. Several parties witnessed the beginning of this work. It is expected that work on this link will be completed, with the current turned on and the lights burning, in less than ninety days."

From the start, REA engineers worked diligently to find methods of building rural lines that were sturdy but inexpensive. Rather than cutting corners on construction, they sought improved methods and their research was rewarded with success. The REA's assembly-line method of building lines was later described in the cooperative's monthly newsletter:

The driver of a staking team would move slowly along the route for a new line. A boy in the back of the truck, equipped with a three hundred-foot rope and a pile of wooden stakes, would throw a stake every three hundred feet. Behind came a man to drive the stakes, a crew to hand dig the holes and the equipment crew, which determined what type of pole to drop off at each hole. Still another crew attached brackets and insulators to the poles. Additional crews came behind to set poles and string wires, hang transformers and install meters. On a good day, it was not unusual to build three miles of line per crew.

For its first few months, Jackson EMC conducted business out of office space rented from J. C. Turner on Lee Street in Jefferson. In October 1938, the co-op moved to Athens Street to share space in a building where Manager Kelly operated a garage with his brother, Ed Kelly. Sarah Hanson was hired as stenographer/bookkeeper, replacing John Edward Lord, and the year 1938 ended with Jackson EMC operating with two employees, Kelly and Hanson. The co-op purchased its first truck in December 1938 from

Jackson EMC's first offices were in rented space on Lee Street in downtown Jefferson. Rob Kelly, left, managed the new cooperative, which started with a small staff.

An early Jackson EMC line truck advertised (on door) the electric cooperative as an "REA Co-op."

University Chevrolet in Athens for $810.85 and, in January 1939, paid $70 for its first typewriter, purchased from Woodstock Typewriter Company in Woodstock, Illinois. In February, the first meters were purchased for $288.20 from General Electric Supply Corporation.

In the ensuing weeks, news spread of electric lines being built into the rural communities of Jackson, Banks, and Madison Counties, and desktops at the co-op office in Jefferson stacked up with applications from residents of Clarke, Barrow, Gwinnett, Hall, and Lumpkin Counties, all asking to be included on Jackson EMC lines. The cooperative eventually expanded its service territory to include the five additional counties. The board amended the co-op bylaws and increased board membership from seven to nine directors with each county represented by one director, except for Jackson which was assigned two.

Energized Lines Bring Light to the Country

As work progressed on the Georgia 83 Jackson project, or Project A, the next two line projects, Projects B and C, were approved with construction funds set aside by the REA; Mathis Construction again was hired for the projects.

Barely more than ninety days after groundbreaking ceremonies, Project A was completed and Jackson EMC's first lines were energized on April 10, 1939. Representing the power supplier, L. M. Shadgett of Georgia Power Company flipped the switch to turn the power on at the EMC's first substation at the Jefferson Water Works plant. "Many witnessed the energizing ceremonies, including city neighbors, farmers and visitors from other areas," Kelly would later recall. The families who received power from the first energized lines were jubilant, and some held parties to celebrate. At the ceremony, Westmoreland announced: "The discovery of sulfuric ether as an anesthetic by Crawford W. Long and the endowment of Martin Institute by William Duncan Martin were events of transcendent importance in the history of Jefferson, but not greater than the carrying of electricity to the rural communities of Jackson County."

Rural residents came from miles around to celebrate the energizing of Jackson EMC's first power lines on April 10, 1939, at the cooperative's first substation in Jefferson. On hand for the momentous occasion were, from left, Lonie Seagraves, director; Rob Kelly, manager; William Alexander, J. C. Head, Rupert Talmadge Farmer, and J. W. Cato, directors; J. W. Jackson, county extension agent; Johnny Wheeler, engineer, J.B. McCrary Engineering Company; and W. A. "Bill" Mathis of Mathis Construction Company, which built the first lines.

Jackson EMC member J. G. Brown recalled the day the lights came on:

I was sitting in my farm home in the Hull community and shall never forget when the Jackson EMC first turned on the electric power. What a thrill! We had lived all our lives on the farm in a dark, cold house. The people in our community were not content to live in the dark… We requested a power line to serve our area, but the requirements were set so high that we could not meet them. Jackson EMC came to our rescue and gladly served us… we shall not forget that rural electric cooperatives served us with electric power when no other source would.

Albert Stone worked for Mathis Construction Company when he helped build the first span of power lines in 1939. "I'll never forget that day in April when the lights were turned on for the first time," he recalled. "We started stringing wire in Jefferson; then we moved to Commerce and eventually to Winder. It was a long process, and the idea of having electricity for the first time was a very big deal."

Albert Stone, left, helped build original power lines strung across Jackson EMC's service area in 1939. Journeyman lineman Jeff Chandler met the early employee in 2004 when Stone visited the co-op to reminisce about its early days.

In the late 1930s and early 1940s, mules were often used to pull wire and poles when constructing the electric system. Even into the 1960s, mules pulled wire in locations not accessible by trucks, as demonstrated by lineman Bobby Daniels.

As a young man growing up during the Great Depression, Stone was used to hard work when he started building lines for twenty-five cents an hour. He recalled his first day on the job: "I remember six of us riding on the back of a flatbed truck. We dug the first hole at the Jefferson station. The guys who dug the holes went first; digging six holes a day, six-feet deep. The pole setters came, and then we started stringing lines at the first hole."

In the early days, linemen sometimes used mules to pull wire, a task that could be dangerous, according to Stone who described one fateful day when the crew was stringing wire under another utility's lines. "Somehow, the lines crossed into each other and electrocuted two of our mules," he said. "We were saddened by the loss but also fortunate that it wasn't one of us electrocuted."

Linemen dug holes by hand, climbed poles, and depended on each other to get the job done. "The spring and summer months weren't too bad," said Stone, but winter was another story. "We rode in a late model Ford with no heater. Most

The sight of Jackson EMC line construction crews raising power poles was welcomed throughout the rural countryside of northeast Georgia.

of us were on the back of the truck, and we often had to ride about twenty-five miles to get to work. Those were some hard days in the bitter cold."

Woodrow Wilson, a Jackson County resident who lived just outside of Nicholson, also worked with Mathis Construction to build the co-op's original lines. He recalled working on Project C that ultimately took Jackson EMC lines near Dahlonega. Wilson started out on a right-of-way crew before switching to hole digging where he had the opportunity to earn extra income. The job was a tough one with workers digging deep holes with a spade and then spooning out the dirt. "If we hit rock, we tried boring and then left the rest for the dynamite crew," said Wilson. "We went in first, the right-of-way crew followed us, and then the line crew." Mathis paid twenty-five cents an hour to laborers who, by the time Wilson joined on, were expected to dig seven six-foot holes in an eight-hour workday; men were paid thirty cents per hole for any extras they dug. Wilson averaged nine or ten holes per day but once dug eleven in eight hours. He remembered only one man bested his record: "Doug Martin beat me by one hole (when he) dug twelve in one day."

Most, but not all, families were eager to obtain electricity and were grateful for the linemen who brought it; some saw it as an encroachment too close to their property. "I remember one guy who didn't want us to string the lines near his home, so he cut the wires and poles down with an axe," Stone recalled. "He destroyed several days' worth of work in a matter of minutes."

While the new power system was being constructed, Jackson EMC entered its second significant difference of opinion with the REA, this time concerning rates. Using Jackson EMC's projections on customer density and average usage, the REA had set $2.25 as the

Above: Early right-of-way crews cleared brush to make way for lines and dug holes for power poles using a variety of long-handled shovels, including spoons that were curved on the end to dip dirt from the hole, and spades, which were used to dig holes six feet deep.

Left: Linemen Robert Edwards, Tom Harris, George McGinnis, and Cecil Venable, the cooperative's first and only hot line crew for many years, worked together on Jackson EMC's original power lines.

JACKSON ELECTRIC MEMBERSHIP CORPORATION
JEFFERSON, GEORGIA

Oct 24, 1939
Date

For the Month of Oct   Rate   Rate Classification A.

C. L. Thurmond,
Jefferson Ga.

PRESENT METER READING	827	Net Charge if Paid by the 10th	Gross Charge
LAST METER READING	703		
NUMBER OF K. W. USED	124		
SCALE OF CHARGES	Number Minimum 25		
	K.W. for $2.22	5 73	
	K.W. @ 3.55c		
	K.W. @ 3.33c		
	K.W. @ 2.22c		
	K.W. @ 1.65c		
TOTAL FOR LIGHTS			
MERCHANDISE			
TOTAL		5 73	5 7

No discount will be allowed unless this bill is paid at office of the Corporation in Jefferson, Ga., by 5 o'clock on the 10th day of month. Service will be discontinued to customers not paying bill by 15th, and a charge of $2.00 shall be made for reconnection.
Failure to receive bill does not waive discount. We are not responsible for remittances made through the mails not reaching the office in due time.
No receipt will be given unless this bill is presented.

A bill from the cooperative's first year of business, this October 24, 1939, statement to C. L. Thurmond of Jefferson was marked paid on November 10. With tax included, the bill totaled $5.75 for one month's power usage.

minimum bill for the local co-op's members. Jackson EMC, striving to provide the lowest rate and highest quality for its members, requested the minimum rate be set at $2 to keep in line with the minimum charged by neighboring electric cooperatives, including Walton EMC in Monroe and Hart EMC in Hartwell. On November 30, 1938, Westmoreland wrote the REA: "…if a rate is set by the Administration which is more than the rate fixed by cooperatives adjoining this project, it is going to be bad business."

The REA eventually obliged, and Jackson EMC set its first retail rates at $2 for up to twenty-five kilowatt-hours (kWh) of electricity consumed in homes, on farms, and by businesses; the minimum bill for churches and public buildings was $1 for the first twelve kilowatt-hours. Beyond the minimum charges, per kilowatt-hour rates decreased as more electricity was used. The cooperative's first billing was to ninety members for a total of $122.65; the average bill was $1.36, with an average of twenty-two kilowatt-hours consumed. Costing significantly less than the $2,000 per mile private utilities had estimated it would take to build lines, the first Jackson EMC lines were constructed for $956.50 per mile. By December 30, 1939, the cooperative served 994 members on 394 miles of power lines. With fewer than three members per mile in May 1940, the average bill was about $2.40.

Building a Business

In June 1940, Jackson EMC moved into its first permanent headquarters, built behind the co-op office in Jefferson on property purchased in November 1939 for $400. O. P. Cochran, a general contractor from Elberton, constructed the new headquarters for $7,041. The two-story building faced Athens Street and featured décor and colors in compliance with the REA, which sought uniformity among all the country's electric membership corporations. Members of the board's building committee, J. C. Head, Lonie Seagraves, and Johnny Booker, were paid $50 each for overseeing construction of the new office, which included an assembly hall with seating capacity for sixty-five people. Within months of moving into the new facility, the co-op allowed the Jefferson Woman's Club to hold a cooking demonstration there. It

The Athens Street headquarters, from behind, featured two stories and room for expansion.

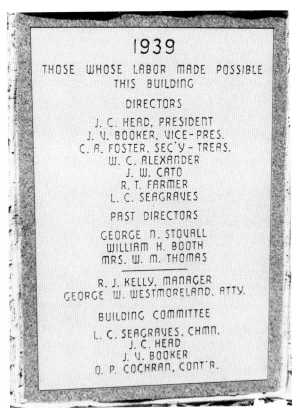

Above: Members of the Jackson EMC Board of Directors were memorialized in a plaque placed at the handsome new headquarters facility.

Top left: Jackson EMC completed construction of its first headquarters in 1940 and moved operations to the new facility that summer. Facing Athens Street, the structure was built with Elberton granite and considered one of the most beautiful buildings in Jefferson.

Left: Work performed by Jackson EMC employees enabled rural homes to be equipped with electric service.

was an early sign of things to come as Jackson EMC would continue throughout its history to make meeting space available for community use.

Meanwhile, line construction continued. Project B involved extending 284 miles of line into Hall, Gwinnett, Clarke, Banks, Barrow, and Madison Counties; most of the lines were completed and energized by late 1939. Project C called for building 224 miles to serve members in Gwinnett, Jackson, Hall, and Lumpkin Counties; while most of these lines were energized in April 1940, parts of the project were delayed due to inclement weather and were not completed until that summer. The co-op's second substation was constructed at Oakwood and energized in early March 1940. By the time Projects A, B, and C were completed in August 1940, Jackson EMC served members on 690 miles of electric lines in eight counties, as follows:

Jackson: 131.75 miles	Banks: 82.75 miles
Madison: 119 miles	Gwinnett: 81.75 miles
Barrow: 112.75 miles	Lumpkin: 45.25 miles
Hall: 100 miles	Clarke: 16.75 miles

Jackson EMC management recognized in its first months of operations that additional funds would be necessary to enable co-op members to wire their residences and plumb their homes and farms. On November 4, 1938, the REA granted the cooperative almost $7,000 as a supplementary loan to help members purchase wiring, plumbing, and appliances. In 1941, another $20,000 loan was provided by the REA to help members purchase electrical items. Three Jackson EMC directors formed a finance committee to approve the individual loans, which covered 80 percent of member cost for wiring, lighting fixtures, and plumbing systems. Hard-strapped for cash as the Great Depression ended, rural residents and tenant farm families welcomed the loans.

After the first lines were energized and those who had not signed up for service saw their neighbors enjoying the benefits of electricity, they signed on for power as well. But the cooperative could not grow based on the number of members alone; it would take increased electricity usage to generate enough income to pay back REA loans incurred to build the system. A family's first electric purchase was almost always for lights. The lone

An electric feed grinder was a welcome addition on rural farms.

bulb hanging from a drop cord in the center of a room became an iconic symbol for the advent of rural electricity. After lights, the first small appliance purchased was typically an electric iron to replace the heavy wedge of iron used to smooth clothes or an electric radio to replace the battery-operated model. Those items alone, however, would never generate enough electricity to sustain the rural electric program; as their lender, the REA pressured the nation's electric cooperatives to increase not only their number of members but also their kilowatt-hour sales by convincing members to purchase more electric appliances and farm equipment.

Even before the first lines were energized, Manager Kelly ordered literature and film strips to promote electricity usage, including five hundred copies each of "A Bathroom for Every Farm" and "Lighting Equipment for the Farmer and Farm Home" and one hundred copies of "Planning for Farm Wiring." The REA sent cooperatives suggestions for economical electrical gifts, urging members to "Give the Gifts that Keep on Giving." Brochures encouraged farmers to "turn loose the power of electricity on the farm" by purchasing electric milkers, pumps, grinders, brooders, and milk coolers.

On August 24, 1939, with the cooperative paying for mailing, *The Jackson Herald* published a special issue devoted to rural electrification. Distributed to 2,500 current and prospective members, the edition was financed by appliance dealers and manufacturers interested in the co-op's success, which could impact their own success. Kelly included a question and answer column about the cooperative, and the issue featured the history of REA and Jackson EMC, the local rate structure, and photos of employees and directors.

The cooperative eagerly accepted assistance from REA and Georgia Power Company. Because Jackson EMC purchased its electricity from Georgia Power, the private utility benefited when the nonprofit cooperative sold more electricity. In September and October 1940, the co-op utilized Georgia Power's farm and home traveling demonstration coach who, each weekday for those two months, presented demonstrations on appliance and equipment use to groups in the Jackson EMC service territory.

Jackson EMC held its first annual meeting of members on February 10, 1939. Perhaps exhausted from two years devoted to forming the cooperative, Board President George Stovall and Directors William Booth and Mrs. W. M. Thomas came off the board and were replaced by new directors J. W. Cato, John V. Booker, and C. A. Foster. Booth would later rejoin the board and eventually serve as the cooperative's general manager.

JACKSON EMC BOARD MEMBERS

County	Director	Year on Board	Year off Board
Banks	W. C. Alexander	1938	1979
	Thomas Wilson	1979	2006
	John Mitchell	2006	Current
Barrow	John V. Booker	1939	1970
	Ernest McLocklin	1970	1998
	Chuck Steele	1998	Current
Clarke	Hubert Moore	1940	1941
	E. R. Hodgson	1941	1966
	E. Baxton Cook	1966	1977
	Balfour Hunnicutt	1977	2011
	Alton Thornton	2011	Current
Gwinnett	Harold Poole	1940	1941
	L. C. Kilgore	1941	1961
	Jones Webb	1961	1964
	Troy Sharpton	1964	1990
	Otis Jones	1990	Current
	Lynn Price	2007	Current
Hall	J. W. Cato	1939	1948
	Otis L. Cato	1948	1976
	Ray Jones	1976	Current
Jackson	J. C. Head	1938	1946
	William H. Booth	1938	1939
	Mrs. W. M. Thomas	1938	1941
	Rupert T. Farmer	1938	1963
	C.A. Foster	1939	1941
	William H. Booth	1946	1969
	H. L. Harman	1963	1969
	Aaron McKinney	1969	1991
	Bill Carpenter	1970	Current
	Charles Gorham	1991	2013
	Shade Storey	2013	Current
Lumpkin	A.D. Pierce	1941	1959
	Haywood O'Kelley	1959	2007
Madison	George Stovall	1938	1939
	Lonie Seagraves	1938	1961
	Thomas Nelson Stovall	1961	1965
	C.Lowell Manley	1965	1968
	Paul Burroughs	1968	2004
	Rodney Chandler	2004	Current

Above: A helper on the Hoschton farm of John V. Booker collects eggs and checks a time clock on an electric feeder in this circa 1957 photograph. Booker, one of Barrow County's early representatives on the Jackson EMC Board of Directors, put electricity to use in his chicken house as soon as it became available.

Left: Since Jackson EMC was chartered in 1938, thirty-eight men and women have served on its board of directors. One director, William H. Booth, served two separate terms. Jackson EMC was among only a few cooperatives in the nation to include a woman on its original board; Mrs. W. M. Thomas helped canvass the community for early members and served as a charter director.

The co-op's second annual meeting, held at the Jackson County Courthouse on February 9, 1940, attracted 142 registered members. REA Engineer Frank Peebles updated members on the progress of line construction. Thelma Wilson, a utilization specialist with the REA, demonstrated how to use an electric roaster to cook a pound cake and ham, which, along with thirty-four electric appliances, were given to members as prizes, beginning a tradition of prize-giving that continues at annual meetings today.

In late 1940, directors changed the annual meeting date from February to the third Friday in May and, on May 16, 1941, the cooperative held its third annual meeting at its new office building on Athens Street; 188 members attended and 127 were represented by proxy. Manager Kelly used charts and graphs to show members the importance of increasing electricity usage. Mary Lokey, REA home economist, demonstrated how to prepare meals with hot plates and other small appliances in the new facility's model kitchen. Tennessee Valley Authority specialist J. L. Calhoun demonstrated how to use well pumps. Members at the annual meeting viewed the film, *Power and the Land*, a motion picture produced by the REA and viewed the year before by area extension agents and Jackson EMC directors and employees at the Roosevelt Theater in Jefferson.

At annual meetings thereafter, REA and other specialists demonstrated to members how to use electric appliances in the home and electric-powered equipment on the farm.

On October 20, 1941, the REA Farm Electric Show was staged on J. H. Lyle's farm just north of Winder. The largest display of its kind to tour the US, the extravaganza featured two circus tents filled with exhibits and, on the midway, demonstrations of feed grinders, farm elevators, silage cutters, pumps, motors, and more. REA home economists conducted "electrified homemaking" demonstrations showing farm wives how to use electric appliances. Thousands from northeast Georgia attended the nationally renowned event.

Early Employees

At the July 1941 board meeting, Jackson EMC directors voted to put employees on a forty-hour workweek with overtime pay at time-and-a-half. Hourly rates were approved for linemen, including J. H. Carter Jr., hired in August 1939 as the co-op's first lineman. Carter would make seventy-five cents an hour while linemen and helpers with less experience would receive a lower rate. Lewis Vandiver and Gus Davis, both hired in January 1941 as helpers but promoted to linemen by July, would make an hourly wage of forty and thirty cents, respectively. A total of 1,907 consumers were billed in 1941 with the monthly bill averaging $3.19.

Ruth Evans Carter had completed a business course in typing and shorthand and was working in Atlanta in 1941 when she received a letter from her mother telling her to come home because Jackson EMC Manager Rob Kelly wanted to hire her. She was twenty years old when she joined the staff as billing clerk in February and proud to report for work at Jackson Electric, the name old-timers called the cooperative in its formative years. The young billing clerk had grown up in Dry Pond, outside of Jefferson, and her family lived on Maysville Road where some of the first Jackson EMC lines were strung. She recalled with clarity the day her family received electricity. "I was working at the beauty shop, and I drove home that night," she said. "I saw the light. It was so much fun to have electricity… That's the most wonderful thing that ever happened to the country people."

Along with lighting, her father, Alvin Evans, had purchased the family's first electric appliance, a refrigerator that was plugged up and ready to run when electricity arrived. "And he put in an electric water pump, and fixed us a bathroom, and then he got mama an electric churn—and all that, real quick when electricity came," Carter recalled. Going

One of the first construction workers at Jackson EMC, Gus Davis was hired as a helper in January 1941 and promoted to lineman six months later.

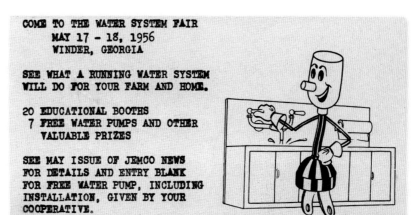

COME TO THE WATER SYSTEM FAIR
   MAY 17 - 18, 1956
   WINDER, GEORGIA

SEE WHAT A RUNNING WATER SYSTEM
WILL DO FOR YOUR FARM AND HOME.

20 EDUCATIONAL BOOTHS
 7 FREE WATER PUMPS AND OTHER
   VALUABLE PRIZES

SEE MAY ISSUE OF JEMCO NEWS
FOR DETAILS AND ENTRY BLANK
FOR FREE WATER PUMP, INCLUDING
INSTALLATION, GIVEN BY YOUR
COOPERATIVE.

JACKSON ELECTRIC MEMBERSHIP CORPORATION   MAY, 1956

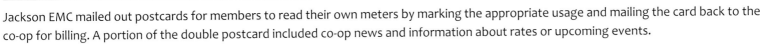

Jackson EMC mailed out postcards for members to read their own meters by marking the appropriate usage and mailing the card back to the co-op for billing. A portion of the double postcard included co-op news and information about rates or upcoming events.

Farm families were eager to receive electricity and helped the cooperative by reading their own meters, as demonstrated here by Mrs. Robert Hill of Winder.

Lafayette Mobley served as office manager and bookkeeper at the cooperative until 1942. He and coworker Bea Anchor stand in front of the new headquarters on Athens Street in this June 26, 1940, photograph taken shortly after the new facility opened.

to work two years later for the company that provided her family with electricity was like wearing a badge of honor. With a starting salary of $45 a month, hers was a decent paying job at one of the few companies where women made as much as men. As one of only four office employees, she joined Kelly, bookkeeper/office manager Lafayette "Fayette" Mobley, and Wilda Wardlaw, who had replaced Sarah Hanson as Kelly's secretary and stenographer. Usually only three were in the office though, according to Carter. "Mr. Kelly stayed out with the boys and out on the line a lot," she said. "He'd come in with work clothes on, his boots and everything." After helping build lines during the day, Kelly worked in the office at night, devoting almost every waking hour to building the business of the young cooperative.

Carter's first job was printing out meter cards on a mimeograph machine. "We mailed out cards and let everybody read their own meters," she said, describing the "double postcards" that prompted members to mark their meter usage on one side and send that portion back to the co-op office for billing. The other half of the card contained a message that differed from month to month, whether reminding members of billing methods or urging them to attend annual meetings.

A New Way of Doing Things

The first four years of operation at Jackson EMC had proven successful as the cooperative grew in terms of membership, staff, system capacity, and net value. The greater value, though, could be recognized by viewing the brightly lit homes of rural Jackson and surrounding counties where the dim light from low-flame kerosene lanterns before had barely illuminated the northeast Georgia nights.

Thelma Little was about ten years old when "two men and a lady" visited her family's home to talk with her father about getting electricity; however, World War II delayed line construction in her community, which didn't receive power until shortly before the war ended. The wait was worth it for the girl who grew up on a farm, picking cotton in the fall and chopping it in the spring. She helped her mother cook two meals at midday on the wood-burning stove, saving one for suppertime, leaving the stove and house to cool off by bedtime, if then. On hot summer evenings in Georgia, relief from the heat came only by raising windows or waving funeral home fans. Little's family ate what it raised from the garden and on the farm, including two hogs her father killed each fall and a yearling calf raised for beef. The family's radio used a big black battery similar to a car battery. "When it ran down, we took it to the service station to get it recharged, so we didn't run it too much," said Little. "It's good memories, and I'm glad I lived through it, but I don't miss it."

When electricity finally came, her family could keep their new electric-powered radio on longer, listening to the *Grand Ole Opry*, *The Shadow Knows*, *Little Orphan Annie*, and *Ma Perkins*. "You felt like you were expanding," said Little. "You could listen to the news and knew more about what was going on in the world."

The first electric receptacles at farm homes were those at the base of the light that dropped from a cord in the middle of a room. Farm wives positioned ironing boards under the lights, plugging electric irons into the overhead receptacle, the iron's cord restricting their reach. Little said her husband "was a pretty good electrician," so she soon had receptacles installed in other places in her house, enabling her to move from the confines of the light receptacle. Getting her first electric stove "was just like living in a fairyland," according to Little. Her mother kept a wood stove even after obtaining an electric one because she was afraid the electricity might fail. "I wasn't scared of electricity, but one of my neighbors said someone in their family didn't like electricity; said he could taste it in his butter," Little recalled, surmising that perhaps the butter had lost the taste he'd been familiar with when keeping it cool in creek water.

While electricity lightened the load, it did not do away with manual labor. Little's first electric washing machine was a wringer model that required elbow grease. "It had a round tub with an agitator in the middle and two rollers," she said. "You'd let clothes wash, then pick them up piece by piece, run through the wringer, then slosh in the rinsing tub and run back through the wringer. And you still hung them out on the line to dry."

For Francine Tolbert Dillard, born 1918 in Madison County, electricity brought marvelous appliances like the electric range and churn, but one commodity made possible with electric power outshone them all: "The bathroom made all the difference in the world," she said. Day or night, rain or shine, a trek through the yard to the outdoor privy had been mandatory in the days before electric pumps pushed water inside to fill sinks, tubs, and toilets. Dillard's family kept a kerosene lantern by the door to take on nighttime trips to the outhouse.

Ann Holcomb's family was among the first to join Jackson EMC. Holcomb grew up on Jefferson Road, the youngest of seven children of Rufus and Vassie Ann Lavender, in the house her father built in 1900 from lumber sawn off the family's ninety-acre farm. Living on a farm, the family never lacked for food, or for work. Rufus Lavender had a reputation for growing dandy watermelons and cantaloupes, which he carried into town to sell. Holcomb recalled picking strawberries and

For many farm families, the well pump, which brought running water into the house, was the most anticipated piece of electric equipment because it enabled indoor plumbing, making outhouses a thing of the past.

Ann Lavender Holcomb was seventeen years old before electricity came to her family's Jackson County farm. She recalled catching a blazing-hot kerosene lamp chimney, similar to the one she held here, to save it from shattering on the floor.

Jackson EMC Superintendent Rob Kelly attended the twelfth annual REA conference at Lafayette Hotel in Washington, DC, held July 22–27, 1940. Here, REA Deputy Administrator Robert Craig addressed superintendents at the meeting as REA Administrator Harry Slattery looked on. The chart behind Craig revealed how European countries were ahead of the United States in terms of rural electrification.

milking the cow before she went to school each morning; in the evenings, she and her siblings circled the dining room table to study school lessons by the light of two kerosene lamps. Times were tight, and even as a child Holcomb understood the importance of frugality. She was eight years old when the chimney from a kerosene lamp she was carrying dropped; she instinctively caught the hot glass, cradling it in the crook of her arm, burning her skin as she lowered it to the floor. "I caught it with my arm because I knew it was hard times," she said, recalling the burn on her tiny arm. "I caught it and just held it, because I didn't want it to break."

She would be seventeen years old before electricity, via Jackson

EMC, came to the farm in 1939, replacing kerosene lamps with electric light. "I just remember how nice it was to have a drop cord, and a switch on the wall, and maybe a plug," she said, recalling the family's new electric radio. "We'd sit around and listen to Henry Aldridge, but that was something new. We didn't waste much time."

After all, on the family farm, time was the most precious commodity. It took time to work the land, to prepare, to plow, to plant, then pick, and to do it all over again, season by season. When electricity finally made its way into the rural communities of northeast Georgia, farmers and their wives were amazed at the time they could save by using electric appliances and farm equipment. Purchasing electric power was like buying time.

"Rural people, gaining faith and confidence, lifted themselves out of the muck and mire of the dark ages into an era of prosperity and improved living conditions," Manager Kelly said when recalling the cooperative's early years. "Not only were the farmers able to pay for the electricity they brought themselves, but they began to see how to use this electricity to make their farming operations easier and more profitable."

In time, rural electricity put town and country people on more equal ground. "City people cooperated with farm people because it meant business for them, selling stoves, churns, farm equipment," said Kelly's daughter-in-law, Imogene Kelly. "That's when the South began to come out of its slump, when electricity was put across the land."

Rural electricity promised to lighten the load for rural residents upon whom the Great Depression had heaped additional burden. But another obstacle to prosperity on the home front was lurking.

A simple incandescent light bulb was a thing to behold for young children who experienced electricity for the first time. Families on Jackson EMC lines almost always purchased lights as their first foray into electricity. During Lighting Improvement Week in Banks County in the fall of 1958, Banks County High School student Barbara Brown's 4-H lighting exhibit demonstrated the wonder of electric lighting to elementary school students, from left: Donna Garrison, Myrna Jean Hill, Patsy Meeks, Elaine Worley, Frankie Gowder, Barbara Smith, Susan Carter, and Gail Martin.

Chapter Five
Barbed Wire and World War II

"When the hour arrived, whoever did whatever he was supposed to do, whatever it was, and the 100-watt bulb located on the ceiling, in the exact center of the room, exploded with light. No one said anything. The light was blinding, a small sun in a new universe."

—Terry Kay
Author of *The Year the Lights Came On*

With the Great Depression barely in the rearview mirror, World War II consumed the first half of the 1940s. As with electric cooperatives throughout the United States, Jackson EMC's steady growth came to a limp as the war got underway.

Between January 2, 1939, and the summer of 1940, more than seven hundred miles of power line had been constructed through the co-op's service territory. As the US entered into World War II, fewer vital materials were available for constructing the electric system, such as transformers, meter equipment, aluminum, steel, copper, and creosoted southern yellow pine poles. During the war, there were no extensions other than short ones made from lines already strung. To acquire electricity at that time, members had to demonstrate that receiving electric service would assist in producing food, fiber, or animal fats that would contribute to the war effort.

Although the first three construction projects had run relatively smoothly, Project D was a different story, deterred first because of other new electric cooperatives competing for supplies and then sidetracked four years by World War II.

Copper wire was preferable for constructing power lines in the 1940s and Jackson EMC did its best to keep it in stock, a goal that became increasingly difficult as copper was deemed crucial to the war effort, as evidenced by the aluminum wire on this early truck.

Opposite page: As a much-told story goes, in the absence of adequate wiring materials during World War II, Manager Rob Kelly led an initiative to run electricity into Gwinnett County on barbed wire. By utilizing wire traditionally used to keep cows in, Jackson EMC set the stage for progress in what became its high-growth district in later decades. This photograph of pasture and fence was made in 1957, in the shadow of Walker Mountain, at the Murrayville farm of F. W. O'Kelley, a Jackson EMC member.

Many everyday items were diverted to the war effort during World War II, including steel and copper wire. Jackson EMC employees joined in the effort by loading the co-op rubbish truck with materials that could be recycled for wartime use.

Upon reviewing initial plans for Project D in 1940, the REA informed Jackson EMC directors that thirteen more Georgia applications were ahead of theirs. It should have come as little surprise. Since Roosevelt created the REA, farmers had rushed to organize cooperatives and in five years, forty EMCs had formed in the state. Chartered January 6, 1936, Rayle EMC in Washington was Georgia's first electric cooperative; in November 1940, Coastal EMC (now, Coastal Electric Cooperative) in Midway became the fortieth to incorporate. It would be five years and one world war later before the state's last two electric co-ops were organized, Coweta-Fayette in Newnan in 1945 and Tri-State in McCaysville in 1948. Jackson EMC was the twenty-seventh of Georgia's forty-two electric cooperatives to form and one of thirty-three chartered within a three-year span from 1936 to 1938.

As the state's cooperatives scrambled to build lines to rural residents clamoring for electric power, they competed with other utilities to acquire supplies. Their competitive skills barely mattered as World War II ensued and supplies increasingly went to the war effort. On June 5, 1941, the REA sent a memorandum to all US electric cooperatives notifying them there would possibly be a shortage in various types of material. "We can substitute certain non-essential materials for house wiring and service entrances," the memo read, noting that material considered "essential" would be diverted for use in the National Defense Program. Two months later, the REA notified Jackson EMC that $146,000 had been allotted for Project D. Jackson EMC's board had requested hard-drawn copper conductor for constructing the system but, because copper was becoming increasingly scarce, agreed to accept galvanized steel wire.

President Roosevelt established the War Production Board (WPB) in early 1942 to prioritize and ration materials. Copper was one item most sought for both electric system construction and the war effort. Copper wire was the preferred conductor for most electrical wiring, including overhead electric transmission lines; likewise, copper was invaluable in war, where copper wire was used in everything from shipbuilding to wiring for radio transmissions. Even bullets called for copper.

By February 1942, REA engineers said copper was no longer available to the cooperatives. On April 14, 1942, Jackson EMC received notice from the federal agency that absolutely no materials would be made available to any new construction projects other than those specifically linked to the war effort and extension to members that met strict criteria. "We are in an all-out war against the Axis, and I know that you will gladly put forth every effort to win this war," REA officials informed electric cooperatives.

Eventually, the REA not only stopped approving EMC requests for construction but asked some of the budding cooperatives, including Jackson EMC, to return materials. In July 1942, Jackson EMC received the following correspondence from the federal agency: "In view of the REA policy to suspend all construction on REA financed projects for the duration of the war, it is suggested that the cooperative consider the cancellation of your contract for the construction of Project D and discuss with you any materials that may have been shipped to the project areas for such construction." Jackson EMC was asked to inventory items in stock so the War Production Board could arrange to purchase the excess material.

Jackson EMC was an early supporter of youth activities like 4-H, which had clubs in schools throughout the co-op's service territory.

Supply acquisition wasn't the only segment of business upset due to the war. At least two of Jackson EMC's early employees, M. L. Mobley and Wilda Wardlaw, left the cooperative in 1942 to take better paying jobs at the Brunswick shipyards, one of sixteen US ports where cargo vessels were constructed to assist Allied forces in Europe.

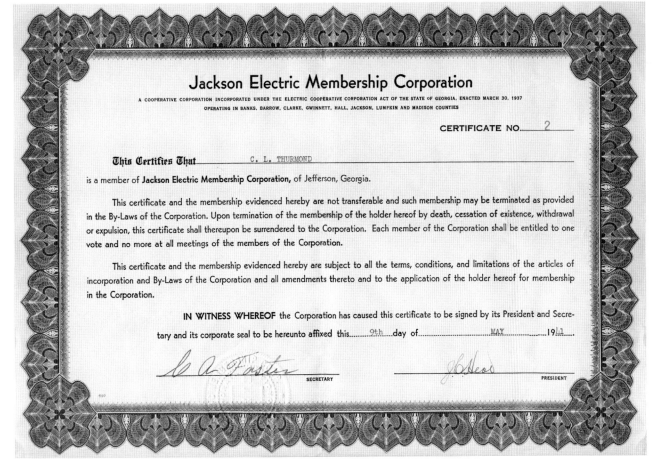

Jackson Electric Membership Corporation

A COOPERATIVE CORPORATION INCORPORATED UNDER THE ELECTRIC COOPERATIVE CORPORATION ACT OF THE STATE OF GEORGIA, ENACTED MARCH 30, 1937
OPERATING IN BANKS, BARROW, CLARKE, GWINNETT, HALL, JACKSON, LUMPKIN AND MADISON COUNTIES

CERTIFICATE NO. 2

This Certifies That   C. L. THURMOND

is a member of **Jackson Electric Membership Corporation**, of Jefferson, Georgia.

This certificate and the membership evidenced hereby are not transferable and such membership may be terminated as provided in the By-Laws of the Corporation. Upon termination of the membership of the holder hereof by death, cessation of existence, withdrawal or expulsion, this certificate shall thereupon be surrendered to the Corporation. Each member of the Corporation shall be entitled to one vote and no more at all meetings of the members of the Corporation.

This certificate and the membership evidenced hereby are subject to all the terms, conditions, and limitations of the articles of incorporation and By-Laws of the Corporation and all amendments thereto and to the application of the holder hereof for membership in the Corporation.

IN WITNESS WHEREOF the Corporation has caused this certificate to be signed by its President and Secretary and its corporate seal to be hereunto affixed this....9th....day of....................MAY....................19.41.

SECRETARY   PRESIDENT

Joining Jackson EMC as a voting member in 1938 when the co-op was formed cost $5, the same amount it costs for membership in 2013. Many early members kept their certificate of membership, a symbol of prestige in the formative days of rural electricity.

Ruth Evans Carter remembered "economizing on gas" by carpooling to work with Morgan Pounds, an early employee who planned easements and prepared maps as the co-op's only staking engineer for many years. Pounds had worked with Georgia Power Company for ten years before coming to work at Jackson EMC and was recalled by numerous members as the man who first brought electricity to their home or farm. "Times were hard in the 1930s and people were sure glad to get electricity," Pounds recalled. "They'd pay as much of the $5 membership fee as they could and sign a note for the rest."

After Wardlaw's resignation, Dorothy Merk was hired in 1942 to fill the position of secretary to the manager. Two years later, her sister, Janette Johnson, joined the staff as records clerk and would work for the cooperative for thirty-eight years. Johnson recalled new construction was put on hold during World War II due to lack of material. To ease the burden for members, the board of directors adopted an emergency measure allowing homes without service to receive electric power through a neighboring house already served by the cooperative. A special rate adopted for the dual service remained in effect until 1955.

Manager Kelly sought other ways to get around the supply shortage. His daughter-in-law, Imogene Kelly, recalled a conversation with Frances Staton, who replaced Merk as Kelly's secretary in 1945 and would work as secretary for all four of Jackson EMC's managers. The cooperative served some but not all of Gwinnett County's rural areas during the war, according to Staton, when a group of Gwinnett residents visited Georgia Power and nearby electric cooperatives to request service. Like Jackson EMC, the other electric providers were short on supplies and told the would-be customers they would have to wait until the war was over. But Kelly, exuding the same can-do spirit organizers utilized when forming the cooperative, found a way around the lack of traditional copper or steel wire.

"He used barbed wire to run electricity to some of the areas of Gwinnett County," said Imogene, who recalled asking her friend, "Are you sure, Frances? I thought barbed wire was to keep cows in."

Morgan Pounds, Jackson EMC's first and for a time only staking technician, staked out paths to run power lines across barren land, dense woods, and mountainous countryside.

The barbed wire was only a temporary fix in hard times and had to be replaced as soon as adequate supplies were available, but it helped Jackson EMC extend service into Gwinnett County areas that ultimately became home to the largest concentration of the co-op's members. If copper or steel had been in big supply in the 1940s, or if Kelly had not resorted to barbed wire, perhaps another electric cooperative would have beaten Jackson EMC to Gwinnett and benefitted from its eventual growth. "Probably Jackson Electric wouldn't be in Gwinnett County now if it hadn't been for him having the foresight to stretch his money and stretch the supplies and meet the demand," said Imogene. "If they'd waited 'til after the war, someone else would have taken it."

Throughout the war years, Georgia Electric Membership Corporation, formed in 1940 as Georgia Rural Power Reserve Electric Membership Corporation, assisted the state's electric cooperatives in reducing their costs by purchasing electricity, appliances, and supplies in bulk. In its first year, the association netted a 22 percent reduction in wholesale power rates from suppliers, effectively reducing costs for Jackson EMC and the other co-ops.

Farm families were eager to obtain electric appliances, especially refrigerators to preserve the produce they raised. Second from left, Myron Luttrell, a home economist with W. D. Alexander Company, explained the advantages of electric refrigeration to new co-op members.

In a 1942 letter to Steve Tate of Amicalola EMC in Jasper, Manager Kelly wrote of Jackson EMC's "sincere thanks to you for your untiring efforts which have been displayed since you became active in the fight for the REA cooperatives in the state as well as the United States." Tate had served as president of Georgia EMC and was instrumental in organizing the National Rural Electric Cooperative Association (NRECA), formed in 1942 to represent before Congress interests of the nation's electric cooperatives. Tate served as the first NRECA president. "Our job has only begun," Kelly's letter continued. "With the cooperatives forging forward as they have been and with the war now on us, construction at a standstill, we must all pull together and hold the gains that have been made, and after the war, launch out for even greater things… After the war, REA will be one of the foremost organizations and will be one of the first which will launch out in readiness to extend electric service and appliances to rural areas which are so much in need of them for health and food for our nation."

One Kilowatt Hour

—with a man guiding its power

Can milk 20 cows twice
Can churn 70 pounds of butter
Can elevate 250 bushels of grain
Can hoist 3 tons of hay
Can saw one-half to one cord of wood

—for just a few pennies

REA-served farms used about 600,000,000 kilowatt hours of power during 1942. Did the kilowatt hours you bought do a war job on your farm in 1942? Will the kilowatt hours you buy in 1943 serve Uncle Sam, as well as you and your family?

Check this list of _average_ consumption figures in kilowatt-hours, of various pieces of farm equipment.

EQUIPMENT	CONSUMPTION		EQUIPMENT	CONSUMPTION
Electric fence	7 kwh per month		Barn ventilator	2½ kwh per cow per month (variable)
○ Fly screen or trap	5 kwh per month		○ Bottle washer	½ kwh per 1,000 bottles
Grain grinder	1 kwh per 100 lbs.		Brooder	½ kwh per chick raised
Poultry house lighting	5 kwh per 100 birds per month		Clipper (for horse or cow)	⅒ kwh per hour of use
Poultry water heater	1 kwh per day		○ Corn husker-shredder	30 kwh per 100 bu. corn husked
○ Sheep shearer	2 kwh to shear 100 sheep		Corn sheller	1 kwh per 30 bu. shelled corn
Tool grinder	⅓ kwh per hour		Cream separator	½ kwh per 1,000 lbs. milk
Ultra-violet lights for poultry	10 kwh per 100 hens per month		○ Milk cooler	30 kwh per 10 gals. milk daily, per month
Utility motor (small ¼ hp)	½ kwh per hour		Dairy water heater	1 kwh per 5 gallons of hot water (145 degrees F.)
○ Utility motor (3 and 5 hp)	1 kwh per hour		Ensilage cutter	1 kwh per ton
Water pump (deep well)	1½ kwh per 1,000 gallons			
Water pump (shallow well)	1 kwh per 1,000 gallons			

RURAL ELECTRIFICATION ADMINISTRATION, U. S. DEPARTMENT OF AGRICULTURE

U. S. Govt. Printing Office

To show what electricity could achieve on the farm, the REA routinely published literature aimed to educate farmers on the powerful contributions of one kilowatt-hour.

Along with supply shortages, storms delayed progress of the young cooperative. The first major ice storm to damage the system occurred on March 2, 1942, when a morning snowfall caused as much as six inches of snow to accumulate in Jackson County, followed by rain and freezing temperatures that produced ice. In some areas, the snow was so deep it had to be shoveled to the roadside before the co-op's trucks could travel through. Damage included trees toppled over lines, breaks in conductors, and broken poles. The main lines were repaired and reenergized in relatively short time, but with the small crew responsible for all maintenance and repair work, it would take about six months to repair all of the system's damaged power lines.

In keeping with the cooperative's bylaws, Jackson EMC continued to hold annual meetings through the war years. While construction of new lines stalled, the REA continued to diligently work for the electric cooperatives, striving to solidify legislation that would enable them to better serve the rural people. On September 21, 1944, the Pace Act became law, ensuring a 2 percent interest rate for those borrowing REA money and setting a loan repayment period of thirty-five years. Congressman Stephen Pace of Georgia wrote the significant legislation that, by establishing the low interest rate, would enable more farmers and farm wives to leave backbreaking chores behind as they hooked up electric water pumps and washing machines.

With passage of the Pace Act, all was in place for local cooperatives to resume expanding rural electric systems when the war ended. At Jackson EMC, the demand to build lines weighed heavy on employees like Charlie Pinion who, after serving in the Army Air Corps during the war, joined the co-op staff in 1946 as a laborer making fifty cents an hour. "It was a battle," said Pinion, describing the post-war grind at Jackson EMC. "The co-op was only seven years old, money was tight, and it was hard to get materials because of the war. We worked overtime and Saturdays trying to get electricity to the people."

Above: Jackson EMC employees, seated, including Melrose Roberts in the foreground, register members for the 1949 annual meeting of members, held August 20 at the Jackson County Courthouse in Jefferson.

Left: Dr. Pierce Harris, pastor of First Methodist Church in Atlanta, was the keynote speaker at the August 20, 1949, annual meeting.

Members packed the Jackson County Courthouse for the 1949 annual meeting. The large attendance prompted the cooperative to hold future annual meetings on the grounds of co-op headquarters in downtown Jefferson.

Storms, he recalled, wreaked havoc on the fragile system. "There were times in both winter and summer we'd leave the office in Jefferson and not get back for three days," he said. Fewer than ten outside employees worked with barebones equipment to do a job that, according to Pinion, would never have been accomplished without co-op members pitching in to help construct the system. "We'd be out building lines and they'd bring mules and help us set poles and string wire," he recalled.

Clarence Wages also joined the Jackson EMC staff in 1946. Hired making forty cents an hour, he worked as a staking engineer, marking spots where poles were to be placed, and checked voltage at sites in all eight counties served by the co-op. "I'd drive a hundred and twenty-five miles a day from the lower end of Madison County to the upper part of Lumpkin County," he said.

Electricians like Harold Holcomb were in high demand in the post-war years. According to his widow, Ann, the licensed

At the 1951 annual meeting, Hall County Director Otis L. Cato, left, and George Stovall, first president of the board of directors, burned a $157,000 note, symbolizing the first loan repaid by Jackson EMC. The loan was paid twelve years in advance of its due date, setting a precedent the cooperative maintained for years to come.

Above: Construction crews in 1953 prepared to head out for a day of building lines throughout the co-op service territory. Line construction workers built the electric system and did maintenance work; district managers were responsible for installing meters.

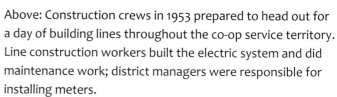

Left: Manager Rob Kelly points out progress on the system at an early substation.

electrician and plumber wired and plumbed many houses in the Athens area following the war, charging $10 per house for his labor.

Within four years of the war's end, the number of electric cooperatives in the US had doubled, while the number of members connected more than tripled, according to the NRECA. Almost 90 percent of American farms lacked electricity when the REA was formed in 1935; by 1953, the statistics had reversed, with more than 90 percent of the nation's farms receiving electricity. By April 1954, Jackson EMC was providing electric service to approximately 11,500 members. In 1939, members of the new co-op on average

Billing department employees in July 1954 worked feverishly to prepare margin refunds to mail to members. Employees include Mary George McCain, Melrose Roberts, Mrs. A. W. Tolbert, Martha Jean Elrod, and Mrs. Jimmy Tompkins.

used twenty-two kilowatt-hours of electricity per month; by 1954, they used 238 kilowatt-hours monthly. To keep up with the increase in members and their increased use of electricity, Jackson EMC "heavied up" their distribution lines to enable delivery of the higher voltage required to operate the extra electric appliances and farm equipment. By 1954, the co-op had added four substations to serve its growing membership, and two more were planned. The service territory had expanded to include a small portion of Franklin County.

Jackson EMC, like its sister electric cooperatives, had toiled to achieve what private utilities had deemed impossible: reliable electric service to rural families at affordable prices. But throughout the nation, co-op members referred to their electric provider as "the REA" rather than "the EMC." Kelly sought to set the record straight, reminding members that the Rural Electrification Administration was a federal agency established to make loans to cooperatives and other entities for extending electric service into rural areas. "This cooperative is a private enterprise and is not owned or controlled by the government or holding company," Kelly said.

Although the REA had been established as one of Roosevelt's New Deal programs, it operated more as a bank than an emergency relief agency. Its interest-bearing, self-liquidating loans made electrification possible for rural families, but theirs was not a gift. From the beginning, the REA was the banker and the EMCs were borrowers who paid back loans with interest. Perhaps the electric cooperatives were indebted

to the REA, but they were beholden to their members, those who owned interest in the not-for-profit entities, the very consumers to whom electricity was delivered.

By 1954, Jackson EMC had adopted as its motto a slogan used by numerous electric cooperatives: "Owned by Those We Serve." "Much hard work and effort has brought us this far," Kelly wrote in April that year. "So let's continue and keep this cooperative *owned by those we serve*."

Above: Jackson EMC's logo featured Willie Wiredhand and the cooperative's slogan.

Left: Manager Rob Kelly and Billing Clerk Melrose Roberts display farm and home electric rates at the September 1955 annual meeting. The rate reduction went into effect in 1956, with the price for power decreasing from seven cents per kilowatt-hour for the first twenty-five kilowatt-hours to five cents per kilowatt-hour.

Chapter Six
Building the System

"Lenin once said that Communism is just Socialism plus electricity. Well, that may be, but this convention can with far greater truth proclaim that Democracy is Faith plus electricity. When those two precious commodities are put together, then you have the stuff of which freedom is made."

—The Very Reverend Francis B. Sayre Jr.
Dean of the Washington Cathedral
1959 annual NRECA convention

Robert Judson "Rob" Kelly served as Jackson EMC's first manager. Hired by the cooperative August 10, 1938, he held the top post until his death on May 1, 1965. A tribute article in the cooperative's newsletter summed up Kelly's twenty-seven years of service as the builder of the business that is Jackson EMC: "Rural electrification was his life, his joy, his dream."

Constructing an electric distribution system from scratch was his mission.

Kelly's main role in the cooperative's infancy was to coordinate efforts of county agents and community leaders to sign up new members and secure right-of-way easements to build the first lines. He also held meetings to explain the function of the new organization to members and prospective members.

"Jackson Electric Membership Corporation could not have hired a better man than Robert J. Kelly," Editor John N. Holder wrote of the manager in a 1939 *Jackson Herald* article. "Besides being a skilled and accomplished engineer, he is a man of business sagacity and looks carefully after the finances of the corporation."

Those who worked with him recalled a man dedicated to making the cooperative a success. "Mr. Kelly was just as nice as could be," said Ruth Evans Carter, who

Above left: Blondean Kelly, center, wife of manager Rob Kelly, worked with the cooperative for twenty-five years, often accompanying her husband at night to hold a light for him while he worked outages. Her retirement was celebrated in 1963 with fellow employees Frances Staton, secretary to the manager, and E. E. "Gene" Thurmond Jr., who served as manager of member services from 1959 to 1967.

Above right: Robert Judson "Rob" Kelly served as Jackson EMC manager from the cooperative's beginnings in 1938 until his death in 1965. This 1940s photo shows him in front of the co-op headquarters on Athens Street.

Opposite page: Linemen Robert Edwards and Cecil Venable worked to build the electric system which, in 1958, included 2,659 miles of line serving almost 14,000 members.

sometimes joined Kelly and his wife, Blondean, for workday lunches at their home, located three doors up from the co-op office in downtown Jefferson. Mrs. Kelly was active in building the business, working without pay in the early days and sometimes accompanying her husband on after-hours calls. "At nighttime when there were outages, she would go with him and hold the lantern or a light for him to work" while restoring service at the pole, said their daughter-in-law, Imogene. Blondean Kelly worked part-time in the co-op's mailing department from 1938 to 1963.

After the cooperative was organized, word of mouth was instrumental in expanding electric service. When neighbors saw farm families next door enjoying electric-powered stoves and refrigerators and recognized how convenient it was to receive electricity, they were eager to sign up as well, even if they had been holding out before. Some holdouts who equated electricity with lightning had to witness the wires working safely at their neighbor's home before they bought into the new program.

Foster Seabolt served as the first manager of the Gainesville District.

A. D. "Doug" Wilkes was the first to lead the Neese District.

Jackson EMC District Managers

Gainesville
Foster Seabolt, January 1953–March 1964
Charles Overman, March 1964–April 1966
Eugene R. Collins, July 1966–June 1967
Derl Hinson, September 1967–April 1969
Charles Sims, June 1969–March 1970
LeRoy Truelove, June 1970–March 1993
Bill Sanders, April 1993–present

Lawrenceville/Gwinnett
Henry Pinion, November 1952–January 1967
Dick Mills, January 1968–October 1970
O. L. Powell, December 1970–December 1977
Roger Willis, May 1978–December 2009
Randy Dellinger, January 2010–present

Neese
A. D. "Doug" Wilkes, December 1952–February 1981
Marvin White, June 1981–June 1990
Kenny Beck, August 1990–July 2010
Jean Mullis, July 2010–present

Jefferson
Don Stewart, December 1991–December 2010
Scott Martin, December 2010–present

Since the first of four district offices was established in 1952, eighteen district managers have led operations.

Henry Pinion served as the original manager of the Lawrenceville District, in later years called the Gwinnett District.

The Gainesville District office opened in January 1953 in this small building. Two other district offices had opened in late 1952, at Neese and Lawrenceville. Each original district office building was about this size.

Manager Rob Kelly, left, points out to Director Otis Cato a new metering point built to handle the growing load on co-op lines. New steel switching structures with automatic voltage regulators and oil circuit reclosers were installed at the 1965 construction in Gainesville.

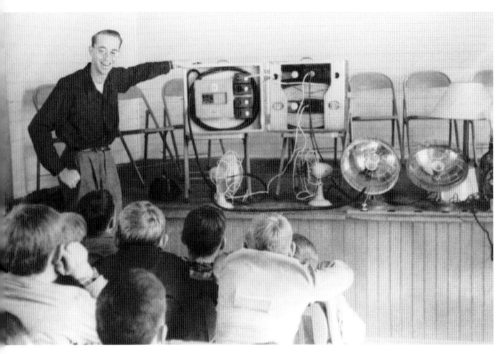

Above: William Fletcher was hired in 1952 as the co-op's first farm electrification advisor, charged to teach men and boys about using electricity on the farm.

Right: Danielsville resident and co-op member Sam Porterfield, right, conferred with Farm Electrification Advisor Jack Aultman when he needed to rewire his farm in order to meet increased electricity demands. Placing a new meter pole at the center of his load demand and upgrading from a 60-amphere to 100-amphere meter entrance to serve his home, pump house, and three chicken houses dropped his monthly power bill from $19 to $13.

After the war, construction of new lines picked up with intensity, and the accompanying increase in members led Jackson EMC to establish district offices. The first, in Lawrenceville, opened in early 1952 on Collins Hill County Road. On December 1, 1952, a district office opened at Neese, and the following month, the Gainesville District office opened for business. The district offices operated weekdays from the first through the tenth of each month to give members a convenient location to pay power bills and apply for service and to put co-op employees closer to the jobsite when repairing lines.

The increase in members called for expanding communications and, in November 1952, the first issue of *Jemco News* was published, announcing the co-op's new power use department. Its employees were Evelyn Harris, hired the month before as the first home electrification advisor and charged with teaching women on Jackson EMC lines how to use electric appliances, and William Fletcher, the first farm electrification advisor, employed to teach men how to use electricity on the farm.

To pique readers' interest, *Jemco News* each month included ten members' account numbers printed within its four pages; members who spotted their account number were mailed a $1 check. The award eventually rose to $5. Willie Wiredhand, the cartoon mascot of the REA, routinely graced the pages of the publication, reminding members that electricity brought on wires was their helping hand. Because obtaining electricity had become not only fulfillment of a desire for a commodity but a status of pride and prestige, early newsletters

Beloved REA mascot Willie Wiredhand, greeted here by the thrilled daughter of a Jackson EMC member-family, made home visits to show off small electric appliances like hand-mixers, coffee pots, and cookers.

Affectionately referred to as "The Jemco Ladies," part-time workers came to the co-op each month to place address labels on *Jemco News* in preparation for mailing to members. Assisting with the task were, from left, Mrs. Una Hammock, Blondean Kelly, and Mrs. Billy Culbertson. Therese Legg and Elinor Boyd were two more Jemco Ladies.

With the introduction of the co-op's power use department and *Jemco News* monthly newsletter, electric kitchens on EMC lines were celebrated, like this one enjoyed by Mr. and Mrs. Bobby Blackwell of Homer, featured in Jackson EMC's 1957 annual report.

published names of new members who joined the cooperative. To congratulate those who used electricity to its fullest advantage, and to encourage other members to do the same, the newsletter routinely featured homes on Jackson EMC lines. In the first issue, the new home of Mr. and Mrs. Lewis Sailors in the New Virgil community of Jackson County was celebrated. Their six-room brick house featured two baths, a heating system, lighting, and electric appliances including a range, refrigerator, washing machine, and dishwasher that "will make this home a joy," according to Harris, who served as the newsletter's first editor. For the first few years of its publication, the role of *Jemco News* editor rotated among recent graduates of the University of Georgia. The newsletter soon expanded to eight pages with monthly features that included columns by the home and farm electrification advisors and co-op manager and a "Community of the Month" section spotlighting communities that worked progressively to improve conditions for their residents.

In 1952, Jackson EMC launched a ten-year expansion program after a system survey conducted the previous year indicated more facilities were needed. In 1953, construction began on four new substations and 107 miles of power lines, additions necessary to maintain full capacity power to all members.

In April 1953, Jackson EMC ranked fourth among the nation's electric cooperatives with its stellar safety record. The Employers Mutual Insurance Company honored the cooperative for accumulating 400,000 man-hours worked without loss of time due to an accident. Within days of the announcement, the streak of good fortune abruptly ended on April 13 when Lewis Shirley touched a 7,200-volt power line while working at a pole on Brockton Road. Age twenty-four at the time of the accident, Shirley had worked at Jackson EMC since

Jackson EMC linemen started wearing hard hats in 1958. This 1962 crew included, from left, J. O. Nabors, Calvin Carey, Cecil Venable, Billy Crowe, Charlie Pinion, and Douglas "Ponchie" Beck.

The co-op purchased its first bucket truck in 1964. Since there were few bucket trucks for several years, line crew workers continued to climb poles routinely.

Members of the Jackson EMC Board of Directors worked diligently to meet the needs of members, even when it meant visiting local fields to assess the soil and farming situation or confirm the best place to install the next section of power lines.

1946. His tenure as lineman would end as his injuries necessitated amputation of his right arm, but he would continue his employment with an office job and eventually became manager of operations.

To ensure safe working conditions, the cooperative followed REA guidelines that called for consistent safety training. Safety instructors visited Jackson EMC each month to remind line workers of safety regulations and procedures through talks and film presentations. The company's efforts were ramped up even more following the June 25, 1958, death of Billy Joe Wilbanks, a lineman remembered by his peers as "as one of the most friendly, likable persons who ever donned climbing boots on anybody's line crew." Relative Billy Wilbanks, who joined the Jackson EMC staff in 1961, recalled the accident: "When you climbed a pole back then you had spikes, and when Billy Joe stretched up to lock his belt, he hit the primary power line with the top of his head. No hard hat on. The next week they had hard hats." (In 2013, Wilbanks remains the only fatality at Jackson EMC. Along with Shirley, two more linemen lost limbs due to electrocution, Luther Wilkes who in 1955 lost his left arm and Douglas "Ponchie" Beck who lost both arms after a 1970 accident.)

In the fifties, before bucket trucks, linemen climbed poles every time new service was established or when storms damaged lines already constructed. As the years and the industry progressed, the introduction of hard hats, rubber gloves, bucket trucks, and other specialized gear and equipment raised the level of safety achievable by line workers and, within a few years, Jackson EMC was again awarded with safety commendations.

A significant reason for the cooperative's early success was its board of directors, according to Manager Kelly, who described the directors as "substantial and well-to-do people in their county and community who have made a success in their own business and likewise have given much of their valuable time to the proper operation of Jackson EMC." Since banding together to create the cooperative, the board members had continued to dedicate themselves to obtaining rural electricity for their communities. For the many hours they devoted to the task, they received only a small stipend for attending meetings and minimal mileage for the travel that incurred. Originally elected to one-year terms, the board in 1953 lengthened the term of service to three years and staggered the terms with three of the nine directors up for election each year. All directors attended annual meetings of Georgia EMC and a strong delegation travelled each year to NRECA's annual convention.

Joining Forces to Obtain Power

Along with routine management of the corporation, directors paid close attention to the political climate, ever ready to act when necessary to protect members' interests. One of their first tests came in the early 1950s when private power companies opposed attempts of Georgia's electric cooperatives to build transmission lines from Clark Hill Dam. Per congressional legislation, municipalities and cooperatives had preference rights on federal power generated at the Savannah River hydroelectric project. At Jackson EMC's 1953 annual meeting,

Georgia EMC Manager Walter Harrison accused private power entities of using a "tremendous cheap propaganda campaign" to label REA-funded electric cooperatives as "creeping socialism." After the meeting, an October 1953 editorial in the *Gainesville Daily Times* used a tongue-in-cheek approach in responding to the charge: "According to the Republican administration, we have a bunch of 'creeping socialists' in our neck of the woods. There are 11,000 of them, all subscribers to and members of the Jackson Electric Membership Corporation." The editorial went on to describe Jackson EMC as "a group of people who have joined forces to borrow money and supply themselves with electricity… it is not a subsidized outfit and has no price favoritism from Washington. By congressional policy, it does have the edge over public utilities in that it has a priority on government-produced power. But that's all. It's a cinch we would not have the health and prosperity we now boast without electric power co-ops and we doubt that we could continue to expand that prosperity if something should happen to them."

Like electric cooperative across the nation, Jackson EMC formed a Minutemen organization in 1958. Its members were charged with helping the cooperative share legislative concerns with co-op members. The group was named after Minutemen of the Revolutionary War who sounded the alarm when necessary and adhered to the words spoken in 1775 by Captain Parker: "Stand your ground. Don't fire unless fired upon, but if they mean to have a war, let it begin here." Admiring a plaque with that directive are, from left, Rob Kelly, manager; Phil Landrum, congressman; William Booth, board president; and Otis Cato, director.

For two more years, rural electric leaders called on their state legislators and senators to help them gain preference power at Clark Hill Dam. The local battle was supported by national leaders, namely NRECA Executive Manager Clyde Ellis who in 1954 defended the co-ops by saying: "REA has never lost a dime on a loan to a rural electric cooperative or power district. Some of them are having quite a struggle, but they are paying off. Consider that the farmers have borrowed nearly $2 billion to provide themselves with electricity, and that they are repaying cash on the barrelhead with interest and without loss to anyone… The farmers have chalked up perhaps the finest repayment record on their REA loans that has ever been known in the history of the world." In 1955, the *Atlanta Constitution* expressed the economic impact of electric cooperatives when it reported that "for every dollar loaned by the government to REA cooperatives, their members have spent $4 for electrical wiring and appliances."

In May 1956, the five-year controversy was settled when contracts for Clark Hill power were signed, enabling Georgia's electric cooperatives and municipalities to purchase power from the US government, which in turn paid Georgia Power Company a wheeling fee for transmitting the power. To assist the co-op in negotiating future political concerns, Jackson EMC members formed the Minutemen, an organization which met quarterly; similar organizations met throughout the nation to defend the rural electrics. Balfour Hunnicutt, who eventually became a member of Jackson EMC's board of directors, joined the auxiliary organization as a teenager and canvassed his community informing neighbors how they could get electricity.

Eventually, the electric cooperatives gained another defender in Washington, DC. At the NRECA's annual meeting in 1959, Jackson EMC employees and directors were pleased when then-Senator John F. Kennedy said: "The job ahead for REA supporters is to get the private power lobby out of the Government. You are not the recipients of some Federal charity—a charity which is to be cut off when the recipient is no longer poverty stricken. On the contrary, you are doing an essential job at the request of the Congress for the benefit of the entire nation—and it is the nation which is grateful to you."

Spreading the Word

Jackson EMC routinely publicized its service area, as in 1954 when it produced a sixteen-page brochure in partnership with local chambers of commerce and civic groups. The area was promoted as "rapidly moving toward industrialization after having diversified its agriculture." More than a thousand copies of the brochure, created to attract new industry, were mailed to all forty-eight states, inviting business officials to visit. "Living conditions are better; per capita income is greater," Manager Kelly wrote of the stable condition of northeast Georgia. "These and many other things contributing to a richer and fuller life have been dependent upon electricity. So it is with pride that Jackson EMC helps."

Its outreach was in line with the marketing and public relations emphasis the cooperative had used since its earliest days, starting before it was chartered, when word of mouth was the tool utilized to gain members. As surely as the cooperative had worked its first fifteen years to build a power system, its employees deliberately worked to build a positive rapport with members,

Rural electricity was credited with affording a diverse economy by powering local businesses like Hawkins Peach Orchard peach packing plant in Jackson County, circa 1956, where Joe Sims, left, and Carlton Wheeler worked by the light of a drop-cord bulb.

aware that their continued cooperation—and increased usage of electricity—was necessary to grow the local electric business.

By the mid-fifties, the word-of-mouth marketing method had given way to publications, incentives, and meetings. *Jemco News* and other publications updated members on what their electric cooperative had to offer. Incentives were advertised to provide ways of adding electric appliances at affordable prices, ensuring electricity use for the cooperative and enhancing business for area appliance dealers. Meetings were held with members, appliance dealers, government officials, and neighboring electric cooperatives on issues ranging from how to best cook a turkey in an electric oven to gaining power supply from generating facilities.

By the late fifties, televisions had become a standard electric appliance enjoyed in most homes throughout Jackson EMC's service area.

Jackson EMC rose as a leader among electric cooperatives, routinely inviting employees from other co-ops to take part in workshops, like a two-day pole inspection conference held in 1955 with seven electric cooperatives represented. In January 1956, Jackson EMC hosted ninety appliance dealers and distributors to share ideas about the potential market in its service territory. A few months earlier, the cooperative had taken advantage of that market by signing a joint-use telephone agreement that allowed a local phone company to use Jackson EMC poles

Exhibiting an eagerness to share information, Jackson EMC often led workshops attended by employees of neighboring cooperatives, including a farm meter pole seminar held in 1955.

Renovations at Jackson EMC headquarters in 1955 included an expansion that housed offices, a small auditorium, and a demonstration kitchen and laundry room.

for attaching telephone lines; likewise, the EMC would use some of their poles. The offer would be extended to other phone companies as well, providing increased phone coverage throughout northeast Georgia.

By February 1955, the amount of electricity provided by Jackson EMC had doubled every four years since the cooperative's founding, due in part to the fact that the average number of appliances for the home had increased from nineteen to fifty-four. A survey of co-op members revealed the appliance most popular in the area was the electric refrigerator; 80 percent of member-families owned one.

The year 1955 was hailed as the cooperative's most successful year to date. Renovations at the headquarters in downtown Jefferson were completed with a small auditorium that featured a modern electric kitchen and laundry for demonstrations. The growing membership, at almost twelve thousand, compelled the co-op to contract with the Remington Rand Company to modernize its consumer filing system which had out-grown office space. By December 1955, the cooperative had reduced rates twice since forming, from an average cost of 7.7 cents per kilowatt-hour in 1939 to two cents per kilowatt-hour.

In the first quarter of 1956, Jackson EMC was selected by the REA to take part in a pilot project, the Power Use Promotion, which partnered appliance dealers and electric cooperatives with a national advertising

The 1956 Power Use Promotion partnered appliance dealers with EMCs to advertise electric appliances. Jackson EMC took part in the promotion by helping members pay for wiring when installing new appliances. Here, members inspect new General Electric appliances at the 1956 annual meeting.

campaign to drive appliance, and consequently electric, sales. For consumers purchasing their first range, water heater, clothes dryer, or water pump, the cooperative would assist in paying for installation wiring. By mid-1956, more than two hundred appliances had been installed on Jackson EMC lines via the promotion. In addition, the cooperative, through REA, offered loans with a 5 percent interest rate to finance renovations and expansions of agricultural, commercial, and industrial projects.

By 1957, Jackson EMC's consistent growth necessitated expanding operations at the district offices. With an REA loan of $1.28 million granted just before Christmas that year, work began on system improvements, including new line construction and new or renovated district offices. In the summer of 1959, an open house was held at each district office, which from then on would open for business each weekday with deposit boxes available for after-hours payments.

In 1959, an open house was held at new office facilities in each district, where after-hours deposit boxes were installed to provide added convenience for members. Deborah Dawkins demonstrated how the boxes were used.

In 1960, a brick
addition at the
headquarters
facility in Jefferson
included new offices
and a lobby.

Jackson EMC invited
members to an
open house on
September 11, 1960,
at the expanded
headquarters in
Jefferson where a
lobby and offices
were added to
provide faster
and more efficient
service. Greeting
attendees were,
from left (wearing
badges), Directors
Lonie Seagraves
and William Booth
and Manager
Rob Kelly, in the
doorway at right.

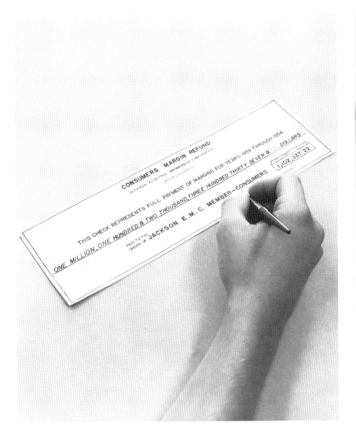

Even while the cooperative was expanding its
facilities and power system, it consistently repaid, with
interest, its REA loans. By May 1960, Jackson EMC had
borrowed approximately $5 million from the REA but
had repaid its first six loans ahead of schedule, at least
one a full twenty-two years before its due date. Equally
impressive was its record for returning margin refunds
to members; these refunds consisted of surplus above operating expenses of the not-for-profit
corporation. By July 1963, Jackson EMC had reimbursed to members more than $1 million
and boasted the highest margin refund record of any electric cooperative in Georgia. The co-
op refunded its first margins in the form of "free" electric bills to members in December 1950
and July 1951; in 1953, Jackson EMC started mailing checks to members, the amount per each
calculated by the family's power usage during the time period for which the reimbursement
represented. While the enviable financial records of the cooperative could be attributed to its
board, equal merit went to its manager.

"Mr. Kelly was a very thrifty man, which is what the company needed at that time because
things were very difficult," said Bill Carpenter, a member of the board of directors whose fifty-
one-year association with Jackson EMC began when Kelly hired him in September 1962 as
editor of *Jemco News*.

Work of the Line Crews

What some considered thrifty, others sometimes deemed penny-pinching, especially early
line workers eager for the day when improved equipment would ease the task of digging holes
and setting poles, a job still done by hand with spade and spoon, drill and hammer, or dynamite

Above left: Each year, Jackson
EMC refunds margins (surplus
above operating expenses) to its
members. By 1963, the co-op had
returned more than $1 million to
members and had the highest
margin refund record of any electric
cooperative in the state.

Above right: Bill Carpenter has been
associated with Jackson EMC for
more than half a century. He came
to work at Jackson EMC in 1962 as
editor of *Jemco News* and, after
resigning from his job as manager
of member services to go into full-
time ministry, joined the board of
directors in 1970.

In July 1955, workers on the hot line crew included, from left, Gus Davis, Jack Little, Luther Barnes, Billy Cobb, Billy Baird, and J. O. Nabors.

Billy Culbertson, left, and Jack Thomason were early Jackson EMC line workers on the Neese District crew.

Ice and snowstorms presented the greatest difficulties for electric utility workers like Clarence Wages who worked this storm in 1958.

A Letter From Your MANAGER

R.J.Kelly

R. J. KELLY

Your Cooperative is in its 25th year of providing service to those who in 1939 thought of adequate electric service as only a dream. At that time only 3½% of the families living in the rural areas outside the municipalities in our state had electric service.

The usefulness of electric service was visualized by many but the task of extending lines into the rural areas with rates the users could afford was an overwhelming problem. It was also difficult to determine the *best* method of extending electric service to sparsely settled locations.

FDR's Dream

Our late President, Franklin D. Roosevelt, while at Warm Springs, Georgia, some 28 years ago, envisioned a way to provide funds so that electric power could be extended at a reasonable price to rural people.

From the day in 1939, when the Jackson E.M.C. began, your Cooperative has grown to cover an eight county service area with approximately 18,000 member-consumers. We now have nine substations located to deliver the required level of voltage to the consumer meter.

WW II Slowed Progress

For several years after organization and beginning of construction, much had to be done about securing applications for membership, getting the required membership fees, and planning the right-of-way where lines were to be located. The trend of progress was slowed during World War II years when materials were not available.

The small group that pioneered the work in those days never realized the potential that would be available in the future years for users living in our area. They had only planned to use electricity for lights, electric irons, radios, and possibly refrigerators. Since that time, consumption of electric power has increased as a wide array of electrical appliances has been added. Through the years member-consumer usage has increased, but rates have decreased.

JEMCO NEWS Began in 1952

Well do I remember at the Annual Meeting in 1952, our president, William H. Booth, announced to the Cooperative membership that plans were being made for publication of a Cooperative paper to be distributed to all members. At that time we were hesitant as what the content of the paper should be. I quote from the first issue, *"This is your newsletter, so if the items we print are not in accord with what you want, please let us know as we want to keep it interesting and informative."*

Since that time, we have tried to bring you through the JEMCO NEWS (as it was named by one of our readers in Winder, Georgia), information on the best use of electric power, material to help you keep your appliances and farm equipment at the best operating level, and general news of your Cooperative's work.

One item which we have carried on throughout the years of publication is the publishing of ten account numbers chosen at random over the geographical area served by the Cooperative. These numbers are located on the pages of the newspaper to be recognized by the reader. If the reader notifies the office by a given date, that reader is mailed a check for $1.00.

These past 25 years have been years of growth for your Cooperative. Your assistance in making this growth possible is greatly appreciated.

2 ● JEMCO NEWS ● April, 1963

Jemco News
117 Athens Street
Jefferson, Ga.

Vol. 11 ● April, 1963 ● No. 7

R. J. KELLY, *General Manager*

BOARD OF DIRECTORS

W. H. BOOTH
Jackson Director
President

W. C. ALEXANDER   J. V. BOOKER
Banks Director   *Barrow Director*
Vice-President   *Sec.-Treas.*
E. R. HODGSON   JONES WEBB
Clarke Director   *Gwinnett Director*
O. L. CATO   HAYWOOD O'KELLEY
Hall Director   *Lumpkin Director*
T. N. STOVALL
Madison Director

T. D. STOREY
Staff Assistant
C. ELMO WALLER, *Office Manager*
J. FLOY BULLOCK
Engineering Services
L. W. SHIRLEY
Electric Operations
E. E. THURMOND, JR.
Member Education & Public Relations

JEMCO NEWS

Published monthly by the Member Education and Public Relations Department of Jackson Electric Membership Corporation and mailed to all members and consumers of this rural electric cooperative. Ideas and suggestions welcomed from readers. Subscription rate: 50 cents per year. Second class mail privileges authorized at Jefferson, Ga.

EVELYN HARRIS
Home Service Advisor
BILL CARPENTER
Editor

Is this your account number? J79-32-5-30

JACKSON
ELECTRIC MEMBERSHIP CORPORATION

OPERATING REPORT

	Feb., 1962	Feb., 1963
Consumers	16,720	17,506
KWH Sold	8,565,260	8,290,090
Average KWH	523	481
Amt. Billed	$150,826.15	$160,131.12
Average Bill	$9.18	$9.30
Minimum Bills	1432	1524
Miles of Lines	2,862.43	2,899.51
Consumers Added	58	62

ON THE COVER

The top scene on the cover shows the ground breaking ceremony which signaled the beginning of the construction of the Jackson E.M.C. on January 2, 1939.

The lower scene is the energizing ceremony for the Jackson E.M.C.'s first 100 miles of line on April 10, 1939. Left to right are: L. C. Seagraves, R. J. Kelly, W. C. Alexander, J. C. Head, R. T. Farmer, J. W. Cato, J. W. Jackson, John Whealler, and W. A. Mathis.

Is this your account number? L79-140

Jemco News kept members informed of progress in the cooperative's service area.

that was kept on company trucks. In 1953, only two line crews were employed by the cooperative. New hires started out on the ground, fetching supplies for the men who climbed poles. After learning the job of the lineman, the helpers, or ground men, were promoted to line workers who set poles, dug anchor holes, put in anchors, and strung lines. The cooperative's first line truck, a hydraulic pole-setting truck, was purchased in 1964 along with a three-quarter ton truck with a six-man cab, which enabled the co-op to utilize more men per crew. Up to that point, most line crews consisted of three workers—a lead lineman, lineman, and helper. The line crews "caught trouble," the lineman's lingo for responding to outage calls. Their trucks were equipped with radios on which they received outage and construction calls.

Storm work, always troublesome, was especially difficult in the 1960s when equipment was minimal. An ice storm during the holiday season in 1962 was particularly severe in the Gwinnett District with manpower limited and equipment scarce. The storm started the night before Christmas Eve and the crew did not return home until the day after Christmas. As with many storms, employees often had to put the same line up twice after ice re-accumulated, causing it to fall again, or a nearby tree laden with ice fell across it. During the worst storms, the electric system that line crews had worked for years to build came crashing down all at one time.

Years of line construction were destroyed with the creation of Lake Lanier which, when filled due to completion of Buford Dam on the Chattahoochee River in 1956, washed over a racetrack and grandstands, numerous houses, a golf course, and acreage once crossed by miles of electric power lines. While lake water covered land previously developed, the lake sparked new development of homes and lakeside communities calling for line construction.

The creation of Lake Lanier in 1956 resulted in the loss of years' worth of electric line construction.

Lake Lanier provided new opportunities for development as homes and neighborhoods began to spring up around it in the 1960s.

Appreciation Expressed

The can-do work ethic of the co-op's employees made Jackson EMC a self-sufficient company. Employees did all their own printing, building maintenance, meter and transformer repair, right-of-way clearing, line construction, blueprinting, photography, data processing, and maintenance for their fleet of twenty-seven vehicles, handling even major repairs like engine and transmission overhauls. The in-house handiwork of its employees served the cooperative and its members well by shaving expenses.

The community at large took note. The August 14, 1952, edition of *The Jackson Herald* lauded Jackson EMC's progress and praised Kelly as "a great leader, a loyal citizen and the man with a dream." Further acknowledgment came from *The Jackson Herald* in October 1961 when N. S. Hayden reported that 99 percent of those living in Jackson EMC territory received electric power, a far cry from the 3 percent who received it in 1938. "Its building is one of the beauties of Jefferson and its personnel are working members of civic and religious groups in all communities," Hayden wrote. "The efficiency with which the corporation conducts its business and the pride in the service which it renders cannot help but rub off on its member-owners who reflect this pride in their attendance and active participation in the corporation's activities."

Expanding his influence, Kelly joined fifty-four business and agricultural leaders from throughout Georgia in April 1962 on a nineteen-day European goodwill tour through Belgium, Hungary, Russia, Poland, and East and West Berlin. After his return, Kelly often spoke of the tour and presented a slide presentation about the European countries to school students and civic groups, noting the poverty and lack of industry there.

Above: Expansion of power lines through the rural environs of Jackson EMC territory was a continuous task as evidenced in this 1958 photo. On the ground, lineman Gus Davis (left) and Herman Weldon assist linemen at the pole.

Right: Members of Jackson EMC routinely participated in co-op activities, as illustrated in this photo from 1961.

In the summer of 1962, Jackson EMC staff members received safe driving awards. Honored were, from left, front row: J. L. Langston, George McGinnis, Talmadge Carter, Charlie Pinion, Robert Boyd, Robert Edwards, Jim Ivey, and Gene Thurmond. Second row: David Dorsey, Rob Kelly, Broughton Nabors, Evelyn Harris, Morgan Pounds, Jack Thomason, Bobby Gunter, and Roger Thomason. Third row: Herman Weldon, Eugene Moore, Billy Culbertson, J. H. Jones, Foster Seabolt, Luther Barnes, Clarence Wages, Gus Davis, and Boyd Daves. Fourth row: Doug Wilkes, Henry Pinion, Tom Gainer, and Billy Baird.

While other areas of the world were lacking, at home in Jackson EMC territory improved living conditions seemed to parallel success of the electric cooperative. In 1964, the co-op's engineering staff conducted studies to determine where new stations and larger circuits, transformers, and wires were needed. Employees at the time were converting single-phase lines to stronger, three-phase wires in Jackson, Madison and Gwinnett Counties. The same year, the co-op installed its first computer, an undertaking handled by Manager of Office Services Elmo Waller. In prior years, power bills had been printed off-site by computer at Southern Engineering

Manager of Office Services Elmo Waller installed the cooperative's first computer system in 1964.

Company in Atlanta, returned by bus to Jefferson, and mailed to members from there. Waller brought the cooperative into the computer age after he painstakingly worked for weeks to assemble an IBM punch-card accounting system, a large and bulky mainframe computer that consumed a whole room. Waller said the conversion "took more out of me than any project in my career."

In 1965, facility improvements were completed at the Jefferson headquarters where a 250-seat auditorium was added. A similar auditorium, truck storage, and new offices were added at the Gainesville District office. Growth was on an uptick—at the cooperative and in the communities it served.

On May 1, 1965, Manager Kelly spent the day at Jackson EMC doing inventory, according to coworkers who assisted him in the task. That evening, he died of an apparent heart attack. "It was a shock to everybody because he had worked all day, and people said he was jolly, talking," his daughter-in-law recalled.

Jackson EMC's first manager had been a committed community leader, serving as secretary of the Jefferson Chamber of Commerce and president of the Jefferson Rotary Club. Part of his legacy was that his son, Sam, followed in his footsteps, becoming manager at another Georgia electric cooperative, Slash Pine EMC in Homerville. A tribute to Kelly reported that his life and activities had been characterized by devoted service to his Lord, his family, his fellow man, his community, and to Jackson EMC. By example, he had taught others to continually plan ahead and look forward to reaching lofty goals.

Near the end of World War II, Kelly had envisioned the growth boom that eventually would hit Gwinnett County, and he did all he could to project that vision for Jackson EMC, even when it meant running electricity on barbed wire. His lasting legacy would be his foresight and planning, attributes that opened the gate for phenomenal growth to come.

At the time of Rob Kelly's death, Jackson EMC served approximately twenty thousand members. In 2013, it supplies electricity to more than ten times that many.

Opposite page: Rob Kelly, right, was remembered as a "hands-on" manager who accompanied linemen to the worksite, often pitching in to build the system. Here, he joined Clarence Wages to install a meter at Candler School in Hall County.

Chapter Seven

Teaching a Region How to Use Electricity

"Electricity is but yet a new agent for the arts and manufactures, and, doubtless, generations unborn will regard with interest this century, in which it has been first applied to the wants of mankind."
—Alfred Smee
Nineteenth-century chemist and inventor of the Smee battery

After World War II ended, a new flurry of activity consumed the next few years as power lines were extended, lighting the homes of patient farm families whose applications for service had lain dormant through the war years. By 1952, the directors and staff of Jackson EMC were finally able to catch their collective breath and make the next move. When they created the power use department in October 1952, they set in motion wheels that would move forward the growth of the cooperative, and the paralleled prosperity of the whole region, for decades to come.

From the co-op's beginning, employees had provided basic instruction on how to use electric appliances and equipment, but there had been no one dedicated to seeing that members used their appliances and farm equipment to the best advantage. Home and farm electrification advisors would fill that gap.

Rural electricity afforded lighted, outdoor Christmas displays, providing holiday cheer to the countryside in a way not previously experienced.

Opposite page: Beginning in the 1950s and through the next decade, Jackson EMC's annual meetings were held on the campus of the Jefferson headquarters on Athens Street, under an enormous tent, as depicted in this photo from the 1961 annual meeting.

Home demonstration council groups met throughout the counties served by Jackson EMC in the middle decades of the twentieth century. Jackson EMC home advisors were routine guests at the meetings where they shared know-how on use of electric appliances and tips on cooking, freezing, laundering, and more.

To inform members of the advantages of electric pumps, Jackson EMC joined with Walton EMC and Georgia Power Company in October 1955 to present a Water Systems Fair at Winder. Thousands of area farmers attended to learn how their workload could be reduced with electric-powered equipment.

Electrification advisors traveled the cooperative territory putting on demonstrations on everything from proper lamp lighting, above, to wiring poultry houses. Evelyn Harris, center, showed EMC members of all ages how to wire an electric lamp.

Jackson EMC home and farm electrification advisors routinely drew up wiring plans for members and stressed adequate wiring at annual meetings as in 1955 when they set up this display.

In the weeks leading up to Christmas, lighting and holiday decorating workshops were presented at home demonstration council meetings, high school home economics classes, and for various women's groups in the eight counties served by the co-op. On December 12, Jackson EMC and neighboring Walton EMC held the co-ops' first cooking school in the Lawrenceville High School auditorium for all EMC members and Gwinnett County residents, whether or not they were on EMC lines. The all-day event focused on home and farm lighting and included a freezer demonstration. The grand prize, a Frigidaire range, was won by Marie Maddox, a home economics student at Lawrenceville High whose family still cooked on a wood-burning stove.

At the co-op office in Jefferson, calls were fielded from members seeking help in using their new freezers and ovens, asking questions about lighting and kitchen planning, or seeking assistance in developing wiring plans. The new appliances made possible by electricity seemed mysterious, and sometimes threatening, to those first acquiring electric service. Farm wives didn't know how to preserve food in electric freezers or if eating food that had been frozen was safe. Home economists educated the rural population on how to safely and effectively use the new equipment and, in turn, farm families purchased more of the life-altering appliances.

The January 1953 newsletter reported an early power use department success. Rachel Wall of Barrow County had been stumped on her kitchen remodel. Upon reading the first issue of *Jemco News* and discovering the assistance Jackson EMC offered, she called the co-op and received help in devising a kitchen-wiring plan. Augusta Jenkins, raised on a Madison County farm and schooled at Ila, recalled a Jackson EMC employee visiting her parents' home to show the family how to use the range properly. When she built her own house, Jenkins obtained the co-op's help when placing her electrical outlets. "I had good lighting in my house and it was due to Jackson EMC helping me put the outlets where they needed to be," said Jenkins.

The volume of calls that came in for assistance confirmed the local interest in all things electric and prompted the cooperative to escalate their efforts. The board approved purchase of a station wagon to use for hauling displays when conducting workshops. Help was enlisted from the ladies of Jemco-land, the nickname attributed to Jackson EMC territory soon after the newsletter caught on. Meetings were held in each of the co-op's eight counties, soliciting volunteers to serve as power use leaders in their communities, leading workshops

Power use leaders received specialized training at laundry and other workshops conducted at the University of Georgia and shared their knowledge with neighbors through Jackson EMC communications and Ladies Day meetings.

Power use leaders volunteered to show their neighbors how to effectively and efficiently use electricity to their advantage. Home Electrification Advisor Evelyn Harris, far right, coordinated the program and awarded top power use leaders at the September 1957 annual meeting.

and answering neighbors' questions about electricity. Participation was defined as the patriotic thing to do. The co-op newsletter described the power use leader as "a true American to help her neighbors get the most for their kilowatt dollar and understand their electrical problems." By the end of 1953, more than one hundred power use leaders had volunteered and county leaders were named to coordinate their efforts. Workshops that included freezing and wiring demonstrations and leadership lessons were held to teach the ladies how to effectively pass on electrical information to their neighbors. The power use leaders received additional training at laundry and other workshops conducted at the University of Georgia where factory representatives demonstrated how to use the latest electric appliances.

In its first year, the power use department gave 146 demonstrations, visited 294 homes, and held 152 meetings attended by 5,292 participants. Home demonstration agents, home economics teachers, and appliance dealers helped provide classes to ladies groups and 4-H and Future Homemakers of America (FHA) students. Kitchen parties consisted of small groups learning how to cook with an electric range and smaller appliances. The programs attracted ladies from every corner of Jemco-land, helping to build the reputation of Jackson EMC as an active, helpful cooperative concerned about its members' needs.

The major focus of the early educational programs was on lighting as homes previously dependent on kerosene lanterns or gas for lamp lighting transitioned to electric illumination. Almost always, lighting was the first use for electricity in rural homes, but often not every room in a house included a bulb. Housewives soon realized more light was needed to adequately illuminate the home, so the home electrification advisor taught ladies and youth how to make "pin-up lamps," portable lighting that could be moved around the house to

Left: Home Electrification Advisor Evelyn Harris, back, leads a "Better Sight, Better Light" lamp-making demonstration for area youth in 1964. Jackson EMC's Youth Electric Project reached approximately five thousand young people each year by providing them opportunities to learn about electricity through 4-H and FFA projects.

Right: Jackson EMC annually sponsored a light bulb sales contest with clubs allowed to keep ten cents from each package of bulbs they sold for their organization. Individual winners of the 1960 light bulb sales campaign were, from left, Mrs. Lonie Seagraves, first place winner, of the Sanford Home Demonstration Club in Madison County; Mrs. Truitt Brown, second, and Mrs. W. C. Alexander, third, were both of the Better Homes Demonstration Club in Jackson County.

provide lighting where needed. Georgia Power Company and the University of Georgia Extension Services teamed with the cooperative to host lighting programs. In the 1950s, Jackson EMC offered a fundraising opportunity that improved home lighting while supporting the causes of participating organizations that sold packages of 75-, 100- and 150-watt light bulbs and pocketed part of the proceeds. Sales were encouraged by cautioning mothers about the hazards posed to children studying by the light from low-wattage bulbs.

Popularity of its educational programs led Jackson EMC in 1955 to construct its onsite auditorium, which included an all-electric kitchen and laundry where refrigerators, stoves, and other large appliances were on permanent display. Members were invited to inspect appliances when contemplating purchases, and workshops on laundering and cooking were held with attendants gathering at the co-op. The ladies events typically included a covered dish lunch.

Electricity on the Farm

Just as home electrification advisors helped homemakers, farm electrification advisors worked with area farmers and agricultural organizations to teach proper wiring and wise use of electricity, the "hired hand" that was helping farmers to maintain production in the wake of an exodus of farm workers.

In rural northeast Georgia, farming had been the thread that wove community life for generations. Families had sustained themselves by working the land and, as their farms grew larger, sold their harvest to sustain

Above, inset: Chestnut Mountain Hatchery started out as a small operation in Hall County.

Above: In part due to increased productivity made possible by rural electricity, Chestnut Mountain Hatchery expanded its operations to become one of the area's top producers.

others. For those who lived in the country, the farm was part of daily life, no matter the family's relationship to it. Several had inherited family farms with many acres rich in crops. Others worked in town but came home every afternoon to a small homestead where they milked a cow or two and planted a garden each spring. And there were many who lived on and worked the farm as tenant farmers. For all of them, the farm supplied a livelihood, sustenance, or both.

At the O'Shields' two-hundred-acre farm in Gwinnett County, both livelihood and sustenance were provided. Selena O'Shields Arnold recalled working the family's "cotton and truck farm" with her three sisters. Her parents grew vegetables and raised chickens that her father loaded onto a pickup truck and hauled into Atlanta to "peddle" each Wednesday and Saturday. Arnold often joined her father on the excursions, going door to door in residential neighborhoods along his route. For fun, she and her sisters attended the occasional taffy pulling when not roaming the pastures of their home place at Pleasant Hill, where car dealerships now do business along Satellite Boulevard; then, their nearest neighbors were a mile and a half away. She remembered watching Jackson EMC linemen putting up poles and stringing wire, daily inching closer to her home.

Above: Taking advantage of electric equipment that increased productivity, brooder farms became common sights in Hall County. The co-op offered an electric brooder incentive plan that helped pay for wiring for farmers who switched to electric brooding.

Right: Poultry production of all types, including turkeys, in the 1950s led Hall County to being called the "Poultry Capital of the World."

Retired employee Gilbert Wier said it was 1947 before his family got electricity at their farm where his father raised sheep to produce wool he sold to Sears Roebuck. "When electricity came, he bought electric sheep shears," Wier recalled. "The sheep jumped around the first time they heard the clippers, but it was a tremendous help."

By the mid-1950s, row cropping in northeast Georgia was giving way to chicken farms, especially in Hall County where Gainesville gained a reputation as the "Poultry Capital of the World." Rural electricity can be credited with the rise of the poultry industry: as more northeast Georgia farms obtained electricity, more chicken houses were constructed to take advantage of the modern farming methods that electricity afforded.

As mystifying as has been the age-old dilemma—"Which came first, the chicken or the egg?"—it is similarly difficult to determine what first amplified the poultry industry in northeast Georgia. Was it the increasing number of chicken houses that prompted processing plants to pop up, or did the presence of modern processing plants encourage farmers to build more chicken houses? Perhaps it was a combination of both, plus the innovation of Jesse Jewell, the man most credited with the poultry industry's boom in the mid-fifties and for whom Gainesville's Jesse Jewell Parkway is named. A Hall County native, Jewell pioneered vertical integration in the state's poultry industry, combining all

Co-op linemen, at left, hustle to supply a local egg operation with adequate electricity.

stages of the business into one company that handled production of raw materials, processing, and distribution. His innovations made him a national leader in the poultry industry. His were the first refrigerated trucks to haul chickens produced in Georgia across the continent into California, making Jesse Jewell chickens available to consumers throughout the country. It changed the state's chicken industry, and more poultry followed. Hatcheries set up shop as the industry flourished, producing a stable economy with respectable paychecks, especially in Hall and Lumpkin Counties.

Farm Electrification Advisor Jack Aultman, right, shows a local farmer and new Jackson EMC member how to read the new electric meter at his poultry farm.

Serving later as Jackson EMC's Hall County director, Ray Jones started his career in the poultry industry in 1955 at Crystal Farms in Hall County and, in 1978, joined two others to form J&S (Jones and Strickland) Farms, producing commercial eggs and manufacturing and selling poultry feed. Jones was one of numerous members of the Jackson EMC Board of Directors who lent farming knowledge and expertise to an organization planted in farmland. For just as farming had been the backbone of rural life, farmers in northeast Georgia had been the driving force in establishing Jackson EMC. Almost if not all of the founding directors farmed. William Booth operated a peach, cattle, and cotton farm in Jackson County; William C. Alexander raised beef cattle and hogs in the Hudson River community of Banks County; Rupert Talmadge Farmer raised cattle in the New Harmony community of Jackson County; and Lonie Seagraves raised cattle and row crops on his Madison County farm near Hull.

Directors who followed farmed as well. Barrow County Director Johnny Booker raised beef cattle and poultry and was among the first to use modern electric equipment in his poultry houses. Gwinnett County Director L. C. "Luke" Kilgore raised chickens at his farm near Dacula. E. R. Hodgson Jr. of Clarke County managed a 450-acre farm in Athens and owned a 230-acre grain and cattle farm. A. D. Pierce farmed and ran a country store in Lumpkin County, and Aaron McKinney farmed and operated a ham-curing plant in Jackson County. Ernest McLocklin, who served as vice president of the first FFA club in Georgia, worked as general manager of the North Georgia Production Credit Association and raised beef cattle in Barrow County. An early conservationist, Lumpkin County Director Haywood O'Kelley owned a 550-acre farm where he planted pastures and built ponds to conserve water. Gwinnett County Director A. T. "Troy" Sharpton operated a 300-acre beef cattle and poultry farm and was hailed as the first farmer in Gwinnett County to plant fescue, a "wonder grass" hardy

Left: At the annual power use meeting at the Jackson EMC auditorium in Jefferson in 1960, Myron Luttrell, a home economist employed by W. D. Alexander Company of Atlanta, demonstrated freezing and cooking with electric appliances. The twenty-fifth anniversary of the REA was celebrated that year as the "Silver Jubilee of Rural Electrification."

Below: A skit at the May 26, 1960, power use meeting featured "Mrs. Dreamer," seated at center, tormented by the pre-electric chores awaiting her, like hauling water in pails from the creek, bringing in firewood, and washing clothes with a scrub board.

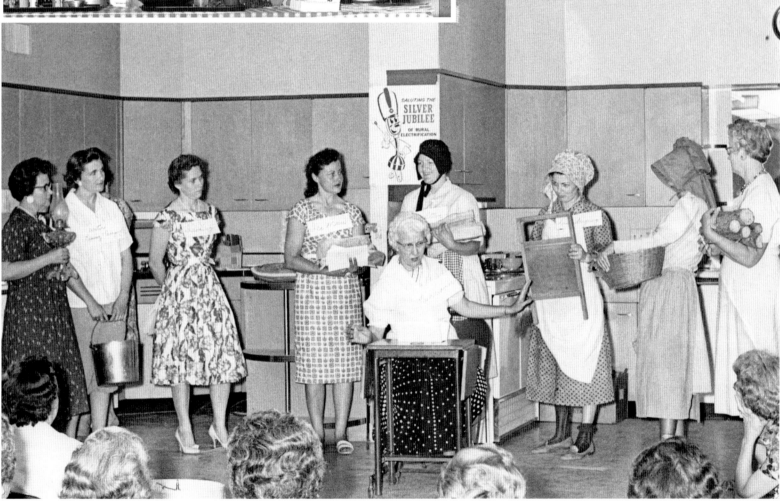

enough to survive the state's harsh winters and hot summers. Like Sharpton, many of the directors were members of their community's Farm Bureau, Farmers Mutual Exchange, Soil and Water Conservation District, and/or Agricultural Stabilization and Conservation Service committee.

Farmer and dairyman Otis Cato joined the Jackson EMC board in 1948, filling the Hall County seat left vacant by the death of his father, J. W. Cato, who joined the board in 1939. A rural electric pioneer who had travelled the countryside urging his neighbors to join the cooperative, J. W. had been accompanied by his son,

Cattle farmer H. M. Peabody of Pendergrass was featured in the 1953 *Jemco News* as a co-op member who adhered to that year's annual meeting slogan of "Let Electricity Work for You" when he crafted a hay elevator to lift bales into his hayloft minus sore muscles and an aching back.

Otis, and instilled in him a love of the land and a call to duty. The younger Cato served on the co-op board until his death in 1976 and was recalled as an innovator in farming methods. On his 450-acre Hall County farm near Gainesville, Otis Cato produced broilers and hens, beef cattle, grain, grass and clover seed.

Dedicated to conservation before it was a buzzword, Cato served as a district supervisor for the Upper Chattahoochee Soil and Water Conservation District for almost forty years and as secretary-treasurer of the Resource Conservation and Development Project in a thirteen-county area in northeast Georgia. He and his family were honored as "Farm Family of the Year" in 1961 by *Progressive Farmer* magazine and the University of Georgia. A master farmer, Cato created pastures where none existed and planted Hall County's first fescue pasture by spending $40 on fescue seed, fertilizer, and lime to turn ten acres of eroded land into green grass. In an area where erosion was common, row cropping that had been popular during the thirties and forties was suffering by mid-century, leading to creation of the Soil Conservation Service to address the issue.

To make a living off the land through the fifties, farmers had to be progressive. Less than two decades after Jackson EMC was organized, the face of farming in the region had changed. Thousands of farm workers had left northeast Georgia farms, and further reduction in manpower was predicted as farmhands left in favor of industrial jobs that paid higher wages. Using more electricity on the farm helped fill the gap. Automatic feeders cut in half the time it took to feed chickens. Electric milking machines reduced by half the time it took for dairymen to milk their herd. Increased use of electricity on the farm eased the work and upped production, like in Jackson County where H. M. Peabody assembled an elevator with an electric motor to lift hay bales into his hayloft. "Without electricity it would be impossible for me to operate my dairy," said Ralph Cable, an Athens farmer who counted on assistance from the co-op's farm electrification advisor when wiring his farm.

Most, if not all, of the cooperative's electrification advisors were University of Georgia graduates schooled in agriculture engineering. In that respect, Jackson EMC was ahead of the curve, hiring college-educated employees to share advanced farming techniques with its members. Supplying electricity was the foremost goal but not the only goal. Jackson EMC was willing to spend the money it took to hire educated people to teach members how to use electricity on the farm and in the home, efficiently and economically. Equipped with ag engineering degrees and Jackson EMC work ethic and experience, most of the electrification advisors went on to become professional electrical engineers, senior staff managers at Jackson EMC, or president/CEOs of other cooperatives.

Through the fifties and sixties, farm electrification advisors worked with the Farm Bureau, 4-H, and FFA clubs and invited men to Jackson EMC headquarters for supper meetings that focused on wiring and water pump education. The co-op advised farmers on what one kilowatt-hour of electricity could power. For as little as one-and-a-half cents, one kilowatt-hour could milk thirty cows or cool ten gallons of milk, hatch four chickens in an incubator, or light a poultry house with one hundred birds for four days.

Above: Men of Jackson EMC territory routinely gathered at the co-op headquarters for supper meetings that emphasized education about farm wiring.

Right: Larry Glass was named Jackson EMC's Outstanding Young Farmer in 1966. The co-op sponsored the young farmer competition to promote farming in the counties it served.

In 1957 and 1958, Georgia was tops in the nation in broiler production. Among the state's thirteen counties ranked as top producers were four in Jackson EMC territory: Hall, Jackson, Lumpkin, and Gwinnett. A 1950s advertising campaign claimed to the nation that "Wise Buyers Choose Georgia Fryers." To assist local producers, Jackson EMC held promotional campaigns with the cooperative helping pay the cost to wire chicken houses, as long as the layout was followed as planned by the co-op. To promote farming, Jackson EMC held an "Outstanding Young Farmer" competition.

Reaching Members in Multiple Ways

Farmwives through the fifties and sixties attended cooking schools sponsored by the cooperative in partnership with manufacturers and organizations like Frigidaire and home demonstration groups. Homemakers packed Jackson EMC auditoriums to witness demonstrations by top home economists who showed attendees how to roast, bake, and broil with electric appliances. Usually, an entire meal was prepared with guests invited to sample the results. Typically, the recipes were as simple and straightforward as the farm women who filled most of the seats at the cooking schools. To show members

Jackson EMC joined electric cooperatives across the nation to promote living better electrically through the Medallion Home Program, which featured a gold or bronze medallion awarded to members whose homes met specific criteria in wiring, lighting, insulation, and appliance standards.

Mr. and Mrs. W. H. Kesler watched as Farm Electrification Advisor Jim Carlton placed a gold medallion plaque at the front door of their new home in Gainesville, circa 1960.

how the ideal kitchen displayed at cooking schools could be obtained in their homes, Jackson EMC sponsored open houses, with assistance from members who welcomed neighbors into their electrified kitchens during the co-op's annual Show of Homes.

In 1958, the cooperative joined in the electric industry's national Medallion Home Program campaign designed to raise living standards by increasing efficient residential electricity use. The program featured a bronze or gold medallion awarded to builders or homeowners whose newly constructed houses met or exceeded lighting, wiring, insulation, and appliance standards. The overall purpose of the program was to stimulate

The co-op played a significant role in local youth education by contributing materials and leading workshops for Future Farmers of America, Future Homemakers of America, and 4-H clubs. Kicking off Jackson EMC's 1958–59 Youth Electric Project were, from left, H. E. Hemphill, Madison County High vocational-agriculture instructor; Evelyn Harris, co-op home electrification advisor; Paul Chastain, district 4-H agent, Athens; Betty Thrasher, home economics teacher, Jackson County High School; and Sara Carnes, home demonstration agent, Jackson County.

construction and sales of new homes with electric features, and some who achieved gold medallion status were featured in *Jemco News*. The Otis Skelton family of Winder was awarded Jackson EMC's first gold medallion in 1959 and was featured in that year's Jackson EMC Show of Homes.

Jackson EMC teamed with the Georgia Department of Commerce and Georgia Institute of Technology in the late fifties to conduct industrial development workshops in Madison and Banks Counties, which had been counted among Georgia's rural counties with decreasing populations. Jackson EMC's willingness to step forward in times of crisis to address community concerns would be replayed over and over in years to come.

In 1959, each of the co-op's district offices—Gainesville, Neese, and Lawrenceville—went from opening ten days a month to maintaining full-service hours

Barbara Brown, daughter of Mr. and Mrs. Wilton Brown of Homer in Banks County, put together a prize-winning lighting exhibit for the 1959 Jackson EMC Youth Electric Project and went on to become the state's first National 4-H Club electric project winner.

each weekday with a permanent staff. When the district offices needed help to keep up with the demand for new electric service, they called the headquarters office in Jefferson, which sent assistance when they could spare workers and equipment.

Jackson EMC routinely applauded its members who made their mark in the community. One family's members, in particular, were mentioned often in the co-op newsletter—the Mays Venable Sr. family of Jackson County's Brockton community. Among their achievements, Mrs. Venable was named one of eight national 4-H alumnae, Mr. Venable was a director of Georgia Farm Bureau and president of the Jackson County Farm Bureau, daughter Joyce was president of the Georgia 4-H Club Council, daughter Patricia was a national 4-H winner, and son Mays Jr. was the first-prize winner in the 1957 Jackson EMC Youth Electric Project. Other Jackson EMC members noted for achievements were Barbara Brown of Banks County, whose work in the cooperative's Youth Electric Project led her to become Georgia's first National 4-H Club Electric winner, and Mrs. Lonie Seagraves, named Georgia's Homemaker of the Year in 1962. The widow of Jackson EMC director Lonie Seagraves, she served many years as a power use leader and helped organize the Northeast Georgia Area

Mr. and Mrs. Lonie Seagraves stand amazed at the family cat atop their electric power pole. Mr. Seagraves was a founding director of Jackson EMC and his wife was an active power use leader and Georgia's Homemaker of the Year in 1962.

Planning Commission. Upon receiving her award, she said, "There was a time when mothers concentrated just on their family, but a real homemaker today must be concerned with her neighbors and the welfare of the community as a whole."

The Annual Meeting of Members

Of all its initiatives and events, none was more anticipated than the co-op's annual meeting. As did EMCs throughout the nation, Jackson EMC depended on annual meetings to gather the sufficient number of voting members to handle important business decisions. The first annual meetings were held at the Jackson County Courthouse and later at the headquarters in Jefferson. The early meetings were mostly business, with perhaps a talk given by the manager and a few prizes distributed. As the co-op's membership started to grow after World War II, so did the number needed to achieve a quorum, thereby necessitating an increasingly attractive program to entice members to attend the all-important business session. Electric appliance and equipment dealers were invited to exhibit and demonstrate their products. Entertainment was introduced in the form of talent competitions, and an electronic-talking Willie Wiredhand amused children and adults alike. Appliance dealers sponsored a cake baking contest and members were invited to bring a picnic lunch to enjoy with friends and family on the co-op grounds. A giant circus tent was pitched to ward off heat from the August sun.

Left: Held August 18–19, the 1950 annual meeting invited members to learn about electric range cooking from Crosley's famous "talking range," which was on display at the co-op warehouse along with many other appliance and equipment displays.

Myrtle Gross, home economist for Crosley Distributing Corporation, performed an electric range cooking demonstration at the annual meeting in 1951. Annual meetings through the next two decades featured displays of water pumps, irrigation equipment, egg coolers, home electric appliances, and other electric equipment.

The 1950 annual meeting featured a Case tractor display and a tractor-driving contest. Congratulating contest winner Norman Nunn, standing on tractor at steering wheel, were, from left, kneeling: M. P. Smyth, Dick Storey, Frary Elrod, and H. W. Perkerson. Standing: Paul Crawford and F. C. Staton.

Annual Members Meeting on August 18-19,1950

Case Tractor outside display. Seated left to right: M.P. Smyth, Dick Storey, Frary Elrod, H.W. Perkerson. Standing left to right: Paul Crawford,F.C. Staton and Norman Nunn winner of tractor driving contest seated on tractor.

The board of directors at this 1950s-era annual meeting included, from left, E. R. Hodgson, William C. Alexander, Rupert Talmadge Farmer, Lonie C. Seagraves, George W. Westmoreland (attorney), Otis L. Cato, John V. Booker, and L. C. Kilgore.

A talking Willie Wiredhand entertained youngsters at early annual meetings, including this one in 1959.

Winners in the 1955 cake baking contest held at that year's annual meeting were, from left, Carolyn Barnett, Mrs. Webb Williams, Mrs. J. L. McMullan, Mrs. D. J. Fuller, Mrs. Broadus Cash, Mrs. W. H. Porter, Mrs. H. C. Baird, and Mrs. O. B. Hale.

Jackson EMC pitched a gigantic tent to accommodate the growing attendance at annual meetings, which by 1961 had grown to include more than four thousand members and guests.

Each year, directors and management reviewed attendance at the annual meeting in order to plan for the next year's event, keeping in mind what might best attract members to attend. In 1953, a beauty contest was introduced with Miss Jackson EMC crowned to represent the organization in the community and at state and national pageant competitions. Judges considered beauty, poise, talent, and homemaking ability. In the twelve years the contest was held, one winner, Brenda Parham, went on to claim the title of Miss Georgia

Annual meetings through the 1950s began with registration at the back of the co-op headquarters in Jefferson where employees were kept busy checking the official member roll in order to assure proper registration.

Electrification in 1964. Marion (Legg) Mahaffey, Miss Jackson EMC of 1957, eventually worked in Jackson EMC's member services department as a home electrification advisor.

Significant modifications were made to the annual meeting in 1957 when the date was moved from August to September and a barbecue lunch was provided to all attending. By moving the meeting to a cooler month and offering families a free meal, the directors hoped to attract enough members to this meeting, even more important than usual because the cooperative's twenty-year charter had to be renewed by member vote in order for business to continue. The event was expanded to two days with the beauty contest held on Friday night, along with a youth rally for students who had participated in the Jackson EMC Youth Electric Project. Both the youth project and beauty contest would be judged on Friday night with winners announced during the business session on Saturday. A driving rain threatened to foil the

The 1956 annual meeting was a joy for both adults and children, including the youngsters shown here. Employees' children, some barefooted, feasting on barbecue chicken were, from left, Ernest Harris of Winder, Joe and John Booth of Apple Valley, George Henry Pinion of Lawrenceville, Greg Poss of Jefferson, Skipper Williamson of Athens, Billy Booth of Apple Valley, and Milsey Seagraves of Hull.

Melba Yarbrough, student at Madison County High School in Danielsville, was crowned Miss Jackson EMC at the 1961 annual meeting by the 1960 pageant winner, Andrea Lyon. Eighteen young ladies vied for the title with runners-up including Beverly Dailey of Commerce and Pat McElroy of Hull; McElroy went on to win the crown the following year. In the twelve pageants held from 1953 to 1964, Miss Jackson EMC winners were, in chronological order, Kathryn Waters, Ruth Westbrook, Mairee Massey, Mildred Bone, Marion Legg, Peggy Samples, Trudy Thompson, Lyon, Yarbrough, McElroy, June Davis, and Brenda Parham. The final winner, Parham, claimed the title of Miss Georgia Electrification in 1964. Marion (Legg) Mahaffey, Miss Jackson EMC 1957, eventually worked in the co-op's member services department as a home electrification advisor.

Board President William Booth awarded prize money to winners of the 1957 Miss Jackson EMC Beauty Contest, from left, finalist Mary Grace Carruth, Miss Jackson EMC Marion (Legg) Mahaffey who later worked at the co-op, and Karen Wardlaw.

Almost five thousand youth in 4-H and FFA clubs participated in Jackson EMC's Youth Electric Project in 1964. Cash awards to seventy winners in the eight counties served by Jackson EMC totaled $965. The annual project was conducted in cooperation with the University of Georgia Extension Service and its county and home demonstration agents. Winners were announced at the co-op's annual meeting.

plans, but approximately two thousand members attended the event, enough to approve renewal of the corporation's charter. Georgia EMC Manager Walter Harrison, a state and national rural electrification leader and friend of the co-op, was guest speaker, as he was at several of Jackson EMC's annual meetings. The Reverend E. H. Collins, pastor of First Baptist Church in Winder, was master of ceremonies, a role he filled for many years.

A fundraiser for FFA students who cooked the chicken, the barbecue lunch was a huge success and largely considered responsible for boosting annual meeting attendance, which by 1961 had grown to more than four thousand members and guests. While the free barbecue and fixings continues to be a mainstay of annual meetings, other components of the yearly event have gone by the wayside, including church choir contests that were popular in the 1960s but were eventually phased out and replaced with professional groups like the Chuck Wagon Gang, Florida Boys, Lewis Family, and the Kingsmen.

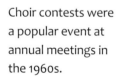

Choir contests were a popular event at annual meetings in the 1960s.

Mrs. H. P. Mealor of Commerce was the grand-prize winner at the 1952 annual meeting. Her prize was a Hotpoint Electric Range donated by eight Hotpoint dealers in Jackson EMC's service area.

The long-standing tradition of serving barbecue chicken prepared by FFA members began at the 1957 annual meeting when thousands of barbecue plates were served to members and their families.

Retired Extension Service agent Pat Bell recalled annual meetings of the 1960s and 70s as the "social event" of the era and likened them to camp meetings of old. "They were the best attended thing in the county," she said. "None of my home demonstration ladies would miss a Jackson EMC annual meeting or a cooking school. The talk at home demonstration club meetings was about the annual meeting because they gave away the best gifts, you got to eat, you got to see people, and you got to meet people. It was the place to be, for goodness sakes, and still is."

On September 18, 1965, a standing-room-only crowd attended the annual meeting where a special tribute was made to the late Rob Kelly. Prior to the manager's death the previous May, Jackson EMC's power use leaders had gathered recipes from members for a cookbook they published later that year. Kelly had his doubts about the cookbook, according to his daughter-in-law. "He thought everybody had cookbooks because Mrs. Kelly had all kinds of them in her kitchen," said Imogene. "He was afraid they were going to be stuck with a bunch of cookbooks."

Watts Cookin' on the Line? debuted in December 1965 as a spiral-bound, two-hundred-page cookbook available for $2. The cookbook's primary function was to serve as a fundraising project for clubs and churches in Jackson EMC's service area. The co-op set the advertised price based on costs and discounted that cost to clubs and churches, with the difference being their profit.

For all that Rob Kelly had been right about, from negotiating complicated power contracts to predicting future growth in Gwinnett County, he was wrong about the cookbook. By 2013, more than 100,000 copies of *Watts Cookin' on the Line?* had been sold, and the popular cookbook was slated for its fifth reprinting.

Manager Rob Kelly, center, turned the ticket barrel for a youngster to pull out the winning tickets, which were read by Rev. E. H. Collins who served as master of ceremonies at numerous Jackson EMC annual meetings.

Chapter Eight
Building Member Relations

"Is it a fact – or have I dreamt it – that, by means of electricity, the world of matter has become a great nerve, vibrating thousands of miles in a breathless point of time?"

—Clifford Pyncheon

Fictional character in *The House of the Seven Gables* by Nathaniel Hawthorne

1851

Over its seventy-five-year history, Jackson EMC has benefited from the varied strengths and talents of its four top executives, the men who steered it through the evolution of rural electricity. It can be said that each man was right for the time, starting with Rob Kelly who, by all accounts, was a rural electric pioneer and hands-on leader who helped create the cooperative and its efficient electric system.

In between Kelly's death and hiring of the cooperative's second manager, the board's vice chairman, Otis Cato, served as acting general manager while a permanent manager was sought. After leading the co-op for eight months, Cato returned his focus to his farm when the new manager was hired.

Otis Cato, vice president of the Jackson EMC Board of Directors and interim manager between Rob Kelly and William Welch, looked over plans for expansion that began in 1965 at the Jefferson headquarters.

Opposite page: Country stores like H.A. Langford General Merchandise in Holly Springs were places to shop for groceries and hardware and spots for gathering to discuss politics or which nearby community would be next to receive rural electricity.

William Welch became Jackson EMC's second manager in January 1966 and was known for emphasizing communications with co-op members.

William S. "Bill" Welch joined Jackson EMC as the cooperative's manager in January 1966. Raised on a farm in Laurel, Mississippi, where his father produced broilers, Welch was familiar with the poultry industry that had taken hold in northeast Georgia. A graduate of Mississippi College, he had worked eleven years with Humble Oil Company and Gulf Oil Corporation before beginning his career in rural electrification as assistant to the manager of Pearl River Valley Electric Power Association in Columbia, Mississippi. He left his home state to work with the REA as operations field representative for the State of Indiana and, in 1964, moved to Washington, DC, when promoted to member services officer, the post he held before moving to Georgia to head Jackson EMC.

Upon starting his new job, Welch said, "I will strive to continue the type management Jackson EMC has had in the past, making it one of the largest and fastest growing electric cooperatives in the nation." By then, Jackson EMC was serving 21,146 members on 3,093 miles of line as Georgia's second largest electric cooperative. While Jackson EMC's first manager had worked to engineer a reliable system of electric service, its second manager would strive to build the cooperative's relationship with its members.

"Rob Kelly was an engineer; Bill Welch was a public relations man," said Bill Carpenter. "Being an electrical engineer, Mr. Kelly was developing the service, the engineering and operations. Mr. Welch had worked in the rural electrification program with statewide organizations and had a real strong background in public relations, member relations. Bill Welch knew about people and put that together to make Jackson EMC a people place."

In his first months as manager, Welch credited the staff when the cooperative received high marks from the REA for reliability and continuity of service. Since electric cooperatives began, they had struggled to keep pace with the private utilities, often working on shoestring budgets to build power systems sometimes lacking in

Longtime Jackson EMC employees Morgan Pounds, left, and Floy Bullock, manager of engineering, check out the new metering point added in 1964 to serve co-op members in northeast Madison County. Pounds was one of the co-op's first employees and the only staking engineer for many years. Numerous members recalled him as "the man who first brought electricity" to their home or farm. Bullock worked at Flint EMC in Reynolds for eleven years before joining Jackson EMC in 1960; he was the first engineering graduate to manage the engineering department, which he led until his retirement in 1988.

Jackson EMC celebrated its one-thousandth total electric home in June 1966.

reliability. Continual service had been years in the making as co-ops across the country strived to gain funds for and then built new or "heavied up" power lines to adequately serve their expanding memberships. At Jackson EMC, preventive maintenance programs, pole testing, right-of-way clearing, meter and transformer testing, and application of long-range engineering and annual work plans were utilized to lend reliability and serve the co-op's escalating needs.

In June 1966, Jackson EMC switched on the power to its one-thousandth total electric home. The total electric marketing program begun five years earlier had grown phenomenally since 1961 when nine members first chose to use electricity as their only means of heating the home and powering appliances. The co-op built kitchens and placed appliances in local high schools and sent home service advisors to teach home economics students proper appliance use and safety. Home service advisors also visited elementary schools to teach students about wiring and electrical safety, gave demonstrations to garden clubs and home demonstration councils, and planned and prepared for the co-op's annual meetings.

A major expansion of the cooperative headquarters was completed in 1966 with a larger auditorium featuring seating capacity of 250 and additional workspace for the engineering department and linemen along with more parking space.

Additional office space made possible with the expansion was welcomed by office staff, including co-op secretaries who, in 1968, completed a ten-week course offered through Gainesville Junior College, an endeavor that reinforced Manager Welch's commitment to education and continuous employee training. Attending the training led by instructor Louise Holcomb, far left, were (from left) Carol Aaron, Janie Love, Janet Garrett, Sara Bell, Rita (Gunter) Legg, Judy Taylor, and Frances Staton.

While work of the home service advisors traditionally had revolved around homemaking skills, introduction of the Medallion Program meant they were increasingly called on to sell electricity. All along, home demonstrations and cooking schools had served to interest homemakers in new appliances that, once purchased, added to the co-op's electric load. But in the mid- to late-1960s, as REA loans became increasingly difficult to obtain during the Vietnam War era, cooperatives depended on more electricity sold to generate revenue, and home and farm service advisors were charged with promoting power sales.

In the last half of the sixties, the push to total electric was stronger than ever, but some co-op members were wary of using only electricity in their homes, as compared to all gas or a mix of the two. Perks offered by the cooperative calmed their fears. One incentive included a one-cent per kilowatt-hour charge for total electric homes where two meters were placed—one for heating and air, which carried the one-cent per kilowatt-hour charge, and another which kept track of other electric consumption. Member service advisors and co-op draftsmen helped members with wiring and lighting plans, pointing out the most desirable places for switches and lights, and they created kitchen plans with appliances, receptacles, and switches strategically placed.

Manager Welch must have been heartsick at the 1966 annual meeting when members complained about the long lines they waited in to receive their barbecue chicken plate. Special aims were taken to thwart a repeat and, after the September 1967 annual event, Welch reported that four thousand plates were served to

Employees recognized at the 1965 annual meeting were, from left, front: Joan Tompkins, Evelyn Echols, Roger Thomason, Robert Boyd, Floy Bullock, H. O. Parks, Judy Taylor, and Janie Love. Back: Calvin Carey, Billy Culbertson, David Dorsey, Dickie Fleeman, Bobby Gunter, Robert Harris, William Holland, and Franklin Nichols.

Jackson EMC was the first in its communities to provide outside security lighting, which it started offering to members in May 1959 to enable safe and efficient farm operations and to light driveways and walkways at night.

The co-op installed outdoor lighting for a $3 monthly fee. Within the first month of offering the new service, a dozen member-families had outside lights installed and more had applied for the service that provided ample light to brighten yards at night.

consumers and guests in only forty minutes. By the late 1960s, the annual meeting had returned to a daylong event. Youth Electric Project awards were presented, Jackson EMC's Outstanding Young Farmer was named, dozens of door prizes were distributed, and the grand-prize winner in the annual prize drawing chose between an electric range and freezer.

In 1968, attendance at the annual meeting was the largest to date. The cooperative added almost two thousand meters that year, marking the largest annual increase yet and leading Welch to ramp up construction maintenance programs, pole inspection and treating, right-of-way clearing, and routine line upkeep. The highest amount in margin refunds ever distributed in one year, $256,644 was reimbursed to members in 1968, and Jackson EMC was credited with having the highest and most consistent refund record of any rural electric cooperative in Georgia.

While Jackson EMC grew steadily, even three decades after the co-op was formed, a resident occasionally received electricity for the first time. Velvie Harrison lived in Pendergrass when she finally obtained electric power in 1968. She started out slowly, retiring her kerosene lamp in favor of electric lighting while she continued to cook on a wood stove, warm her home with a fireplace, and sew with a foot-pedal machine. While Harrison had just begun to bring electric lighting into her home, others in northeast Georgia were purchasing security lights to brighten their yards at night.

The Jackson EMC Board of Directors in 1967 included, from left, Haywood O'Kelley, C. Lowell Manley, H. L. Harman, Otis Cato, William Booth, Johnny V. Booker, W. C. Alexander, A. T. Sharpton, and E. Baxton Cook.

Throughout much of Welch's tenure as manager, he and the board of directors struggled to secure additional loans to meet the numerous requests for electricity during what amounted to Jackson EMC's first major burst of growth. Never before had loan funds been so restricted and difficult to secure as they were due to inflationary trends and the Vietnam War, which strained the nation's coffers. Electric cooperatives were asked to limit system improvements that called for extra financing, and the REA requested that co-ops repay loans early, if possible, and use "reserves down to a bare minimum" before requesting additional funding.

Jackson EMC received national recognition in January 1965 for its work to help members live better electrically when the National Electrical Manufacturers Association (NEMA) presented the co-op with first place honors for an outstanding job in planning and conducting a program of sales promotion and service. Member Education/Public Relations Director Gene Thurmond, left, accepted the award from NEMA Secretary of Consumer Products R. D. Smith at NRECA's twenty-third annual meeting in Miami Beach, Florida.

As co-op directors worked to obtain financing, Manager Welch built up the staff, putting into place a revised wage and salary plan and adding a training program with a continuing education component. From its earliest years, the cooperative had strived to hire the most educated and experienced workers available. Many held college degrees, many of those from the University of Georgia in nearby Athens. With the philosophy that continued success depended on the quality of its employees, Welch improved onsite training and started an education program coordinated with local colleges and vocational-technical schools. This concentration on education was part of a ten-year "forecast on future growth and needs" that Welch devised in his first months as manager. His plan also called for upgrading equipment by obtaining the best quality machines available. While Welch was manager, the cooperative purchased additional bucket trucks and hydraulic diggers that were put to use by appreciative linemen who until 1964 had done the bulk of pole setting and line extension by hand.

Welch put equal attention to improving office procedures, specifically in terms of financial planning, reporting functions, work plans, and budgets. Under his leadership, operations were expanded at the Gwinnett District and installation of a modern computer system was completed. Using advanced equipment to streamline construction and maintenance work saved the co-op money while increasing productivity.

By April 1969, Jackson EMC served 25,000 meters with every indication its membership would continue to increase. In May, the co-op turned on power to its two-thousandth total electric home.

Shortly after, Manager Welch announced his resignation. He would return to Laurel, Mississippi, to work for Howard Industries, Inc., a manufacturer of

In the last half of the 1960s, the board and management strived to provide line crews with the tools and time they needed to "heavy-up" electric lines in order to supply co-op members with fewer and briefer interruptions in service. At work here are, from left, on the ground: Darrow Carruth, Herman Weldon, and Gurnie Bell. On the pole: Calvin Carey and Billy Crowe.

Dedicating a new metering point in Gwinnett County in 1965 were, from left, Jackson EMC Manager of Engineering Floy Bullock, Gwinnett County Commissioner Ray Morgan, Lawrenceville District Manager Henry Pinion, and Jackson EMC Director A. T. Sharpton.

electric transformers, as national sales manager for rural municipal electric systems. Welch noted that his decision to leave northeast Georgia had not been an easy one. He applauded co-op employees for their cooperation, loyalty, and job dedication and claimed himself a better man for having associated with the board of directors. In his brief but busy three-and-a-half years in Jackson County, he had served on numerous boards and had been president of the Jefferson Chamber of Commerce, which named him Citizen of the Year in 1968.

In leaving, he urged directors, employees, and members to support and promote their cooperative. "Make no mistake about it, Jackson EMC has tremendous potential—in growth, in service and in total area development. At the same time, though, it has problems—some of which are bordering on the critical side. Adequacy of growth capital takes first place on this list."

Bill Welch died March 21, 2011, in his native Mississippi at the age of eighty-one. In the view of many who worked with him during his 1966–1969 tenure at Jackson EMC, Welch was a progressive leader who sought to strengthen bonds between the cooperative and its members while attracting new members, especially new businesses, to the cooperative's service area. The time he served as manager was relatively short but remarkably strong in terms of steering the cooperative in a positive direction.

William Welch, shown speaking at an annual meeting, served as manager of the cooperative from January 1966 to the summer of 1969 and was remembered as a progressive leader who sought to strengthen bonds between the co-op and the communities it served.

Chapter Nine
Growing Pains

"The plain message physical science has for the world at large is this, that were our political and social and moral devices only as well contrived to their ends as a linotype machine, an antiseptic operating plant, or an electric tram-car, there need now at the present moment be no appreciable toil in the world."

—Herbert George "H. G." Wells
Author of *The War of the Worlds*

The August 1964 issue of *Jemco News* featured a photograph and caption that would be prophetic. The photo showed a section of interstate highway under construction just south of Commerce. The caption read: "History will almost with certainty report that Interstate-85 was one of the great stimulating forces which helped to spark the phenomenal industrial growth of our area."

Almost fifty years later, the completion of Interstate 85 in the 1960s stands as the single greatest igniter of the astounding growth that consumed northeast Georgia into the twenty-first century.

Building the four-lane interstate through Atlanta to Greenville, South Carolina, was part of a massive nationwide project begun in 1956 with passage of the Federal Aid Highway Act. President Dwight D. Eisenhower signed the bill into law, recognizing the highways as necessary for the national defense. If the country were invaded, the US Army would need dependable roads to transport troops. The act authorized $25 billion to build 41,000 miles of an interstate highway system to provide interconnectivity throughout the nation. At the time, it was the largest public works project ever undertaken in America.

For many months, highway workers reshaped urban landscape and rural farmland through Atlanta into South Carolina to construct Interstate 85.

Opposite page: Construction of Interstate 85 in the mid-sixties proved to be a turning point for commercial and industrial growth in northeast Georgia. Part of a nationwide project, building the four-lane highway changed the landscape as it coursed through the center of Jackson EMC territory.

The interstate highway system brought with it truck stops at various exits. The first one served by Jackson EMC was Pure Oil Company Truck Stop, which opened in 1968 at the Pleasant Hill exit in Gwinnett County.

The sign here points to the second Holiday Inn to be served by Jackson EMC, completed in 1968 at the Lawrenceville-Suwanee exit off Interstate 85. The first Holiday Inn was built one year earlier at the Commerce exit.

Interstate Industrial Park was the first industrial/commercial venue to break ground in the area after completion of Interstate 85. The first inhabitants at the Gwinnett County location included J.I. Case Tractor, Adcom Metals, and Johnson Motor Lines.

Panasonic Corporation was another early addition at Interstate Industrial Park, the first such park in Jackson EMC territory to sprawl alongside the new interstate highway.

By the summer of 1965, new business and industry had popped up north of Atlanta, automatically it seemed, to create an expanding north Georgia economy. For the remainder of the decade, new stores and industries seemed to shoot up like bean sprouts. At interstate exits north of Atlanta, motels and truck stops were planted to take advantage of the new traffic. At I-85 and Highway 441 near Commerce, the new Holiday Inn, served by Jackson EMC, touted electric resistance heating coupled with an air-conditioning unit to provide the latest in comfort. Truck stops were a novelty spawned by the new interstate system that brought eighteen-wheelers through before-uncharted territory. The Pure Oil Company Truck Stop at the Pleasant Hill exit off I-85 in Gwinnett County opened in 1968 to offer truckers a one-stop shop where they could sleep and eat while their vehicles were serviced; Jackson EMC proudly announced the new business was a total-electric member.

By 1970, Interstate Industrial Park in Gwinnett County consisted of 164 acres of prime property along I-85 at Beaver Ruin Road inviting manufacturers to set up shop; Panasonic Corporation, J.I. Case Tractor, Adcom Metals, and Johnson Motor Lines obliged and, in turn, received their electricity from Jackson EMC.

The growth, and the potential for more to come, was good news for northeast Georgia where, in the three decades between 1920 and 1950, the counties served by Jackson EMC had lost population. Manager Welch attributed the outmigration to the declining number of farms, a phenomenon that had led many rural families to relocate to nearby cities. While farming as an occupation continued to decline, the population stabilized by the mid-fifties and, as the number of industries moving to northeast Georgia increased, so did the population. In Winder and Barrow County, for example, population rose by 10 percent from 1950 to 1960.

An Uptick in Growth

In the early sixties, industries slowly started moving into the area surrounding Jackson EMC headquarters. Landing even a small industry was a major achievement in the agriculture-dominated communities. A few small textile plants started to develop, and the ones already operating, like Jefferson Mills, began to expand. By 1967, Gwinnett County boasted six industrial parks, a new airport to serve executives flying in for business at those parks, and new homes where families attracted to the good-paying jobs settled amidst reputable schools and recreational facilities. The myriad of opportunities brought by the exponential growth was not lost on Jackson EMC's board of directors as they assessed the state of their communities.

To accommodate the growth, the cooperative set to work converting more of its smaller single-

Substations were added as demand for electricity grew. Director W. C. "Will" Alexander, right, and Operations Superintendent Harold Harbin, left, looked on in 1973 as Line Foreman Robert Edwards prepared to flip the switch at a new substation near Commerce.

phase lines to larger capacity three-phase lines to support the increasing power load. Old power poles were replaced, and new poles and line were strung into communities once cotton fields. New substations were built and existing ones improved as the once-rural territory transformed into a mix of rural and suburban environs. The transformation at Jackson EMC and in areas served by electric cooperatives throughout the country created radical changes in cooperative membership. By the late sixties, more than half of the billing of rural electric cooperatives was to rural and suburban non-farm consumers. An entire generation had never cleaned a kerosene lamp or cut wood for a wood stove.

That reality would have been inconceivable less than three decades earlier, when the cotton and barely-scraping-by dirt farmers of northeast Georgia toiled from sunup to kerosene lights out. In the years since Jackson EMC was organized, electricity had changed the way farmers worked and women did chores. Now, just as electricity had brought to the country conveniences long enjoyed in the city, a new highway system promised to link cities to rural communities, bringing the two even closer together by facilitating growth and allowing people to commute.

Along with smaller industries moving in, the addition of new residents prompted retail development. Where depopulation had negatively impacted the area, suddenly there was population growth. Northeast Georgia became the land of opportunity. The growth was evidenced in new industries, new homes, increased retail trade, and record-breaking demands for new schools. Central Gwinnett Industrial Park opened in Lawrenceville. As a result of snaring new industry, Banks County's Maysville community was named the most outstanding community in the 1965 North Georgia Community Development Program. In 1965, area merchants enjoyed one of the busiest sales years since World War II, and city and county governments worked feverishly to keep up with the need for public services. The same year, Jackson EMC extended electric lines to more than 1,600 new houses.

This first burst of growth would foreshadow things to come.

At Gainesville, the pace quickened as new industries located, including Dixieland Hatchery and Southeastern Freezer. Whereas Jesse Jewell had stimulated the local economy by transporting chickens outside the county, the new interstate highway promised to bring opportunity into the area. The local banks were prepared to seize the opportunity and shape it into substantial benefit for their communities. Along with elected officials, bankers were the decision makers who moved the community forward.

To stay ahead of the development, the staff at Jackson EMC devised a ten-year plan to assure electricity would be in good supply as usage increased and, in 1966, the co-op built one hundred new miles of line to accommodate growth. An engineering and mapping firm was hired to survey the cooperative's electrical facilities and produce a more efficient mapping system. High school and college students were hired for part-time jobs after school and during the summer to assist with the increase in construction. In the late sixties, the cooperative supplied underground service for the first time to a subdivision, Westgate Park near Athens.

High school and college students were hired for part-time jobs to help Jackson EMC keep up with an increasing workload due to its expanding communities. Part-time employees included, from left, Jeff Davis, Earl Tompkins, Buck Tolbert, Larry McNeal, and Rod Johnson.

Jackson EMC began offering underground electric service in the 1960s, earlier than most electric cooperatives. The aesthetically appealing service was favored by many businesses and industries. By the 1990s, the cooperative employed high-tech methods to replace high-voltage underground cable, in special cases using a trenchless digger to bore holes that new cable was fed through. More recently, journeyman linemen Craig Etris, left, Russ Dowdy, center back, and Jason McElwaney, kneeling, attempt to locate an underground fault using a "thumper," a device utilized to find faults on 25,000-volt cable. Linemen listen to hear the thump and then dig at that location to repair the fault.

Along with offering residential members assistance with lighting, heating and air plans, kitchen layouts, and remodeling schematics, Jackson EMC increasingly courted commercial accounts by assisting local chambers of commerce in promoting their communities. In 1968, the cooperative published a brochure titled "Power for Industrial Progress," describing its ability to serve industries with reliable electricity while showcasing the co-op's service area and its larger commercial customers. In October of that year, Jackson EMC joined seventy of Georgia's banking and industrial representatives on a Red Carpet Industrial Tour of Gwinnett County to show off its industrial parks.

With the growth boom that occurred in the last half of the sixties, Jackson EMC's once rural service area became a hodgepodge of rural and suburban communities. But in Madison County, in tiny towns like Ila and Danielsville, daily life ambled at a leisurely pace and work at the Neese District office remained similar to what it had been for decades.

Rural electric cooperatives, including Jackson EMC, used billboards to advertise to a broader audience.

Life seemed to stand still in some areas served by Jackson EMC, particularly in its northern reaches where rural filling stations like Youngblood Grocery in Chestnut Mountain served as gathering spots for locals through the fifties and sixties.

On the other end of the spectrum, at its southernmost points, new business and industries made themselves at home in Jackson EMC territory. Kubota, a Japanese-based tractor manufacturer, opened its first facility served by Jackson EMC in 1975 and became a long-standing and valued customer.

While life in Madison and Lumpkin Counties remained relatively slow and easy, in growing cities like Lawrenceville and Gainesville, the pace had picked up to a steady trot that, in another decade or so, would evolve into first a gallop and then a downright stampede. At opposite ends of Jackson EMC territory, the district office at Neese, nestled deep in the piney back roads of still-rural Madison County, and the Gwinnett District office at Lawrenceville, on its way to serving numerous Fortune 500 industries, might as well have been on polar ends of the planet.

Standing in the Gap

Ironically, the transition that manifested in the late 1960s had been some thirty years in the making, initiated in 1939 when Jackson EMC first started supplying electric power to rural families. Jefferson already had electricity in the late thirties, as did many small towns that provided electric power to their residents. That's where merchants, doctors, and lawyers lived, amidst a perception of wealth because they had electricity. Over the years, as the co-ops provided electricity to rural families, more parity between the rural areas and the cities was realized, if not financially, at least psychologically.

Electricity or not, differences between city and country folks remained. And Jackson EMC stood in the gap. As a complex corporation staffed with college-educated managers who had grown up on farms, as one of the area's major employers offering well-paying jobs, and as a company tasked with taking their product into the smallest farm houses and the largest corporate offices, Jackson EMC blended the worlds of city and country in a way few companies were able to do. The deep agricultural roots the co-op had planted in the counties it served became eminent as the area transitioned into an increasingly commercial economy. As the area transitioned from agriculture to modern industry, Jackson EMC kept a foot in both worlds and was able to speak both languages.

From Neese to Lawrenceville, Ila to Gainesville, Dry Pond to Athens, the needs, once similar, were as different as Mayberry from Los Angeles. And somehow, more than most companies at the time, Jackson EMC was comfortable in each locale. Its employees were as capable of dealing with executives at Interstate Industrial Park in Gwinnett County as they were with chicken farmers in the Hall County towns of Alto or Lula.

Growing pains were inevitable as Jackson EMC worked to meet the needs of members with increasingly different concerns. In its rural communities, the cooperative continued to support the farmer and his family. In 1969, the co-op held its first Jackson EMC Quality Steer Show at the University of Georgia Coliseum, open

The co-op staged its first Jackson EMC Quality Steer Show in 1969, beginning a tradition that would continue for decades to come. Carolyn Shackelford, the Gwinnett County 4-H student shown here with Jackson EMC Director Haywood O'Kelley, raised the 1976 Grand Champion steer. Her brother Steven raised the Reserve Champion steer that year, and their brother Larry won reserve honors at the 1975 event. They are the children of Mr. and Mrs. Wayne Shackelford of Snellville. An avid supporter of 4-H, Mr. Shackelford served as commissioner of the Georgia Department of Transportation from 1991 to 2000.

Serving educational needs of youth within its communities remained a mission for Jackson EMC as the co-op worked closely with 4-H, FFA, and FHA clubs. The cooperative provided schools in its service area with electric appliances for classroom use, as they did at Winder-Barrow High School where members of the school's FHA chapter sampled their cooking while instructor Yvonne Jett, left, waited to deliver the final taste test, circa 1969.

to all FFA and 4-H youth in the EMC territory. Board President William Booth, a farmer and cattleman, chaired the event and worked with agriculture teachers and county extension agents to stage it. While a steer show satisfied concerns of rural members, in Gwinnett, where new businesses moved in like moths to a flame, the co-op added after-hours dispatchers to streamline communications. For years, members had been provided, via *Jemco News*, with phone numbers of employees to call for emergency service after regular business hours; the new afternoon and evening dispatch services supplied more timely attention to members' needs.

Along with supplying electricity to its members, Jackson EMC worked to provide leadership in its communities. "The biggest problem of this county was its image," said Pat Bell, a Jackson County extension agent who would go on to serve two terms on the Jackson County Board of Commissioners and one as a state legislator. "The county had a bad image, and one of my objectives was to try to do my part in changing the image. Jackson EMC was so far ahead of me it wasn't funny."

Jackson EMC sponsored youth in 4-H, FHA, FFA, and school activities, and employees were encouraged to take part in civic organizations that worked to improve the communities served by the co-op. "Without the leadership from Jackson EMC, we'd not be where we are today," said Bell. "They had tremendous projects and things for the kids in the schools. Their employees belonged to the Rotary Club, Kiwanis Club and Lions Club. They supported the humane society, churches and schools, and helped with building Hurricane Shoals Park. Jackson EMC was always there."

While it supported schools and organizations with volunteer efforts, the cooperative also did its part to boost the local economies, especially in the late sixties and seventies when chambers of commerce recruited industries. During this challenging era, when incoming industry could threaten those established, Jackson EMC directors and employees held steady as role models. Although careful not to be excessively political, the cooperative

sought to inform and educate its members on pressing matters. The rural electrification program had been born of politics and evolved through the years with political support from Republicans and Democrats, from country people and city people, from poor farmers and wealthy citizens. Jackson EMC felt an obligation to actively speak out in support of public issues, policies, and legislative acts which affected the welfare of its progress—and to oppose those things which were detrimental. With the directors and management setting the tone, employees followed and a culture of austerity, hard work, and doing the right thing was developed.

For all its efforts, Jackson EMC's path was not without bumps. In 1969, Board President William Booth alerted members that employees of the cooperative would vote that month on whether or not to seek representation of a national labor union, the International Brotherhood of Electrical Workers (IBEW). Booth believed management could and should provide good working conditions, reasonable wages and salaries, vacation time, holidays, and health benefits by working directly with employees as part of the whole team, without the intervention of a third party. Even so, on September 4, hourly employees, mostly line workers, voted in favor of joining the union.

Along with the opportunities brought by its expanding communities, the challenges at Jackson EMC multiplied as well.

Helping with construction of Hurricane Shoals Park in Jackson County was one of numerous community endeavors supported by Jackson EMC. The county park was completed in 1978.

Chapter Ten
The Tipping Point

"Imagination has brought mankind through the Dark Ages to its present state of civilization. Imagination led Columbus to discover America. Imagination led Franklin to discover electricity."

—L. Frank Baum
From *The Lost Princess of Oz*

Jackson EMC, into the 1970s, continued to grow. The fastest developing areas in its service territory were Gwinnett County along I-85, Hall County around Lake Lanier and outside Gainesville, and the Athens area in Clarke County. The trend, however, would taper off as the decade brought a severe assortment of concerns—recession, inflation, and an energy crisis. By the time Gerald Ford became president in 1974, the upward march of prosperity, evident throughout the nation since the end of World War II, had begun to reverse. The Arab nations' oil embargo of 1973 led to a stock market crash in 1974; inflation resulted and recession took hold.

Left: Jackson EMC provided electric power to a growing number of subdivisions in the sixties and seventies, including this Clarke County neighborhood near Athens.

Right: Colony Mobile Home Park was one of many mobile home neighborhoods that sprang up in all counties served by Jackson EMC in the 1960s. The co-op promoted total electric living in mobile homes just as it did in stick-built houses.

Opposite page: As homes and businesses continued to multiply around Lake Lanier, the cooperative was compelled to string more lines and reroute others to provide electric power to residential and commercial/industrial customers. The lines at this lake crossing in Gainesville are now installed inside a duct bank attached to the bridge structure. Approximately 2,500 feet north of here are power lines that were reconstructed to accommodate the lake backing up; the new construction is almost identical to that pictured here.

Neese linemen, like line workers throughout Jackson EMC territory, worked primarily on line repair and maintenance when growth in northeast Georgia stalled during the mid-70s.

Prior to the embargo, subdivisions were going up, one after the other, and it seemed the soaring growth would never stop. But it did. Construction came to a screeching halt when the economy collapsed. Chains crossed the entrances to subdivisions that were boarded up. Builders went bankrupt. The whole country seemed to come to a standstill.

When utilizing economist Arthur Okun's misery index to assess the 1970s, it's clear that the decade was, indeed, miserable. The index is an economic indicator which presumes that high unemployment coupled with high inflation creates economic and social stress. In the United States, the misery index was at its highest from 1974 to 1981.

While the 1970s is rightfully remembered as a tumultuous time of economic and energy crises, the decade was monumental in setting the course for the growth and well-being of Jackson EMC. In one of the greatest ironies in EMC history, not just Jackson's but throughout the nation, this decade was the period most important for the future of electric cooperatives. Although physical growth stalled for much of the decade, cooperative minds raced in fever-pitch motion to propose ideas that, when carried out, rivaled the Rural Electrification Act in their relevance to the future of rural electricity in America.

Member service advisors Lonnie Hall, center, and Jim Smith, right, worked with local FFA advisors in the 1970s to coordinate various youth projects.

Introduced within a five-year span from 1969 to 1974, the three events that arguably remain the most important in Jackson EMC's modern history include creation of the National Rural Utilities Cooperative Finance Corporation (CFC), which provided the co-op another way to secure funds; passage of the Georgia Territorial Electric Service Act, which protected the EMC's service area from encroachment by other utilities; and establishment of Oglethorpe Electric Membership Corporation, now Oglethorpe Power Corporation, which enabled Jackson EMC to procure power from additional sources.

The Lender

Since its origins, as did all the nation's electric cooperatives, Jackson EMC had relied on the federal government to provide funding via loans approved through the Rural Electrification Administration. For the most part, the loans were made with a 2 percent interest rate. The funding wasn't free, but the low interest rate certainly served as incentive for electric cooperatives to build into the nation's rural communities.

As time progressed, American communities spread outside traditional city limits into EMC service areas, which meant many of the co-ops had to upgrade their electric distribution system to handle the load growth, necessitating a demand for new capital. The only source for electric cooperatives was the REA, and in the mid- to late-sixties, it warned the EMCs that its funding was limited. At the time, an application for a two-year loan based on a two-year work plan might be partially funded, for perhaps one year, which meant a year later cooperatives had to request another loan. The NRECA assigned a study committee to look into the problem and determined the solution was for the cooperatives to create their own lending institution.

The National Rural Utilities Cooperative Finance Corporation (CFC) was formed in 1969 as a nonprofit cooperative to raise funds from capital markets to supplement loans for the EMCs. Now they would not be solely dependent on government loans for their survival, and the CFC enabled them to extend electric power services without waiting for a government entity to approve loan applications.

Susan Rector of Hall County and Barry Cronic of Jackson County were chosen to represent Jackson EMC on the 1971 Washington Youth Tour, sponsored by Georgia EMC and the state's electric cooperatives. An East Hall High School student, Susan was the winner of the 1970 Jackson EMC Youth Electric Project. Barry, a student at Jackson County High School, was the area winner in the Jackson EMC-FFA Electric Wiring Contest and fifth place finisher in the state wiring contest.

The Territory Solution

Although its financing options had increased, Jackson EMC faced a new hurdle when submitting loan applications. Growing uncertainty over which electric provider would serve new subdivisions and industrial parks left the cooperatives in a lurch when applying for loans to extend power into areas that, if something wasn't done to protect the co-ops, could be claimed as service territory by private utilities and municipalities.

Since the late 1930s, the EMCs had been prohibited from serving homes or businesses already receiving central station service, and they were not allowed to extend lines into incorporated towns with population of 1,500 or more; therefore, private utilities and municipalities retained most of their customer base. The rules served well until growth in rural communities began to blur the city limit and territory lines. By the early seventies, some formerly rural areas had begun to resemble suburbia with heavily populated residential neighborhoods, or industrial towns with factories planted where cotton once thrived. Locales once snubbed by private utilities and municipalities became increasingly attractive

Jackson EMC adopted a new look in the 1970s when it incorporated NRECA's new logo into its own. John Stringer, shop foreman, stands by a truck featuring the logo.

to them as industrial parks and new houses went up in Gwinnett County, the growth engine of Jackson EMC. If territorial issues were not resolved, management feared, that growth engine would stall.

By July 1971, concerns over territory had escalated. While the co-ops were prohibited from extending service into certain areas, few restrictions were placed on other power suppliers. The lawful practice of the electric utility "closest to" extending service to a new customer was no longer a practical way to extend lines. The co-op's relationships with other power suppliers were positive, but competition has a tendency to alter many relationships. Jackson EMC felt it needed more assurance that its areas of service would be protected.

In 1973, with pending legislation regarding territory, cities and counties merging, and city limits being extended, the co-ops found themselves faced with the possibility of other power suppliers moving into territory that at present was theirs. Jackson EMC, like other electric cooperatives, determined it should be allowed to keep what it served and protect the territory it might serve in the future.

On March 29, 1973, the Georgia General Assembly passed the Georgia Territorial Electric Service Act, formally defining the territory in which each electric supplier would provide service. Territories would be established under jurisdiction of the Georgia Public Service Commission (PSC), which was responsible for approving each co-op's REA or CFC loans. For the most part, suppliers in assigned areas would continue serving their same customers plus new construction within five hundred feet of its lines; the PSC would assign a supplier to unassigned areas when necessary. All consumers with a 900-kilowatt load, or more, would have the right to choose their power supplier. This "customer choice" provision in the act would prove to be most beneficial to Jackson EMC.

By then the manager of Jackson EMC, William Booth lauded the plan, saying it would prove to be fair to all concerned and would become more important as time went on. "Every supplier will be able to continue their plans with a greater degree of certainty of territory protection," he said. "As we are forced to go into the private money market for loan funds we can do so with greater strength, knowing that a prospective lender will look with favor on the security of the area from whence the revenue will come. There will be problems—differences in interpretation, differences in understanding, etc., but these will be resolved as everyone concerned works in good faith to be fair to everyone else, under the bill."

A year later, Jackson EMC employees were negotiating territories, using the act as a tool to tie down the territory it had. Most of the co-op's negotiations took place with Georgia Power. "It was the first recognition that Georgia Power Company had of where all the co-ops were," said Charles Sims, then manager of member services.

The same territorial act that protected Georgia Power from encroachment by the cities gave rural electric cooperatives permission to bid on certain industrial loads they formerly were not allowed to serve, thus leveling the playing field when it came to competition for large commercial customers. A new era of competition between the private power companies and the co-ops was born.

J. A. Underwood worked for the cooperative for thirty-seven years, from 1949 to 1986, starting his career as a ground man in Jefferson and retiring as line foreman at the Gainesville District. Like other longtime employees who earlier climbed poles and later were hoisted in buckets to do line work, he watched the company grow from a small-time rural electric cooperative to a leading force of progress in northeast Georgia.

Generation and Transmission

With financing and territory concerns calmed, Jackson EMC was left in the mid-seventies with one remaining hurdle: how to ensure a reliable power supply at affordable costs.

Up to that point, Jackson EMC purchased 10 percent of its wholesale power from the Southeastern Power Administration (SEPA), which operated hydroelectric plants. The remaining 90 percent of wholesale power was purchased from Georgia Power Company.

Like other EMCs in Georgia, Jackson EMC had its own contract with the power company, albeit these contracts were typically restrictive. Even more sobering, the cost for wholesale power had tripled in the past five years.

Driven by the growth boom from the mid-sixties to 1973, utilities started building new generation plants to meet the demand. Building the generation facilities would be a challenge for the private power company, and they had begun to realize it would be much more expensive than the last generating facilities constructed. When Georgia Power notified the EMCs that they no longer would be able to provide generation for them, the EMCs set to work searching for an alternative solution.

Above, top: Ice and snowstorms taxed the strength of electric linemen, their equipment, and the entire cooperative.

Above, bottom: Jackson EMC lineman Brett Hurst, now a line foreman, restores power at the pole during an intense ice storm.

Right: Along with restoring power to residences and businesses, electric linemen play a huge role in preparing roadways for travel by removing downed lines, and the limbs that took them down, after ice and snowstorms.

In the midst of national inflation that continued to drive up prices, construction was underway on two coal-fired power plants in Georgia, Plant Wansley near Carrollton and Plant Scherer near Macon. Georgia Power, which had committed to these projects, was beginning to experience financial pains. Simultaneously, they had plans in motion to build a nuclear plant, another costly endeavor, and were required to demonstrate to the Nuclear Regulatory Commission that there were no anti-trust or anti-competitive issues involved. This opened a door for electric cooperatives whose wholesale power contracts with Georgia Power prevented them from serving the largest loads. Anti-competitive issues were certainly a reality, the cooperatives proclaimed.

The swirl of circumstances combined to give the cooperatives an advantage. With the private power company in dire financial straits, the electric cooperatives gained leverage. For ownership in the nuclear plant, coal plants, and transmission business, the EMCs offered to join forces with the private power company. With access to substantial REA funding, the state's electric cooperatives, in effect, bailed out Georgia Power in its darkest hour.

For decades, the EMCs had been dependent on the private power company for their wholesale power needs; the opportunity before them gave them a chance to gain control of their own destiny, an opportunity the independent cooperatives craved. By teaming with Georgia Power to enter the generation and transmission side of the utility industry, electric cooperatives would be ensured an adequate supply of energy, which enabled them to provide members with lower electric rates through an integrated transmission system.

With a host of energy consultants and attorneys assisting the state's electric cooperatives in negotiations, Oglethorpe Electric Membership Corporation was established on August 8, 1974, as a generation and transmission cooperative serving Jackson EMC and thirty-eight other Georgia electric cooperatives that purchased wholesale power from Georgia Power Company. Oglethorpe EMC, on behalf of its member cooperatives, would buy into generation and transmission plants already in existence or planned for the near future. The deal was historic in that it marked the first time a private, investor-owned utility in the United States joined forces with electric cooperatives.

Jackson EMC's board president at the time, Troy Sharpton served as the cooperative's representative on the Oglethorpe board, which was comprised of one director from each of its thirty-nine member-EMCs. By partnering with the private utility, resources were pooled, responsibility shared, and present and future electrical needs were met in a more effective and cost efficient manner.

After obtaining a $600 million REA loan, Oglethorpe EMC bought into power plants throughout the state. By 1980, the EMCs had ownership (30 percent in most cases) in Plant Hatch, a nuclear facility near Baxley, and Plants Scherer and Wansley, the coal-fired facilities.

In the late 1960s and early 1970s issues regarding financing, territorial rights, and power procurement proved paramount for Jackson EMC and its fellow rural electric cooperatives. On January 7, 1975, REA Administrator David Hamil, seated, signed the first Oglethorpe Electric Membership Corporation (later named Oglethorpe Power Corporation) loan, which provided $513 million towards buy-in of Units One and Two at the Plant Hatch nuclear facility in Baxley, Georgia. At the time, the loan was the largest in REA history. Among those who witnessed signing of the agreement were Walter Harrison (left), manager of Georgia EMC, and I. F. "Nash" Murph (center), then-president of the Georgia EMC Board of Directors who became the first president of OPC.

In October 1976, the REA guaranteed a loan of $823 million for investment at Vogtle Nuclear Power Plant in Waynesboro; to date, it remains the largest single loan guarantee in REA history. In 1977, purchase of the Vogtle plant was completed by its joint-owners, the EMCs via Oglethorpe EMC (later renamed Oglethorpe Power Corporation, or OPC), Georgia Power Company, the Municipal Electric Authority of Georgia (MEAG), and the City of Dalton.

Without the capital supplied by Georgia's electric cooperatives, it is doubtful the power plants would have been completed in as timely a manner, if at all. This significant contribution of capital not only helped complete construction of the plants but gave the EMCs ownership in electricity generation and transmission, which leveled the playing field for the cooperatives. Manager Booth was a driving force in the deal, which came with ample opposition from those concerned about entering the nuclear industry and dismay from those who doubted the cooperatives' ability to keep up with Georgia Power, the older, larger, more experienced utility.

For many in the electric cooperative industry, getting into the generation and transmission business by forming Oglethorpe Power Corporation is deemed the most significant move in the modern history of the rural electric industry in Georgia. While the capital costs were great, operating costs were less expensive and allowed the EMCs to keep rates low. Today, with corporate headquarters in Tucker, Oglethorpe Power Corporation has $6 billion in assets and provides electricity to more than four million Georgians. It is the nation's largest power supply cooperative.

And the Beat Goes On

While Jackson EMC's corporate staff was immersed in deals and negotiations during the first half of the decade, construction crews experienced a slowdown. In fiscal year 1973, just prior to the oil embargo that would stifle the national economy, Jackson EMC connected 2,700 new consumers. The following year, new services dropped to 1,975, and in fiscal 1975, only 1,276 new meters were connected. The cooperative was still growing but at a much slower pace than in years prior. During the mid-seventies, the construction staff at Jackson EMC used time that previously would have been devoted to new construction to review and upgrade the system by changing out old meters, repairing transformers, inspecting service wires, clearing right of way, and converting smaller single-phase lines to multi-phase lines with larger capacity. Renovations were completed at each district office, and, in 1974, the co-op picked up service to a small portion of Oglethorpe County, bringing the total number of counties it served to ten.

Using downtime in the mid-seventies to make system enhancements proved fortuitous when growth resumed at lightning speed in the last part of the decade. In May 1978, Jackson EMC connected its forty thousandth member,

A new Day's Inn was completed at the I-85 Suwanee exit in 1974. Another commercial customer of Jackson EMC, the hotel boasted 120 rooms with electric heating and cooling, along with a modern total-electric restaurant.

Left: A mirror at the demonstration table enabled audience members to see how Martha Armstrong, a visiting speaker from another Georgia electric cooperative, prepared dishes and created crafts.

Middle: Marion Mahaffey, left, and Betty Griffith worked as Jackson EMC home service advisors in 1972 and often drafted plans for kitchen wiring layouts, a service the co-op provided to members for many years. Mahaffey, who earned a Gold Medallion Award after converting her own home to total electric, recalled how advisors, on the spur of the moment, drew plans on paper plates and napkins.

Right: Home service advisors through the seventies led cooking demonstrations at co-op headquarters and in district offices. Here, Home Service Advisor Marion Mahaffey presents a program at the Gainesville District auditorium in 1978.

keeping it among the top ten cooperatives in the nation in terms of membership. By 1980, according to US Census records, Gwinnett County had more than doubled its population since 1970, from 72,349 to 165,177. It was the fastest growing county in the state and the third fastest growing in the nation.

The second fastest growing county among those served by Jackson EMC was Madison County, which had increased from a population of 13,517 in 1970 to 17,516 in 1980. The slowest growing county was Banks, which had experienced a 9 percent population increase, from 6,833 in 1970 to 7,448 in 1980. Albeit slower than its neighbors, Banks County was growing also, as evidenced by the addition of a new bank in 1975, the first added there since the Great Depression. It was appropriately named the Bank of Banks.

All areas in Jackson EMC territory were growing in some form or fashion by the late 1970s, including Banks County where the Bank of Banks opened in 1975 as the first new bank in that county since the 1930s.

Chapter Eleven
Building Community

"What is a soul? It's like electricity — we don't really know what it is, but it's a force that can light a room."

—Ray Charles
American musician and pioneer of soul music

Before there was Jackson EMC, there was William H. Booth. Born December 30, 1911, Booth grew up poor on a dirt farm in Oglethorpe County. He worked his way through college, graduating from the University of Georgia in 1933 with both bachelor's and master's degrees in agriculture. Immediately upon graduation, he moved to the Apple Valley community in Jackson County and the same year was commissioned a second lieutenant in the US Army Reserve. A few years later, he joined farmers from Jackson, Banks, and Madison Counties in their efforts to bring electricity to rural northeast Georgia.

For two years, Booth drummed up support to start the electric cooperative and was a founding member of its board of directors. He came off the board at the co-op's first annual meeting of members in February 1939 and served in the US Army through World War II, training soldiers at Fort Benning in Columbus. After the war, he returned to his farm at Apple Valley, where he raised peaches and cattle, and to the Jackson EMC Board of Directors, which he rejoined in 1946. Two years later, he was elected president of the board, a post he held through September 29, 1969, when he resigned as director in order to become the co-op's manager. From June 1969, when former manager William Welch left the cooperative, to late September that year, Bill Carpenter had served as acting general manager.

Although Booth was not an engineer or an accountant, he was a leader. With one foot in the military arena and the other firmly planted in civilian life, the general led with authority in both worlds. As a young man, he had travelled to Washington, DC, in the early days of the REA to negotiate Jackson EMC business. During the 1960s, he worked as state director of the Agricultural Stabilization and Conservation Service (ASCS), a job that honed his political prowess and served

Charter Director William H. Booth served two terms on the co-op's board of directors and fourteen years as its general manager.

him well as president of the Jackson EMC board. He was instrumental in organizing Georgia Electric Membership Corporation and served as its president from 1966 to 1969. Politically connected due to the combination of his military, ASCS, and EMC service, his opinion was well respected in many circles, including the state legislature.

Opposite page: By the 1980s, Interstate Industrial Park, now Gwinnett Industrial Park, was bustling with business growing alongside Interstate 85.

Since 1967, Jackson EMC has sponsored the local EMC-FFA Electric Wiring Contest designed to teach high school students about electricity and wiring and has produced multiple winners on the state level. Often, students who learn oratorical and leadership lessons in these competitions have gone on to serve in the public arena, including Terry England, right, winner of the 1982 wiring contest at Winder-Barrow High School. Today, he serves as a member of the Georgia House of Representatives serving Barrow County. His vocational-agriculture teacher and FFA advisor Blane Marable, left, won the wiring contest earlier when attending Oconee High School.

Electric Living

in the

Space Age

MARCH 27, 1969

Co-sponsored by Home Economics Clubs in Banks, Barrow, Clarke, Jackson and Madison Counties and Jackson Electric Membership Corporation

Ladies Day programs that once centered on cooking with an electric range evolved by the late 1960s to teach "space age" cooking with the microwave oven.

"William H. Booth was an incredible man," said Carpenter. "I never saw a man who could change hats like he did. He was a farmer with a large tract of land at Apple Valley and also a military man, a very staunch Democrat and very politically connected. He'd come from meetings, always in a hurry, open his briefcase, take out what papers he had, and seemed to have total concentrated power. He was able to shut out everything else, whether he'd come from an Army thing, or ASCS, he'd come to the meeting and be totally focused."

Stories abound about the tough-as-nails general at Jackson EMC. As a young University of Georgia Extension Service agent in Jackson County in the early seventies, Pat Bell was anxious when Booth asked to meet with her, but he welcomed her and the 4-H clubs she represented to Jackson EMC, the only place with an auditorium big enough to hold 4-H banquets and events. Throughout her career, Bell received several commendations, but the two she treasured most were awards named for Booth—the Jackson County Chamber of Commerce's William H. Booth Leadership Award and the William Booth 4-H Agent of the Year Award. "These are the two I truly felt like I had earned, and it was because of his leadership that helped me a great deal," said Bell. "He expected excellence, and he developed excellence and leadership with his staff."

Booth took cooperative leadership cues from Walter Harrison, dubbed Georgia's "Mr. Rural Electrification," the legendary rural electric pioneer who helped found Georgia EMC and worked as its manager for many years. Closely acquainted with Harrison, Booth learned from him and absorbed his rural electric beliefs and philosophies. Georgia EMC has named two awards for state rural electrification leaders: the Walter Harrison Scholarship, for high school seniors entering college, and the William Booth Award, recognizing outstanding Extension Service agents.

The first few years of Jackson EMC under Booth mirrored the nation at large: growth was steady as change permeated the times. Booth attempted to acquire the equipment necessary for the line crew and office staff to do their jobs. Described by many as a hands-on manager, he joined his staff as a show of support after ice and snowstorms damaged the lines, often staying out all night with the line crews. He hired good employees and believed in them.

Jackson EMC's emphasis on youth remained strong. The annual steer show was held each spring and, beginning in 1971, the cooperative sponsored two high school students each summer on the Washington Youth Tour, a national leadership training event sponsored by the nation's EMCs. During the seventies, students in Jackson EMC

Home service advisors and member services representatives often visited members' residences to provide advice on everything from wiring plans to waste heat recovery units, like this one installed by a plumbing contractor.

territory honed a rich tradition of winning local, district, and state titles in the EMC-FFA Electric Wiring Contest. Local contests were sponsored by the EMCs to teach youth about electricity, wiring, and electric cooperatives. Georgia EMC and FFA sponsored district and state competitions. Six Jackson EMC-area students took first place in state competition in the seventies and many more area students have won top honors in the years since.

Transitioning to Sales Mode

Named manager of member services in 1969, Charles Sims came to Jackson EMC with a wealth of utility industry experience after working at Georgia Power for twenty-two years. During his tenure, Sims transitioned the member services department from its historically heavy emphasis on home economics and kitchen design to a stronger focus on electric sales and energy efficiency. Selling total electric meant making home visits as in the past but with eyes open for inspecting insulation and wiring rather than demonstrating use of the latest kitchen appliance.

Cooking schools continued, but on a limited basis, typically twice a year. These "Ladies Day" programs often were held in partnership with county extension offices and drew impressive crowds through the seventies. As the years passed, women on EMC lines had thorough knowledge of how to use freezers and dishwashers, but new appliances had come to the kitchen with the advent of self-cleaning ovens and a newfangled appliance that accomplished electronic cooking using microwave energy. The microwave oven prompted workshops across northeast Georgia with homemakers scrambling to learn how to use what people called a "space age" appliance.

Home service advisors and the member services staff provided an extensive array of services, from advising builders on energy efficiency

Employees and their families looked forward to a Christmas party each holiday season and family-style picnics each summer at locations like Fort Yargo and Lake Lanier Island. Enjoying a picnic in 1973 were, from left, clockwise, Mrs. Una Hammock, Blondean Kelly, Billie Edwards, Sue Wier, John and Virginia Souther, and Greg Fields.

Longtime Member Services Manager Charles Sims helped start the Jackson County Chamber of Commerce and served as its first president in 1973. Sims had a reputation as a progressive leader who helped set the stage for not only future growth at the cooperative but throughout the communities served by it. He was known for hiring quality personnel, many of whom went on to lead departments at Jackson EMC or serve as managers of other electric cooperatives.

measures to assisting new industries with their electrical needs. These employees continued to equip consumers with wiring and lighting plans while coordinating youth and adult programs.

The co-op moved its annual meeting from Saturday morning to Thursday evening in 1971 in order to accommodate working members who found it difficult to attend the morning session. With FFA clubs preparing barbecue chicken, the meetings continued to attract thousands.

Also in 1971, residential rates at Jackson EMC were increased for the first time in the co-op's thirty-three-year history. For years, rates had actually gone down due to the greater efficiencies of the larger coal-fired generating plants at the time along with members' increased usage of electricity, which spread the fixed cost over a much larger base. Even with the increase, at approximately 1.8 cents per kilowatt-hour, rates were substantially lower than what EMC members first paid in the thirties when the rate per kilowatt-hour was seven cents. If bills in the 1970s were higher, it was because members used more electricity.

In 1972, electric rates rose again due to increased costs of labor and fuel and the necessity of meeting new environmental regulations. The cooperative understood it was easy for consumers to question the price of electricity—something invisible that can't be worn, weighed, or put in a bucket like gas and water. But the effects of electric power, the tools it energized and the time it saved, were obvious, and the costs paid for the invisible "helping hand" remained relatively low.

As attention turned to energy efficiency and conservation, the power use leader program that had been active for twenty years was replaced in 1973 with the Jackson EMC Women's Task Force, similar to groups created in EMCs across the nation to support their local cooperatives. The Minutemen organization continued to meet and, in 1974, still drew two hundred members and wives to its gatherings. *Jemco News* remained the cooperative's main avenue of communicating with members.

In the early seventies, recognizing the need for combined community efforts toward economic development, Manager Booth asked Sims to start a chamber of commerce for Jackson County. With Jackson EMC leading in its organization, the Jackson County Chamber of Commerce was established in 1973. Sims served as its first president and Charles Dawson, who later retired as the co-op's director of public relations, was the second president. The cooperative's leadership in forming the important organization reflected Booth's desire for Jackson EMC to be well represented in its communities. Jackson EMC gained a reputation for its influential voice and presence throughout its service territory.

Gwinnett and Madison Counties, vastly different today, looked much alike in the 1960s, both predominantly rural with plenty of dirt roads leading to cow pastures. The growth that began in the late sixties would change that. On May 25, 1972, Jackson EMC energized its largest capacity substation to date, the new Beaver Ruin substation in Gwinnett County, with increased capacity to absorb the growth that had begun. Interstate Industrial Park was luring business to the area like fish to a Catawba worm. Jackson EMC's first large customers included General Service Administration (GSA) in Duluth and Gainesville Stone, a rock quarry. The co-op snagged these large customers before the Georgia Territorial Electric Service Act was passed, thanks to the "closer to" policy in effect at that time.

Jackson EMC personnel in Gwinnett County routinely met with large commercial customers to devise power plans, working with state or county governments to make sure building permits, electrical inspections, and easements were in order. One week, it seemed, employees were putting in plenty of overtime hours and then, suddenly, it was like the water was cut off. The oil crisis of 1973 slowed the growth for several years as Jackson EMC struggled with the same economic and energy problems that stifled the nation. Many businesses, including numerous builders, went bankrupt. In 1974, the weakening economy led Jackson EMC to end its wiring program that, for fourteen years, had offered incentives for members.

Gainesville Stone Company, a rock quarry in Hall County, was one of the co-op's first large industrial customers.

In 1975, the co-op asked members to shift appliance use in order to save costs. During summer months, utilities must pay a premium to supply extra electricity to meet power needs at the hottest times of day, typically afternoons. To control this wholesale power cost, Jackson EMC asked its members to use appliances during the cooler mornings or evenings. In the summer of 1977, the co-op reported the shift had helped control wholesale costs. Inflation and the oil crisis, however, kept driving electric rates up throughout the decade when almost every year was punctuated with a wholesale rate increase. From 1973 to 1978, the wholesale cost more than tripled, rising from .9 cents to three cents per kilowatt-hour.

In 1981, Jackson EMC introduced a load management program that amplified its efforts to shift peak usage to cooler parts of the day. Members were asked to allow the co-op to install switches to control central air conditioners and water heaters during the summer peaks. The switches temporarily turned off a participant's air conditioning compressor for about seven minutes every half-hour, from 3 to 8 p.m., mid-May to mid-September, while the system's fan continued to run, circulating air so those inside rarely felt a difference in temperature. In 1984, the cooperative began paying rebates to participants in its load management program, an incentive that invited members to help lower the summer peak demand in an effort to keep wholesale power costs at a minimum. (More than 42,000 load management switches are utilized at Jackson EMC now, resulting in average savings each year of approximately $750,000.)

Adding New Programs and Technologies

During the seventies, when rates rose almost annually, homeowners who had added electric heat a decade earlier often paid excessive bills because their homes were not well insulated. Jackson EMC researched methods for weatherizing houses in order to cut energy costs for members and, in late 1977, introduced its Energy Efficient Home (EEH) program, which replaced the Medallion Program that had been used since the fifties to sell total electric living. Member services personnel worked with builders to ensure weatherization features were included during construction to provide cost-saving, maximum-energy efficiency. By January 1978, about twenty houses in the co-op's service area were being constructed to EEH specifications. The first Energy Efficient Home plaque was awarded to Elsie Webb of Pendergrass whose new house was equipped with insulated windows and electric baseboard and wall heaters—features projected to save Webb about $77 annually, or $266 in today's economy.

With the passing of the Georgia Territorial Electric Service Act, businesses outside municipalities and using nine hundred-kilowatt loads (or more) were allowed to choose their power supplier, and electric cooperatives were permitted to bid on these larger loads. In the fall of 1979, thanks to the new customer choice provisions and the EMC marketing representatives who used them to the co-op's advantage, Rockwell International became the first large industry to select Jackson EMC as its power provider over Georgia Power Company. The new 50,000-square-foot facility in Duluth would house the company's government avionics division.

In 1979, the cooperative made a significant investment in new technology with the installation of a supervisory control and data acquisition system (SCADA), which allowed engineering and operations personnel to monitor and regulate load at substations from a central location, as well as monitor lines and equipment throughout the service area and improve service to members during outages.

The following year, the co-op updated its energy audit program. Whereas prior home visits called for employees to return to the office to analyze data, the new home energy analysis offered immediate answers by way of a nifty computerized device attached to a member's telephone. After gathering data from on-site inspections, customer service representatives dialed a toll-free number, entered the data and, within moments, a robotic voice responded with suggested upgrades and associated costs. Nationally as well, measures were being taken to help consumers make wise energy choices. In May 1980, the Energy Policy and Conservation Act went into effect, requiring eight major appliances be labeled with yellow tags providing information on energy consumption and how appliances compared with their competitors.

While work of the member services department shifted in the seventies from selling electricity to conserving energy, the pendulum had begun to swing back by the early eighties, when the cooperative requested a heat pump rebate program be approved by the REA. Designed to boost kilowatt sales, the program was contrary to what

The co-op introduced its Energy Efficient Home program in 1977 with member services representatives working with builders to incorporate weatherization features into home construction. Hall County builder Gene Darracott was one of many area builders who constructed homes to meet Energy Efficient Home standards.

the co-op, and the industry at large, had been doing while in conservation mode the previous six or seven years. The REA was receptive to Jackson EMC's plowing new ground.

Similar to wiring incentives of years past, the new program offered members incentives to install electric heat pumps that cost less to operate than other central heating systems, even less than the most efficient gas units. Thousands took advantage of the heat pump incentives, the Energy Efficient Home program, and residential energy audits.

Expanding Facilities

On June 9, 1980, the corporate staff of Jackson EMC opened for business in a new headquarters building on Commerce Road, at the Jefferson city limits. The 107,000-square-foot facility had been a year and a half in the making, with Terry Development Company of Athens as contractor. Situated on forty acres, giving the co-op room to expand as necessary, the new building featured ample space for offices; a garage; machine, transformer, and meter shops; covered storage and receiving dock; warehouse; and plenty of parking. The former corporate office on four acres in downtown Jefferson had been adequate for years, but as the co-op began to average adding seven new members each workday, more space for employees to serve them became essential. Today, the former co-op headquarters on Athens Street houses Jackson County administrative offices.

Capacity at Jackson EMC substations continued to increase through the late seventies as more large industries were added to the cooperative's electric load.

Almost four thousand members and guests attended Jackson EMC's forty-first annual meeting at the new headquarters in September 1980. In the twelve months prior, the co-op had added more than 2,100 members and built its new headquarters without raising rates.

Jackson EMC expanded further in May 1982 when it opened a new, 20,000-square-foot facility with a 160-seat auditorium on Swanson Drive in Lawrenceville to replace the Lawrenceville District office on Buford Drive. When this office opened in 1959, the cooperative provided power to fifteen thousand

Jackson EMC launched a comprehensive heat pump program in the early 1980s, offering members incentive to install electric heat pumps. Assisting in promoting the program were developers like Steve Hill, left, and Buzz Curtain of Oakbrook Properties whose homes at Mount Moriah Heights in north Gwinnett County were equipped with energy efficient electric heat pumps.

Jackson EMC board members held a groundbreaking ceremony for a new co-op headquarters on January 5, 1979, almost forty years to the day from when the board broke ground nearby to construct its first power lines in 1939. At the 1979 event were, from left, Upshaw Bentley, co-op attorney; Ernest McLocklin, board vice president; William Booth, manager; A. T. "Troy" Sharpton, board president; and Paul Burroughs, Balfour Hunnicutt, and Bill Carpenter, directors.

The new cooperative headquarters on Commerce Road opened June 9, 1980, and included ample space for offices, garage, machine shops, a covered dock, and warehouse.

members throughout its entire service territory; by 1982, the co-op served almost that many in Gwinnett County alone.

All across Jackson EMC's service area, growth was booming again, roads were being paved, malls built, and power lines were going up. Within a decade, the northeast Georgia communities served by the cooperative had come full circle. From a burst of growth in the early seventies to a stall in the middle of the decade, the area had returned to bustling development into the eighties. The co-op, which had made considerable strides during the downtime, was prepared for the economic comeback—outside, where new power lines and substations were prepared to handle larger loads,

Additional office space made available when the new headquarters opened was welcomed by employees in need of more room for system controls and the cooperative's growing cadre of computers, examined here by, from left, Lawrenceville District Engineering and Operations Coordinator Gary Bullock, Operations Engineer Tommy Childress, and Dispatcher Mike Montgomery.

District offices were expanded as the co-op's membership grew. The Neese office (middle top) was the smallest and most rural district. The Gainesville District office (left) handled operations in one of the cooperative's busiest areas, Hall County, through the poultry boom of the sixties and seventies. The Lawrenceville District office (above) on Buford Drive opened in 1959, replacing a much smaller office the district had worked out of since 1953. A new facility on Swanson Drive replaced this Lawrenceville District office in 1982.

and inside, where modernizations featured a computerized data processing system that integrated systems in all districts and departments.

By May 1982, Interstate Industrial Park, developed by Alvin R. Weeks, included multiple industries that purchased power from Jackson EMC, including Scientific Atlanta, Kubota Tractor, Panasonic, Edison Industries, and Duracell Battery. Others among the first to select Jackson EMC in customer choice situations were OKI Advanced Communications in Gwinnett and Primex Plastics in Gainesville.

Interstate Industrial Park was the premiere address for industry in Gwinnett County, and just as Weeks, as the developer, was a visionary in recognizing the potential for industrial growth, Jackson EMC's marketing department was visionary in communicating the commercial opportunities to co-op members and potential members. During the downtime in the mid-seventies, the cooperative had upgraded

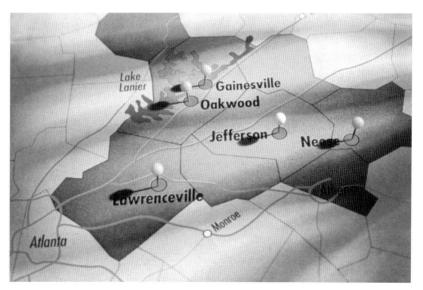

While Jackson EMC served small portions of Oglethorpe and Franklin Counties, most of its territory stretched through eight northeast Georgia counties with three district offices, a headquarters office, and an engineering and operations office strategically located to provide fast, efficient service.

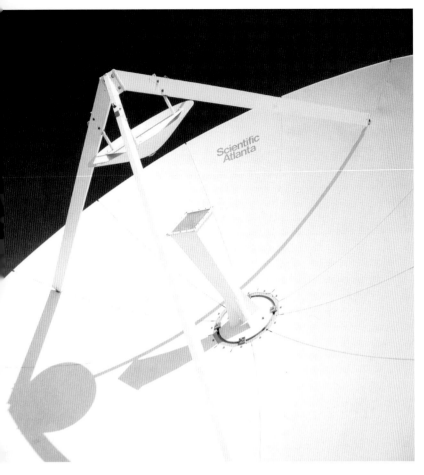

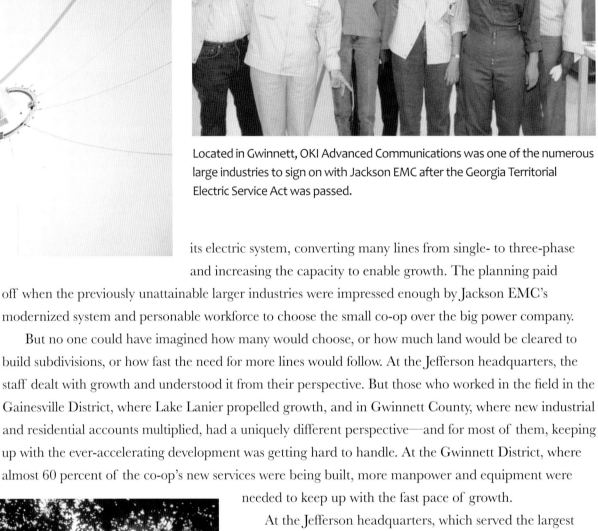

Located in Gwinnett, OKI Advanced Communications was one of the numerous large industries to sign on with Jackson EMC after the Georgia Territorial Electric Service Act was passed.

Scientific Atlanta joined Kubota Tractor, Panasonic, Duracell Battery, and a host of other industries at the Interstate Industrial Park, developed by Alvin R. Weeks as a catalyst for growth in Gwinnett County.

its electric system, converting many lines from single- to three-phase and increasing the capacity to enable growth. The planning paid off when the previously unattainable larger industries were impressed enough by Jackson EMC's modernized system and personable workforce to choose the small co-op over the big power company.

But no one could have imagined how many would choose, or how much land would be cleared to build subdivisions, or how fast the need for more lines would follow. At the Jefferson headquarters, the staff dealt with growth and understood it from their perspective. But those who worked in the field in the Gainesville District, where Lake Lanier propelled growth, and in Gwinnett County, where new industrial and residential accounts multiplied, had a uniquely different perspective—and for most of them, keeping up with the ever-accelerating development was getting hard to handle. At the Gwinnett District, where almost 60 percent of the co-op's new services were being built, more manpower and equipment were needed to keep up with the fast pace of growth.

Komatsu was another large industry Jackson EMC landed in the eighties as a large load customer.

At the Jefferson headquarters, which served the largest geographic territory, there were more trucks. Through the late seventies and early eighties, headquarters daily sent teams of bucket, digger, and pole-setting trucks manned with line crews to the Gwinnett District to assist with line construction there. Even so, the help never seemed to be quite enough to keep up with the multitude of work orders that poured in.

Manager Booth deemed 1983 as the turnaround year for growth. "The year 1983 has been very busy and eventful, particularly in the last half of the year," he said. "Our rate of growth has increased markedly, and we have found it necessary to put forth extra effort to meet the demands. We

A co-op lineman works at the pole in 1982 at the intersection of Pleasant Hill and Club Roads in Gwinnett County.

will continue to build new lines and services as needed, rework existing lines where necessary and build new transmission and substations where required."

On January 8, 1984, General Booth, at age seventy-two, died in his sleep at his Apple Valley home. As a charter director, board member, and manager, he had served Jackson EMC for almost forty years. He was remembered as a man whose life was devoted to improving the quality of life in rural areas. "Jackson EMC was his first love, but he contributed immeasurably to the success of countless other community, civic and youth organizations throughout the area," recalled Sims.

Whether they called him Mr. Booth, Manager Booth, or General Booth, those who worked with the iron-fisted leader remembered him as firm but fair, and wholeheartedly dedicated to rural electricity. His exhortation of, "Service is our only reason for existence," given at the end of any and all meetings with employees, is remembered to this day.

Chapter Twelve
Riding an Electric Wave

"The electric age ... established a global network that has much the character of our central nervous system."

—Herbert Marshall McLuhan
Communication theorist
Known for his studies on the effects of mass media

When Mitsubishi opened its Braselton manufacturing plant in the mid-eighties, cellphones were still referred to as cellular mobile telephones and the new Jackson County industry was set to employ up to 450 people to produce them. Winning the large load was a coup for Jackson EMC and a blessing to area residents accustomed to driving out of town to work in Atlanta or Gainesville. Henry Braselton, grandson of town founder W. H. Braselton Sr., reported there would be no shortage of employees to fill positions at the new plant. "We had eight thousand applicants for two hundred jobs. Gwinnett County is just coming this way," he said. "There's no way to stop it—it's like the ocean."

For the next two decades, waves of growth would roll into Jackson EMC's service territory like the Gulf of Mexico during hurricane season, sometimes splashing, but more often crashing in with a thunderous roar of unbridled but not unwelcomed progress and economic growth. Jackson EMC positioned, then repositioned itself when necessary, to ride the wave.

Road Atlanta opened in 1970 in Braselton as a Jackson EMC customer. As surely as the cars there raced to the finish line, co-op employees raced to keep up with the rapidly increasing demand for new service.

Opposite page: As was predicted during construction of Interstate 85 in the 1960s, the interstate highway brought industry to Jackson EMC territory, along with an increase in population that catapulted the cooperative's membership. Part of what defines Jackson EMC is its location, predominantly along Interstate 85, which bisects the center of its service territory while Interstate 985 runs through the western part of the service area, from Gwinnett County through Hall County. Highway 316 brings business to the eastern side of the territory, from Barrow County to Athens.

Gwinnett County Director A. T. "Troy" Sharpton served as president of the board during much of Jackson EMC's high-growth period.

Right: At one point in the mid-1980s, Jackson EMC installed up to fifty new services a day in Gwinnett County alone, many along Satellite Boulevard where lineman Ricky Frazier worked in 1985.

Gwinnett County Director Troy Sharpton was board president when the growth in his district pulsated like raw nerve endings. The never-ceasing, breakneck speed of expansion was in stark contrast to the simpler, slower times of his childhood on the family farm in Auburn, a small city straddling Gwinnett and Barrow Counties. The growth didn't just take off. It exploded. In the mid-eighties, Jackson EMC employees and contractors installed as many as fifty new services a day in Gwinnett County, most in subdivisions. The pace was staggering. Throughout the cooperative, whether in the field building lines or at a desk drawing plans, employees raced to stay in place. Getting ahead was out of the question.

By late 1984, with a few years' worth of experience competing with Georgia Power for commercial accounts, Jackson EMC was starting to win more than it lost. The early Jackson EMC wins over the larger, wealthier power company were looked upon by many as substantial as David beating the giant Goliath.

Led by dedicated board members and determined personnel since its beginnings, Jackson EMC had long been a well-managed, capable cooperative. For the most part, it had kept pace with progress as well as a not-for-profit, rural cooperative was expected to. Its retail rates were competitive with Georgia Power's, even though Jackson EMC averaged serving only ten consumers per mile of line compared with Georgia Power's thirty-five to forty customers per mile. The co-op's fewer consumers earned it $9,000 per mile, compared to Georgia Power's $40,000 or more, but the cooperative fared well despite that imbalance. It routinely returned margins to its members and extended lines as fast as it could. Most importantly, it kept the lights on.

At the same time, the cooperative was behind in certain areas. While many of the nation's businesses had moved on to computerization, employees in Jackson EMC's accounting office still used handwritten ledgers.

Randall Pugh was hired in August 1984 as the cooperative's general manager, a title that later changed to president/CEO. Pugh had spent his career working in the electric cooperative industry and brought expertise to Jackson EMC that helped the local co-op navigate the massive changes ahead.

Member Services Manager Charles Sims, left, and Manager of Operations and Maintenance Lewis Shirley chat at the co-op's Jefferson warehouse in 1988. Shirley began his lengthy career with Jackson EMC as a lineman in 1952 and lost his right arm in an electrical accident the following year. During his thirty-eight years of service, Shirley witnessed the dramatic growth in Jackson EMC's service territory, was instrumental in the installation of the co-op's SCADA system, and is remembered for his dedication to getting the lights back on after storms.

When the co-op finally purchased its first computer system, employees had to share computer terminals because the high cost for the new technology was deemed too exorbitant. And while the line crews and engineers had adequate equipment to work with, it was not always the most modern or efficient, and there simply was not enough of it to keep up with construction demands.

The limited computer access and aging equipment might have been enough to get by with for a few more years had Atlanta grown south, but the progressive boom headed north, straight into Jackson EMC territory. Nothing could have prepared the cooperative for the almost shocking growth surge that slammed it in the early- to mid-eighties and kept slamming it through the next decade.

Fortunately, some saw it coming.

Jackson EMC Director Bill Carpenter was on the search committee to select the new manager and recalled that about seventy-five people sought the job. "Randall Pugh was the most outstanding applicant we had," Carpenter said, "and time has substantiated the fact that we made a very excellent choice. Randall was our first manager with an accounting and finance background. He had qualities of all the men we'd had—R. J. Kelly: Randall had a good technical background and is quite proficient in operations and engineering. He incorporated Bill Welch's love for customer service, and Jackson now is tops in the nation customer service-wise. And like Bill Booth, Randall's a tough competitor; he plays to win. He's highly respected in the community and has the characteristics of all these men wrapped up in one person."

As manager of Walton EMC, Randall Pugh had witnessed phenomenal growth in southern Gwinnett County and knew Interstate 85 would bring similar growth to north Gwinnett, which was in Jackson EMC territory.

A Plan of Action

When Randall Pugh joined the cooperative as its new president/CEO in August 1984, Jackson EMC was in full-steam-ahead growth mode. A native of Gwinnett County who grew up just outside Buford, Pugh had graduated from UGA with an accounting degree and served two years in the US Army before working at nearby Walton EMC in Monroe for sixteen years, seven as general manager. Upon moving to Jefferson to start his new job, he recognized similarities between the co-op he'd left and the one he'd come to, most notably that Jackson EMC was in line for unprecedented growth, just as its southern neighbor, Walton EMC, had faced in recent years.

"I saw what was happening, knew what the potential was and knew that after Gwinnett it was going to be Jackson, Hall and Barrow," said Pugh. "I think the growth snuck up on people here. We saw that growth at Walton coming first out of Atlanta in the south Gwinnett area. In the mid-to-late sixties, Walton got caught; we didn't anticipate it either, and the growth outstripped our planning and ability to provide the capacity in the system. We learned it the hard way and had some catch-up to do."

Pugh estimated that Jackson EMC was about fifteen years behind Walton in terms of growth and was determined to use what he'd learned there to get, and attempt to keep, Jackson EMC ahead of the curve. His challenge would be to lead the cooperative out of business-as-usual in order to prepare it for the rapidly approaching growth.

Even before his service as interim manager between the death of William Booth in January 1984 and Pugh's arrival in August, Charles Sims had started refocusing his member services team's direction to a more aggressive sales stance, foreseeing that with the flood of new residents and businesses moving into Jackson EMC territory, the sheer volume would dictate rate increases unless meaningful action was taken. By September 1984, net growth in the previous twelve months had increased 97 percent over the prior year. Had the growth not targeted its territory, if the cooperative had progressed at the steady, calculable rate experienced in years past, the need to evolve would not have been warranted. But in the face of substantial change, Jackson EMC had to come up with new ways of doing business.

No single departmental change, facility renovation, or equipment upgrade could begin to meet the challenges that confronted the co-op.

On top of everything else, Vogtle Nuclear Power Plant was gearing up to come on line. Jackson EMC, along with thirty-eight other Georgia electric cooperatives, had invested in the plant in order to secure an

adequate power supply to meet the anticipated growth in the state. While it was the need to become self-reliant in wholesale power generation that led the cooperative to invest in Plant Vogtle, it was the cooperative's growing service area that allowed it to blend more expensive nuclear power into its rate base, while minimizing the impact on customers. Growth was coming; it was a strategic decision to maximize the benefit of that growth by promoting electric sales through electric space heating in homes and signing industrial loads that consume large quantities of power around the clock.

In its favor was Jackson EMC's geography. With its service area bisected by a network of three major highways, Georgia Highway 316 and Interstates 85 and 985, it was an area that nurtured ample industrial, commercial, and residential growth. The cooperative named its service area the "Golden Triangle" and incorporated an image depicting it into the co-op logo. While it was the electric sales growth that led the cooperative to invest in nuclear generation, electric sales, in turn, were key

Interstate Industrial Park was eventually renamed Gwinnett Industrial Park and attracted numerous Fortune 500 companies in the 1980s and 90s.

to absorbing the cost of Plant Vogtle. Therein was the opportunity to maximize the sale of kilowatt-hours—to sell total electric to the explosive residential base and to sign large commercial and industrial loads whose year-round consumption of energy allowed the cooperative to offset Vogtle's fixed cost.

Having experienced the residential growth explosion at his former co-op, Pugh recognized the formula for keeping down costs at Jackson EMC was to maximize the opportunities of adding large industrial loads within its grasp. A few large loads like Rockwell International and Southeastern Freezer were on the system and bringing on more would benefit all customers by keeping rates low.

Promoting total electric living was already in Charles Sims's playbook, and now he had the opportunity to gain market share in large numbers as a result of the record residential construction pace. Promoting heat pumps to residential customers was already a way of life at Jackson EMC; now it became a matter of adapting that sales approach to large-scale subdivisions and apartments.

The aggressive push to court large industries and sell residential total electric would necessitate increasing system capacity, adding employees, and improving outside and office equipment to handle it all. Some directors anticipated growth would come regardless, so the co-op had better bulk up to meet it; others felt it prudent to invest only the bare minimum. What some saw as an opportunity to keep costs down in the long run, others deemed as an excessive outlay of funds in the short-term.

Contractor construction crews set poles in Gwinnett County, a scene common throughout the 1980s and 90s as line construction crews continuously worked to keep pace with growth.

Convinced that increased kilowatt-hour sales would positively impact future rates, Jackson EMC set out to build a balanced load by adding total electric homes and large commercial and industrial customers. To achieve the company's sales and customer service goals, significant effort was spent on revising board policies and operating procedures and in planning for the future. "We made the commitment to increase the capacity of the system to handle the growth," said Pugh. "And it's a good thing we did because when the growth came, it came at a level that was greater than most people, including me, realized it would."

Where farmland and forests once reigned, a metropolitan suburb sprang up. Developers couldn't move enough dirt or build houses fast enough. Jackson EMC was a small company scrambling to keep up. Industrial clients appreciated the co-op's sincerity but questioned its strength and savvy. Developers, who had subdivisions to build, weren't sure the rural electric cooperative was up to the task.

Operations were restructured. Power lines were boosted with greater capacity, from twelve kilovolts to twenty-five kilovolts, to handle more consumers. Facilities were upgraded, additional equipment and utility trucks were purchased, and line workers were added at Gwinnett, Gainesville, and Jefferson. "We had been

Just as the commercial and industrial customer base grew, so did the number of residential customers, who were well-served by Jackson EMC member services representatives such as Leigh Ann Diffenderfer, left, shown assisting customers Joy (Flannagan) Knight and George Flannagan in choosing energy efficiency measures they could utilize to save on power bills.

putting a caravan of trucks, pole trailers, and crews, sending them down I-85 to Gwinnett County to work," said Pugh. "By the time they set up, worked, and then got back here by 4:30, they may have gotten five hours' worth of work in." Managing resources out of the Jefferson headquarters had stifled the cooperative's attempts to keep up. Restructuring so that each district handled its own operations proved more efficient and effective.

By the mid-eighties, the biannual Ladies Day programs that once attracted hundreds of housewives to hear the latest in laundering techniques were called off as attendance dwindled due to more women entering the workplace. Home service advisors who once taught kitchen skills became member service representatives who analyzed electricity usage for members concerned about high bills, explaining to them the difference between perceived high bills—where higher charges were due to more power consumed in extra hot or cold weather, by holiday lights, or increased appliance usage—and true high bills, those that could be resolved by replacing a malfunctioning well pump or switching to a cost-saving heat pump.

Throughout the cooperative, new staff was hired and equipment improved. At the Jefferson headquarters, the restructuring meant beefing up member services and marketing, especially residential and commercial marketing in order to aggressively compete with gas companies for residential members' load and the private power company for customer choice clients. In Gwinnett County, satellite offices were opened to give members easier access to the co-op's services. Line construction crews were constantly building and often worked after hours and on weekends.

Jackson EMC met with more success than failure when courting new accounts due to the exceptional customer service it provided developers and contractors. The cooperative didn't have excess money to throw around, but it could, and did, pitch its good name and its reputation for quality service.

Growing the cooperative to meet the challenges of growth in its communities was often an uphill climb, but Jackson EMC forged on.

A new meter reading program was introduced in 1985 with employees like Jeff Ertzberger using handheld readers to take down readings, which were uploaded electronically to the co-op's new computer system.

A seismic culture shift occurred when employees were called on to abandon typewriters and adding machines in order to utilize computers. The shift would cause a few headaches along the way, but the new technology ultimately improved operations at the cooperative. In 1987, then-Engineering Services Manager Jim Smith analyzed the electric system's growth onscreen.

New Ways of Doing Things

Jackson EMC's staff exuded a can-do, get-it-done attitude that propelled the company forward, even when its workers felt like they were running and going nowhere, especially in Gwinnett County where 70 percent of the co-op's 8,424 new accounts were added in 1985. With almost 70,000 meters in all, Jackson EMC's rapid rate of growth had made it one of the largest electric cooperatives in the nation. To keep pace with the astounding growth, the cooperative that year borrowed $30 million to build new lines and upgrade the system to meet projections for the next two years. At the time, the loan was the largest made to any electric distribution cooperative in history.

Internal and external communications changed dramatically with the introduction of personal computers in 1985. Until then, the only computers utilized at the cooperative were two mainframes that had been installed several years earlier. Jackson EMC's first foray into personal computers accompanied introduction of a new meter reading program.

Since its lines were first energized, Jackson EMC had mailed members monthly cards and depended on them to take their own meter readings. The new plan would utilize field service representatives to conduct monthly meter readings in an effort to decrease errors associated with meter tampering and power theft. When the program launched in 1985, thirty-five field service representatives utilized hand-held devices that read meters and then uploaded the readings electronically to the new computers. Hazards for meter readers ranged from hard-to-reach meters covered in kudzu vines to vicious dogs daring the reps to come close. The job carried a weight of responsibility because the meter reader often served as the face of Jackson EMC for members whose only personal contact with the co-op was seeing the field service representative at their home.

While one of the two first personal computers was for the meter reading program, the other was reserved for employees to learn how to use a personal computer. Entering into the modern age of computers was no small task for the small information systems staff at the co-op, where a huge culture shift accompanied the introduction of new technologies. As a not-for-profit cooperative, Jackson EMC didn't bite off too much at one time when it came to unproven technologies, preferring to first let systems develop and be proven as good business solutions, implementing them in full only after they had passed muster. As computers, software, and associated technologies were enhanced and their prices decreased, the cooperative took on more technology as it tried to keep pace with a world rapidly evolving in the way it communicated.

When the new meter-reading program kicked off in 1985, thirty-five field service representatives—including, from left, Randall Brown, Robbie Foster, Hoyt Winkler, and Darren Copeland—were equipped with hand-held devices to read members' meters.

Serving the Nation's Fastest-growing Region

To the surprise of few Jackson EMC employees, Gwinnett was proclaimed the fastest-growing county in the nation in 1986, a distinction it held for three years in the eighties. Its leaders had developed Gwinnett County with appealing infrastructure, complete with roads, sewer, and water—and land there was inexpensive, creating the perfect formula for development in Georgia's catbird seat for growth.

Perhaps the appeal was too great. In the eighties, so much construction occurred up and down Gwinnett's busy roadsides that workers often felt their lives were in peril. Traffic never ceased along the continuously expanding highways. Co-op crews would build lines, and six months later the highway was being widened again and the newly built lines had to be shifted to the new right of way.

Exacerbating the problem, workers from all the different utilities were on top of each other, all jostling to get their facilities installed. Jackson EMC would put services in, and then gas or phone company subcontractors would cut through co-op underground wires to run their service lines. Neighboring Cobb County had solved a similar situation by allotting space on the roadside for each utility. To bring order to the chaos, managers of the various utilities and county government came together to form the Gwinnett Utility Association, which standardized where each utility would place its equipment. Jackson EMC's Gwinnett District manager, Roger Willis, served as the association's first president.

Top: Gwinnett County's Coers' Corner opened in 1986 at Interstate 85 and Indian Trail Road. Developed by the Coers Company of Atlanta, the first building completed there was the four-story Oakbrook Plaza, which boasted 84,000 square feet of office space. It was among the first multi-story developments devoted solely to office space along Gwinnett's bustling I-85 corridor.

Left: Jackson EMC served more and more apartment complexes as population in its service area exploded in the 1980s. In May 1986, an open house was held at Breckinridge, the newest apartment complex in Gwinnett to be served by Jackson EMC. The four-hundred-unit complex just off Pleasant Hill Road near Gwinnett Place featured an electric heat pump in each apartment unit. The builders were among many who chose to participate in the co-op's energy efficient heat pump program designed to help lower monthly power bills.

The new Canon USA facility was featured in the June 1986 edition of *Jemco News* as one of the cooperative's newest large industrial customers.

While Gwinnett's growth was the most frenzied, other portions of the EMC territory grew as well, including the Gainesville District where Lanier Woods North was the first subdivision with underground lines. As the aesthetically preferable underground service increased in popularity, more developers asked for it and more linemen were trained to provide it. In the last half of the eighties, all linemen were cross-trained to install both overhead and underground power lines.

In 1986, directors and management set specific goals for the year: to increase internal productivity, increase winter load, control summer load, and increase efforts to gain more large commercial businesses and industries that had the choice to select Jackson EMC over other power suppliers. The cooperative achieved its goals and in some cases exceeded expectations. The rate of growth continued to be among the highest of the nation's electric cooperatives. For the first time in its history, Jackson EMC sold more than one billion kilowatt-hours of electricity. Using "The Reliable Choice" as its slogan, the co-op courted big accounts and won them more often than not.

Local gas companies and investor-owned utilities were well versed on Jackson EMC as their competitor, and by the end of the decade, the electric cooperative was making national headlines. Pugh's portrait was featured on the cover of the May 1988 issue of *Rural Electrification Magazine*, the trade publication for the nation's rural electric cooperatives. Inside, a four-page article was titled "Big

Jackson EMC. For all the right reasons.

Rates. Reliability. Technology. Accessibility.
These are the tangible reasons business and industry buy electricity from us.
Another is our people. They are bright, young and proud.
Taking shape in their minds today are the solutions for tomorrow.
Their ingenuity is our trademark.

The Reliable Choice

JACKSON
ELECTRIC MEMBERSHIP CORPORATION

Above: President/CEO Randall Pugh was featured on the cover of *Rural Electrification Magazine*'s May 1988 issue, which focused on Jackson EMC's aggressive marketing strategy for landing large industrial customers.

Left: Jackson EMC adopted the slogan "The Reliable Choice" in the eighties to assure large industrial customers of the cooperative's ability to serve them.

League Co-op: Jackson EMC out-hustles a big power company for Japanese industry." The big power company was Georgia Power; the Japanese industry included Kubota. The article applauded Jackson EMC as one of the first cooperatives in the US to utilize a supervisory control and data acquisition system (SCADA) for load management. Jackson EMC, the article concluded, possessed a "split personality."

"It is both a bedrock institution of rural north Georgia, and a sophisticated player in the urbanization of the New South," the article read. "While Jackson needs to be a caring member of the community, ready to provide service to small-town people, it also needs to be a savvy player in the corporate big leagues. Jackson uses the words 'the company' and 'customers' when addressing industry people, and 'the co-op' and 'members' when talking to residential customers. Pugh is comfortable, and effective, with either audience."

The Residential Angle

To meet Jackson EMC's goal of achieving greater total electric saturation, the cooperative bulked up its residential sales team. The cooperative had just restructured and the excitement of building a workforce, hiring more reps, and creating new programs was intense. The challenge was to place heat pumps in homes to increase total electric saturation. Each day residential marketing representatives beat the bushes in subdivisions, searching out builders and talking with them. Some builders were sold on natural gas, but if one or two key builders in an area would try total electric, others would follow.

Historically a heavy natural gas market, Gwinnett County had fewer total electric homes on EMC lines than other counties in the co-op's territory. In 1992, the total electric saturation of new home construction was only at 9 percent in Gwinnett County, where residents favored natural gas for home heating. In the co-op's more rural counties, total electric saturation was denser, in the 80 percent range in the Jefferson District, 90s in the Neese District, and 70 to 80 percent in Gainesville. The co-op worked hard to up the percentages, particularly in Gwinnett County. The perception that gas was the cheaper fuel made the cooperative's job difficult, forcing it to work harder to get across its story—that electric heat pumps are more than competitive for heating.

Atlanta Gas Light Company was a formidable competitor for residential load, just as Georgia Power Company was for industrial load. To sell electricity via heat pumps and electric water heaters, Jackson EMC would have to promote its product in a strategic marketing plan, just as the co-op originally did in 1958 when it rolled out its first program designed to increase residential electric sales. The Medallion Home program began as a means to award homeowners and builders for meeting or exceeding certain criteria when lighting and wiring new homes. In the sixties, the program steered its focus on promoting total electric homes. In the decades that followed, the co-op modified its home electric sales and energy efficiency programs to reflect changes in the marketplace.

In 1977, Gold Medallion gave way to the Energy Efficient Home program, with residential marketing representatives working with builders and homeowners to ensure energy-efficient weatherization features were incorporated into new home construction; by 1984, the co-op was among the first utilities in the nation to offer financial incentives for members who installed energy efficient equipment.

Jackson EMC presented its Energy Efficient Home Award to Ed and Donna Creel in 1986. Co-op Member Services Representative Luther Wilkes, front center, presented the award while visiting with the Creel family and representatives of their homebuilder, Northeast Builders of Winder.

While the Energy Efficient Home program had been successful, it lacked name recognition, something the cooperative gained in 1987 when it introduced the Good Cents® Home program, a national program promoting energy-efficient construction. Building to Good Cents specifications qualified co-op members for a heat pump cash rebate and ensured lower utility bills and higher resale values. Good Cents was replaced in 1996 with the ComfortHome® program, which paired co-op employees with homeowners and builders to get the most out of electric heat pumps by equipping homes with adequate insulation, precisely sized heating and

cooling equipment, and proper air flow for consistent comfort levels. While Good Cents had been a prescriptive program, with builders given a list of things to do, ComfortHome was a performance-based program that addressed homeowners' top concerns—heat pumps that produced cold heat and electric water heaters that didn't recover promptly.

When state code standards were upgraded to meet ComfortHome building requirements, Jackson EMC, which prided itself in staying at least one step ahead of standards, considered it the ideal time to develop yet another energy-efficient home program. The Right Choice™ program debuted in 2004, giving Jackson EMC its own brand. Right Choice standards are performance-based but call for an enhanced heating and air analysis to determine the efficiency of the heating and air system.

With incentives offered to offset costs, Right Choice homes must pass specific requirements to ensure maximum energy

1958–1977, Medallion Home In effect for almost twenty years, Medallion Home was Jackson EMC's first formal home energy efficiency program. Evelyn Harris, right, presented a Medallion Award to a homeowner who followed program criteria when building her new home.

1977–1987, Energy Efficient Home Hampton Woods Apartments (top) in Gwinnett was awarded Energy Efficient Home honors in 1985. Gwinnett Member Services Representative Lonnie Hall, right, presented the award to John McLean, developer, and Marcia Pettey, resident manager.

1987–1996, Good Cents® Home This was a national program adopted by Jackson EMC to promote energy-efficient construction by offering members a cash rebate when purchasing a heat pump.

1996–2004, ComfortHome® This initiative paired co-op member services employees with homebuilders in a performance-based program designed to get the most out of a home's heat pumps and water heaters.

2004–Current, Right Choice™ Standards for the current energy-efficiency home program are performance based and require enhanced heating and air analysis to judge heating and cooling efficiency.

efficiency and comfort. Right Choice homeowners receive use and comfort warranties, as well as the co-op's lowest residential rates; savings average about 5 percent each month. The preferential rate follows the home, even when it's sold. Star Home Builders constructed the first Right Choice home in 2004 at Shepherd's Crossing in Jefferson. In 2008, the cooperative added the Energy Star qualification to new Right Choice homes and, in 2009, was recognized by the US Environmental Protection Agency with its Energy Star Leadership in Housing Award for promoting energy-efficient construction and environmental protection.

In sixteen years, the Good Cents, ComfortHome, and Right Choice programs enabled Jackson EMC to raise its total electric saturation from about 20 percent system-wide in 1992 to almost 80 percent total electric saturation by 2008.

Along with its various energy efficiency programs for new home construction and remodels, Jackson EMC continued to offer an assortment of energy education tools, including walk-thru home energy audits and, when World Wide Web technology made it available, an online audit allowing members to assess their power bill to study how their energy dollars are spent. Jackson EMC's do-it-yourself energy audit video kit is mailed to as many as fifty members each month and offers low-cost tips for saving on power bills, like changing heating and air system filters or altering thermostat settings. In recent years, a HomePlus loan program offered $1,000 to $5,500 at 0 percent interest for energy efficiency improvements.

While many utilities ratcheted down their energy efficiency programs in the nineties and into the new century, Jackson EMC did not. An extreme dedication from upper management kept the cooperative focused on energy efficiency programs, deeming it the right thing to do to help members. On the energy efficiency front, the co-op would stay ahead of the curve—because it never quit.

The Benefit of Aggressive Kilowatt-hour Sales

Just as it worked to acquire total electric residential customers, Jackson EMC vigorously promoted itself to commercial and industrial customers large enough to choose an electric provider. The cooperative committed to keeping its strong energy sales by courting large industries and commercial customers that kept their lights and machinery working twenty-four hours a day as well as total electric residential developments that pushed the cooperative's load factor to an all-time high.

Beginning in the mid-1980s, a surge of growth that left Jackson EMC scrambling to keep up for the next two decades was accented with signs like these throughout the cooperative's service territory, advertising soon-to-be developments of everything from subdivisions to car dealerships to industrial parks. Preparing for the development of the Banks County Industrial Park (photo at left) were Bank of Banks President George Evans, left, and Milton Patterson, chairman of the Banks County Industrial Park.

The successful sales strategy was staggering in terms of kilowatt-hours sold by customer type. Even though commercial accounts comprised only 7 percent of the co-op customer base by 1999, those accounts supplied 37 percent of the annual revenue, money that allowed the co-op to expand service to all members. The vital importance of this quest for large, high load factor commercial/industrial accounts led Jackson EMC to create the first commercial/industrial marketing department of any cooperative in the nation.

Roy Stowe, left, was director of commercial and industrial marketing and Jim Crawford, a commercial marketing representative, in 1987, at the height of the cooperative's push to win large commercial/industrial loads. In 2013, Crawford serves as vice president of customer/district services and Stowe as vice president of marketing/member relations.

As a rural electric competing for industries accustomed to doing business with huge corporations throughout the United States, the hometown co-op was compelled to improve its image. "If we were going to compete for commercial industrial loads, we had to have a reputation and a positive image, an identity, so people would look favorably on us as a viable power supplier," said Pugh.

It would take time. Linemen who once worked in T-shirts and jeans were fitted with uniforms in order to present a professional image. Antiquated trucks were retired and replaced with newer models. Outfitting line workers with new uniforms could be done in relatively short time, but upgrading an entire fleet of utility vehicles would take longer. Year by year, old trucks were sold and newer, improved models with state-of-the-art equipment were purchased to ease the linemen's work and improve the overall image of the cooperative.

While Jackson EMC was a known force in northeast Georgia, it had to advertise to establish an identity among national and

The grand opening of a new Big Star grocery store in Gainesville was a heralded event as were openings of all new endeavors of commercial and industrial customers served by Jackson EMC.

international industrial leaders. In the marketing department at co-op headquarters, staff worked to advertise the cooperative by way of promotional brochures and videos, which ultimately gained the attention of potential large-load customers who had been accustomed to doing business with only the private electric utilities. Competition between the cooperative and Georgia Power Company for the large accounts was "high pressured, to say the least," according to Pugh. "We had to convince folks that we were serious about giving them reliable service."

To do that, Jackson EMC did what no other EMC in Georgia had done when they started offering underground service encased in concrete to provide additional reliability. Aesthetics were important to quality industrial parks to help them sell their park to tenants. They wanted a utility that helped them preserve the landscaping, so facilities had to be underground and reliability had to be good. Up to that point, underground cable was simply laid in a trench and covered up with dirt. Encasing in concrete cost the cooperative more, but it was necessary early on to convince those leery of rural electrics that Jackson EMC had the ability to provide reliable service.

Jackson EMC was the first electric cooperative in Georgia to offer underground service encased in concrete, a measure it took in the 1980s to enhance reliability in an effort to win large industrial customers along Satellite Boulevard in the vicinity of Gwinnett Place Mall where business boomed that decade. To keep the system operational and dependable, linemen Ben Ivie, left, and Michael Harrison changed out an underground transformer at Satellite Place.

The decision to go after the large loads required a commitment from both the board of directors and management. At stake was the cooperative's ability to take advantage of opportunities with the growth in commercial and industrial business, and some questioned whether it could be done. But the board, management, and employees pledged to do what it took to prove to potential large customers that Jackson EMC could deliver on its promise.

It was a defining moment, and the commitment paid off in short order. In 1988, Jackson EMC won twenty-one customer choice loads with total projected annual revenue of $19 million. That year, the cooperative signed up 72 percent of the large customers who could choose power suppliers in its service area. In Gwinnett County, where the competition between Jackson EMC and Georgia Power Company was the most aggressive, the co-op signed five out of the nine biggest square-footage accounts. That intense spirit of competition was noted in the May 1988 issue of *Rural Electrification Magazine*, which reported, "Jackson EMC is a fierce negotiator for loads when it needs to be."

The cooperative had modernized equipment and facilities and improved its overall image, but its secret weapon, said Pugh, was its employees. "Technically, our competitors can equal us, but they have a long way to go to match our people who will do everything they can to get the job done," he said. "This quality, more than any other, will drive our cooperative ahead of our competitors in our ability to provide the best service at the best price."

A steady strategy of service and accommodation resulted in the cooperative attracting big-name customers. As more accounts were added, more industries took note and were impressed when they found out Jackson EMC's electric system was absolutely reliable and that the cooperative had crews plenty capable of taking care of the largest industries.

A common question from potential industrial clients to the co-op sales staff was: "All things considered, it's a fraction of a penny difference between you and other utilities. Tell me why should I go with Jackson EMC?" The answer was strategic, and sincere: "Because to them you're just a number, and to us you're a valued customer."

Kubota Manufacturing of America remained a valued customer since first choosing Jackson EMC as its power supplier in 1975. When A. R. Weeks launched Interstate Industrial Park in Gwinnett County, Kubota was the new park's first major distribution facility. The Japanese tractor manufacturer became one of Jackson EMC's first large industrial consumers. Eleven years later, when Kubota outgrew its facilities at Gwinnett Industrial Park, it moved to NorthBrook Park, another Weeks development in Gwinnett County; Kubota was the first tenant in this new

Jackson EMC's marketing department worked diligently to tell the co-op's story in order to assure prospective members of the rural cooperative's impressive reliability. A.R. Weeks and Associates and Kubota Tractor were two large customers who vouched for the co-op in glowing testimonials shared in print advertising.

The cooperative landed five anchor stores as customers when the Mall of Georgia opened near Buford in 1999.

industrial park at I-85 and Old Peachtree Road. In 1988, when Kubota opened its first US assembly plant at Industrial Park North in Gainesville, Jackson EMC again was chosen to provide power.

The partnership between Kubota and Jackson EMC continued through the years with co-op representatives touring the company's Osaka, Japan, plant in 1995; performing an extensive energy audit and lighting survey in 2002; and working with the company during numerous plant expansions. In 2005, Jackson EMC was chosen to provide power to yet another Kubota facility, this one in Jackson County. Mickey Lord, Kubota's manufacturing engineering manager, said Jackson EMC was the "only choice" for his company.

"Jackson EMC's service is impeccable," said Lord. "They are the most responsive energy provider I've ever worked with. They are personable, open and take their accounts seriously. They make sure the expectations of the customers are always met."

The early days of trying to sell large commercial customers on the rural electric cooperative produced some losses and lessons learned that led to future wins. The co-op didn't win Gwinnett Place Mall in the early eighties, but when the Mall of Georgia opened in 1999 near Buford, Jackson EMC was selected to provide power to five of its anchor stores—J.C. Penney, Lord and Taylor, Galyan's Trading Company, Dillard's, and Haverty's—plus nearby Target, Wal-Mart, and Lowe's. Signing large customers was a lengthy and complicated process with architects and company executives, but the cooperative's sales teams had earned the trust and respect of the commercial and industrial decision makers.

"I guess we didn't have to go after the large industrial loads, but it would have been imprudent management for us to not take advantage of that opportunity," said Pugh. "We had the opportunities, whereas many of the more rural EMCs might have an opportunity for a customer choice load only once every two or three years, so they couldn't justify building a staff to handle this."

Jackson EMC could, and did.

Navigating the Sea of Change

From 1980 to 1990, Jackson EMC membership more than doubled to ninety thousand. Serving the area from Atlanta to Athens to Gainesville, the co-op advertised the Golden Triangle as the fastest growing region in Georgia and one of the fastest growing in the United States. Gwinnett Place Mall was the crown jewel of the area, with the bulk of economic action occurring within a four-mile radius. Longtime EMC employees had to adapt to meeting with hotshots flying in on jets to roll out plans for mammoth development projects. New subdivisions with 250 homes were commonplace.

The electric cooperative only had itself to blame for the good fortune, Frances Staton concluded upon her retirement after working forty-one years as secretary to the general manager. "Why shouldn't we grow and prosper?" she said in the May 1988 issue of *Rural Electrification Magazine*. "We're the ones to blame, after all. Without us bringing the electricity and lights to the country we wouldn't have had the growth."

In late 1988, Jackson EMC constructed its first microwave tower, utilizing microwave-technology to improve voice and data communications. One of the greatest improvements, and a move that created some of the greatest growing pains, was converting the customer information system, which had been handled with punch cards and machines manned by keypunch operators, to a modern computerized platform. In the long run, conversion to personal computers throughout the cooperative streamlined communications and simplified tasks at a time when anything made easier was welcomed amidst the overwhelming growth. But in the short term, shifting hundreds of employees from using familiar punch cards, typewriters, and adding machines to manipulating computer technology was daunting.

Through the eighties, Jackson EMC positioned itself to meet the future as mainframes gave way to personal computers, marketing shifted from demonstrations to sales, and field service reps took over the task of reading meters. "The eighties had to be defined by the growth, and our commitment," said Pugh. "The growth drove all of our planning. It drove all decision making of both the board and management. We eventually got to the point where we had the resources, we had the people in place, and we had very capable people at the top."

The energy of a company meeting the grand challenges it had set for itself was almost palpable as an enthusiastic and flexible workforce navigated the waters of sea change.

Charles Dawson served as director of public relations during the high-growth eighties and nineties when the co-op's service territory was dubbed the "Golden Triangle." From December 1985 to 1992, Dawson and his staff produced four monthly newsletters, one for each of the cooperative's four areas: Gainesville, Lawrenceville, Neese, and the Jefferson headquarters.

The sight at Interstate 85 interchanges in Jackson EMC territory was the same from exit to exit, revealing the frenetic pace of a rapidly evolving community that never slept at night.

Chapter Thirteen
Building a Reputation

"It is the triumph of civilization that at last communities have obtained such a mastery over natural laws that they drive and control them. The winds, the water, electricity, all aliens that in their wild form were dangerous, are now controlled by human will, and are made useful servants."
—Henry Ward Beecher
Nineteenth-century social reformer

The 1990s, at Jackson EMC as well as electric cooperatives throughout the nation, was the decade of anticipated deregulation. In 1992, when the wholesale side of the business was deregulated, allowing non-utilities to enter the generation business, most electric industry leaders thought the next step would be retail competition. That had happened in the natural gas industry several years earlier, leading to competition there. Throughout the

nation, the political and business consensus was that the same thing would occur in the electric industry. Most utility leaders felt deregulation was a sure bet and that, when it occurred, electric utilities would have to broaden their outreach to survive. That meant diversification by providing non-traditional services, like Internet, telephone, natural gas, or others.

At Jackson EMC, the first provision would be to provide even better service to members. "I told our people from the beginning, if retail deregulation comes, we're going to live or die by customer service," said President/ CEO Randall Pugh. "We have to find a way to become the power supplier of choice for all of our customers, whether they are residential, commercial or industrial."

Jackson EMC began a concerted companywide effort to work towards ultimate customer satisfaction

Co-op members enjoy musical entertainment at the 1993 annual meeting, when Jackson EMC accurately proclaimed itself "A Company to Believe In."

Opposite page: Jackson EMC line workers pull wire for service at a local farm.

Mission Statement

We will meet or exceed our customer's expectations with reliable, courteous, and personalized service. We will provide high quality and competitively priced energy, products, and services by using innovative concepts and technologies. We are committed to the ethical conduct of our business, stimulating the economic growth of our region, enriching our environment and enhancing the quality of life in the communities we service.

Vision Statement

We are a successful, competitive, customer-driven company. We accomplish this by:

Being customer focused

Teamwork and commitment

Professionalism

Positive attitudes

Using state-of-the-art technology

Being flexible

by improving all elements of the cooperative, from the electric system itself to customer service and corporate citizenship. Rural electric cooperatives still had issues with reliability. Minus the deep pockets and long history of the private utilities, the co-ops were borne of grassroots efforts in hardscrabble times, and some matured faster than others. The board of directors and top management determined they would do what it took to make Jackson EMC a thoroughly reliable electric system, equal to private utilities in its capability to supply electricity and keep it humming without interruption.

Proper insulation was advised by Jackson EMC member service representatives as a sure way to save on power bills.

Management and staff hammered out a mission statement that reflected the co-op's intent to enhance its culture of customer satisfaction by striving to meet or exceed expectations of all customers.

To get a handle on where the cooperative stood in terms of customer service, the co-op participated in its first customer service satisfaction survey in 1992 and scored 67, which was not a bad score for utilities at the time, but it wasn't good enough for Jackson EMC. To create a culture where customer satisfaction took priority over every aspect of the business, management started emphasizing customer service to employees, basing the concept on the golden rule: "Treat our customers like we want to be treated."

Two years later, the cooperative embarked on a series of initiatives to focus increased attention on cooperation, teamwork, and customer service. Employees were asked to identify how they could positively impact the cooperative by providing exceptional customer service. Objectives were identified and measures were implemented to improve the customer's experience.

For the first time, membership applications were offered over the phone, removing the requirement that people come by one of the district offices to apply for electric service in person, thus making the application experience more convenient. Changing long-standing traditions like this was difficult at first. But for applicants out of metro-Atlanta used to doing business over the phone, being required to come into an office seemed archaic. As communication systems were put in place and employees trained to handle them, the transition eased. Providing new ways for members to pay their power bill also was deemed essential, and the co-op started accepting credit card payments and gave members the option to pay their bill electronically.

Throughout Jackson EMC, once-rigid rules were modified to give employees more latitude when dealing with members, whether on the phone or in the field. If linemen or field service representatives saw a relevant need while repairing service or reading meters, such as finding a streetlight out, they were given permission to solve the problem rather than simply point it out to members or report it. If a line crew dug a trench to replace cable, rather than cover it up with dirt and head back to the office, they were equipped with grass seed and mulch to leave the area more appealing, and the member more pleased.

"We empowered them to make the customer satisfied, in some cases allowing them to do things we hadn't done in the past," said Pugh. "We knew we could make significant strides in our customer service if we began to address these things. We made a tremendous investment in technology to give us the tools we needed to provide the level of customer service people wanted."

The aim for customer satisfaction determined what technological advances were made, what facilities were upgraded, and what equipment was purchased. Whether it was a new bucket truck to improve operations in the field or upgrading the billing system to improve operations in the office, all were done toward one end result—improving customer satisfaction.

In 1990, Jackson EMC started surveying random groups of members about the co-op issues most important to them. By the mid-nineties, issues addressed by members had led to extension of customer service telephone hours from 5 pm until 9 pm on weekdays and installation of a computerized system to facilitate members reporting outages. Voice mail was introduced, allowing customers to leave messages when employees were in the field.

By May 1993, Jackson EMC was providing power to 100,000 members, a feat shared by fewer than ten of the nation's thousand rural electric cooperatives. While most of the growth through the eighties had been in Gwinnett County, by the mid-nineties it was spilling over into Hall, Jackson, and Barrow Counties. Even in the outlying areas of the co-op territory, growth was imminent, as in Banks County where Banks Crossing featured Tanger's Factory Outlet at the I-85 and US 441 interchange.

Jackson EMC introduced geothermal heat pumps, which were just beginning to be installed in the south as an energy efficient solution in the 1980s. Jackson EMC marketing reps, from left in ties, Roy Stowe, Lonnie Hall, and Kenny Beck, watch the installation of one of the first systems in the area.

After employees were given more latitude in dealing with member needs, customer satisfaction scores started rising. Here, Service Representative Phil Strickland chats with a co-op member.

In an effort to boost the growing membership's sense of ownership in their cooperative, the board of directors in 1995 announced a new way of returning margin refunds, the money left over at the end of each operating year after all bills are paid. Since the co-op started refunding its member-owners, members receiving electric service from 1939 through 1982 had been refunded $24.1 million, with oldest margins paid first. This first-in/first-out (FIFO) method of returning margins was popular among cooperatives because it rewards those with margins invested in the co-op the longest; however, new members had to wait several years before receiving a refund. The new method would benefit new members sooner, instilling in them an awareness of ownership in their cooperative. Instead of receiving only margins from a year in the past, margins would be returned from two years, half from a distant year and half from the previous year. In December 1995, approximately $2 million was refunded to members—50 percent from 1983 margins and 50 percent from 1994 margins.

Implementing these new procedures was testament to the fact that considerable thought had been given to customers' wants and the cooperative's well being.

Expanding and Adding Offices

An engineering and operations facility was constructed at Oakwood in 1990 and a new district office at Gainesville was completed a few years later. An engineering and operations center at Lawrenceville followed, along with renovation of offices there.

Since the 1950s, three district offices had served Jackson EMC communities while the headquarters office at Jefferson handled corporate affairs and provided service to members in Jackson, Banks, and Barrow Counties. In 1992, the Jefferson District office was established on the campus of Jackson EMC headquarters. Customer service was the impetus for the move. The new district office would be dedicated to serving the three counties previously served by headquarters, while the corporate office would concentrate efforts on companywide system plans and projects, as well as providing support to the districts in such areas as information technology (IT).

Mrs. A. T. Sharpton, center, congratulated Diana Mendez, left, of Johnson High School and Jee "Kris" Se Lee, right, of Winder-Barrow High School as the first two recipients of the A. T. Sharpton Scholarship, established in 1994 and first presented in 1995. Jackson EMC and private donors endowed the annual award to memorialize the longtime director who was not able to pursue his own dream to go to college because, in the wake of his father's death, he went to work to support his seven siblings. In turn, he developed a passion for education that lives on at Jackson EMC.

Jackson EMC continued its long-standing tradition of working with youth to enhance their education and career success, as evidenced in 1997 when employee Tommy Evans, left, worked with Shaun Dollins, a West Hall High School student and the third student to participate in the co-op's Youth Apprentice Program.

The new district office opened in March 1992, staffed by about fifty employees, the vast majority from corporate headquarters. The co-op had lost some loads in Barrow County due to a lack of recognition there, so in its first few years of operations, the new district placed concerted efforts on making its presence known. In a relatively short time, a turnaround was realized. When the boards of education recognized Jackson EMC could serve their schools as well as Georgia Power could, the co-op began to sign school loads. About this time, the cooperative hired its first commercial/industrial marketing engineer to ensure new industrial clients received personal service.

One challenge at the new office was the size of the Jefferson District. With the largest geographical area of all four districts, it takes forty-five minutes, minus heavy traffic, to drive between its furthest points. Another challenge was growth. The same growth that had begun in Gwinnett County moved north in the late nineties, causing the Jefferson District to evolve from a slower paced rural locale to one of the co-op's higher growth areas with Jackson, Banks, and Barrow Counties all three attracting new residents, businesses, and industries, including Toyota, Kubota, and Haverty's Distribution.

Deregulation and Diversification

Throughout the utility industry, the buzzword for the 1990s was "deregulation."

In the world of electric utilities, talk of deregulation monopolized most conversations. The wholesale side of the industry was deregulated in 1992, giving non-utilities the option to enter the electric generation business. For the rest of the decade, most utilities were inclined to believe that the retail side of the industry also would be deregulated, and when it was, retail competition would result. Both the actual deregulation of the wholesale market and the anticipated deregulation of the retail market brought changes to Jackson EMC.

Until wholesale electric deregulation, only electric utilities built and owned generating and transmission systems. From its origins in 1939 to 1974, Jackson EMC had purchased most of its electricity from Georgia Power Company. Since 1974, the cooperative had been a member of Oglethorpe Power Corporation (OPC), a generation and transmission co-op that—with Georgia Power Company, the Municipal Electric Authority of Georgia, and the City of Dalton—jointly owned generation and transmission plants in Georgia. For the next two decades, Jackson EMC purchased the bulk of its electricity through Oglethorpe Power; 10 percent or less was purchased from the Southeastern Power Administration, the power marketer for federally owned hydroelectric facilities.

Wholesale deregulation in 1992 created competition among non-utilities that entered the generation business, and lower wholesale prices resulted. Under an all-requirements contract that obligated it to purchase power from OPC, larger cooperatives paid disproportionate prices compared to smaller co-ops in Georgia. To bring down their wholesale costs, the larger cooperatives wanted the ability to negotiate for some of their own wholesale power.

In an effort to control their own destiny, Jackson EMC in 1995 joined other larger electric cooperatives, most in the metro Atlanta area, to declare its intent to withdraw from OPC. To keep from losing its largest cooperative-members, the OPC Board of Directors restructured Oglethorpe Power Corporation into three separate entities and, as a result, Jackson EMC gained access to the nation's bulk supply power market, enabling the co-op to buy power at better prices.

The restructure of OPC created three distinct cooperatives: Oglethorpe Power Corporation, solely a generation cooperative; Georgia Transmission Corporation, which would own, operate, and maintain the integrated transmission system and sell transmission services to the member-cooperatives; and Georgia System Operations Corporation, which would operate the system and schedule generation needs. Jackson EMC would continue to buy part of its wholesale power from OPC, but to acquire better rates, the co-op formed a wholesale

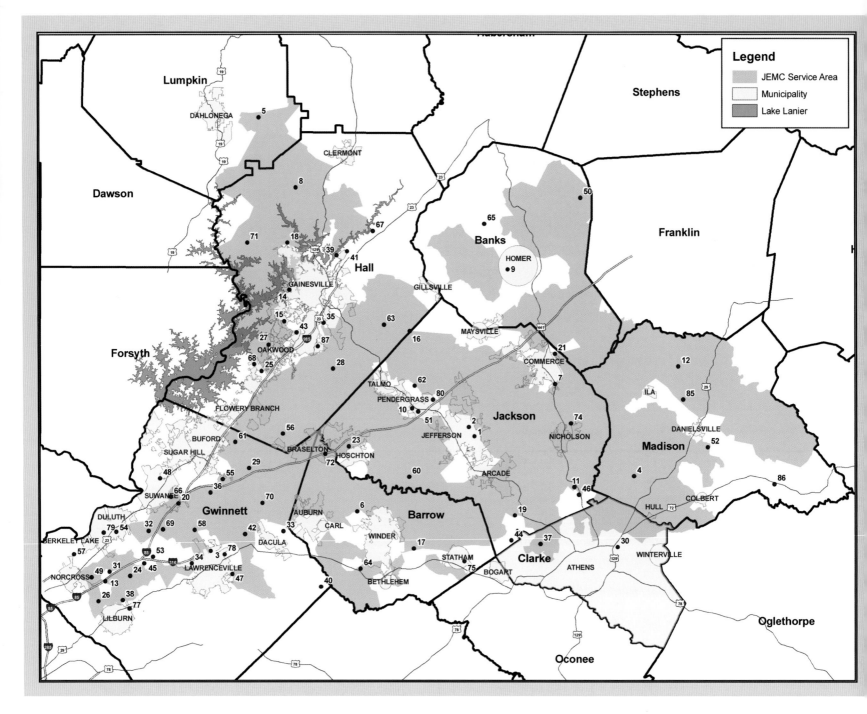

power marketing alliance with other Georgia electric cooperatives including Walton EMC in Monroe, Cobb EMC in Marietta, Snapping Shoals EMC in Covington, Colquitt EMC in Moultrie, and Tri-County EMC in Gray. The new alliance, Cooperative Power Inc. (CPI), would use its combined capacity to leverage better power supply deals, mostly through OPC.

Beginning January 1, 1996, Jackson EMC purchased power from Enron Power Marketing, the Houston, Texas-based energy conglomerate that, at the time, was the largest power marketer in the world. The move saved Jackson EMC members more than $1 million in the first quarter of 1996. The savings were so significant that the cooperative continued its deal with Enron through August, at which time it went with another power supplier, Duke/Dreyfus, which had negotiated a better deal.

Later that year, OPC negotiated long-term purchase power contracts with Morgan Stanley Energy Marketing Group and Louisville Power Marketing on behalf of all OPC members. While most of these power purchase agreements were done through OPC, Jackson EMC entered into a long-term all-requirements power supply contract with Williams Energy in 2001 to provide electricity at fixed rates through 2015.

The dramatic growth of Jackson EMC is reflected in the numerous substations constructed to serve its members as population in their communities expanded. (Map created by GIS Coordinator Bill Zook.)

SUBSTATION NAME

1. Jefferson
2. North Jefferson
3. North Lawrenceville (Lawrenceville)
4. Neese
5. Copper Pine
6. Winder
7. Commerce #4 (Gold Kist)
8. Murrayville
9. Homer
10. Pendergrass
13. Beaver Ruin
14. West Gainesville
15. Oakwood
16. Gillsville
17. Russell
18. Bark Camp
19. Attica
20. Exit 44
21. North Commerce (Commerce)
23. Braselton
24. Northwoods
25. Flowery Branch
26. Singleton Road
27. College Square
28. Candler
29. Rock Quarry

30. Athena
31. Lidell Road
32. Sugarloaf
33. Dacula
34. Lawrenceville #3 (Medical Center)
35. Gainesville #2
36. Ivy Creek
37. Lavender Road
38. North Lilburn
39. Kubota Drive
40. Bold Springs
42. Progress Center
43. Chicopee Manufacturing Company
44. Savage Road
45. Boggs Road
46. Louisiana Pacific Center
47. Lawrenceville #4 (McCart Rd)
48. Suwanee
49. Hopkins Creek
50. Middleforks
51. Nicolon
52. Thomason
53. Herrington Road
54. Duluth
55. Mall of Georgia

56. Spout Springs Road
57. Berkeley Lake
58. Collins Hill
60. Gum Springs
61. Sandy Hill
62. North Jackson
63. East Hall
64. Carter Hill
65. Katfish Korner
66. Avonlea
67. Hagan Creek
68. Lakeside
69. Huntcrest
70. Jim Moore Road
71. Leach Road
72. Sharon Church
74. Nicholson
75. Statham
77. Lilburn
78. Blaze Recycling
79. Sweetbottom
80. Holox
85. New Haven
86. Columbia Farms
87. New Harvest Road

About the time power supply concerns brought on by deregulation of the wholesale side of the electric industry were calmed, anticipation of deregulation on the retail side ramped up to a fever pitch. Deregulation had occurred in California, Texas, New Jersey, and other states, and the consensus in the industry was if deregulation occurred, electric utilities would have to provide additional services in order to survive. Diversification was the survival model, and the question electric cooperatives across the nation asked themselves was, "What do we bundle?"

Dozens of companies approached Jackson EMC in hopes of forming a partnership to sell their products. From dial-up Internet and cable TV to pest control and tree trimming services, the field was wide open. In March 1998, Jackson EMC teamed with VoiceLink, a pager company, to offer local, state, and national paging services. The venture lasted a relatively short time as pagers went the way of the eight-track tape.

In the meantime, Jackson EMC studied the merits of another business alternative as the countdown toward deregulation of the state's natural gas market ticked toward November 1, 1998, the date when the sale of natural gas in areas served by Atlanta Gas Light (AGL) would open to competition. Beginning then, AGL would no longer sell gas to customers but distribute it for marketers. Seeing an opportunity to gain business, multiple energy providers sought to win some of AGL's 1.4 million customers.

Recognizing a prime opportunity for diversification that related to its core business of supplying energy, Jackson EMC partnered with Peachtree Natural Gas Company, based in Roswell, to provide natural gas to co-op members who already purchased it from Atlanta Gas Light. Going into the gas business seemed like a no-brainer at the time since AGL customers, due to deregulation, would be forced to choose a new gas supplier; if they failed to choose a supplier within a given timeframe, the Public Service Commission would dictate one through random assignment. Of AGL's million-plus customers, thirty-five thousand lived in Jackson EMC territory, giving the cooperative a ready base of potential customers. Not allowed by law to own or sell natural gas, the electric cooperatives could market it for someone else for a royalty and fee; Jackson EMC, known for its marketing savvy, already had in place staff well equipped to handle billing and customer service for natural gas.

That November, Jackson EMC and other electric cooperatives entered the natural gas business and, within weeks, brought thousands of new customers to Peachtree Natural Gas, most from the Gwinnett area. The surge was phenomenal. Jackson EMC members who bought natural gas from AGL and had to choose a new supplier chose the electric cooperative they knew and trusted. Within ten months, Peachtree Natural Gas had secured about twenty thousand former AGL customers.

Before a year had passed, the immediate success of Peachtree Natural Gas ultimately led to its demise. Required to pay for gas upfront, the business grew more quickly than anticipated and could not keep up with the advanced payments. This situation created a negative cash flow from the start, leaving Peachtree unable to capitalize its business. Had it grown slower, it may have worked.

By fall 1999, Peachtree Natural Gas was bankrupt and Jackson EMC was out of the gas business. However, another venture the co-op pursued during this anxious period of deregulation worries and diversification concerns would fare much better.

Vince Raia has served as president of EMC Security since the home security company launched in 1998.

EMC Security

At the same time Jackson EMC was getting into the natural gas business, it launched another enterprise in an effort to further diversify. Jointly, Jackson EMC and its neighboring co-op, Walton EMC, formed a home security business, EMC Security, in autumn 1998. Its selling point would be inexpensive home security monitoring that required no annual contract. In October 2006, GreyStone Power Corporation, based in Douglasville, joined as a partner in the cooperative-owned business.

EMC Security was born from surveys that Jackson EMC and Walton EMC conducted asking their members what additional services they would like from their electric cooperative. Home security ranked at the top of the list. After searching for a manager with experience in the field, Vince Raia was hired as president of EMC Security. Raia came to the new business from

Above: EMC Security operates with about eighty employees from headquarters at 55 Satellite Boulevard in Suwanee. Representatives from the company's three owner-cooperatives serve on the board, including Randall Pugh, Roy Stowe, and Greg Keith of Jackson EMC; Ronnie Lee and Marsha Shumate of Walton EMC; and Gary Miller and Jim Hunter of GreyStone Power.

Right: Along with home security, EMC Security provides advanced wiring, home theater, medical alert, and other services.

Southern Company where he had headed their security company, Power Call; prior to that, he worked with several of the nation's largest home security providers.

A for-profit company owned by not-for-profit cooperatives, EMC Security's earnings are invested back into the company with additional profits returned to the cooperatives, which ultimately return those earnings to members in the form of margin refunds. When it opened in 1998, EMC Security charged customers a $15.95 monthly monitoring fee; the rate was raised to $16.95 the following year and has remained the same for the fourteen years since. The company requires no annual or multi-year contract as do most similar businesses, making it unique in the marketplace.

In 2009, EMC Security moved from its original location at 955 Hurricane Shoals Road in Lawrenceville to a larger facility at 55 Satellite Boulevard in Suwanee. The company paid cash for the new building and remains debt free in 2013.

Along with security and fire protection, the company offers advanced wiring, central vacuum, home theater, and whole-house audio and video systems. Its commercial division accounts for about 15 percent

Employees at EMC Security offer person-to-person service to all customers and potential customers, while a central station call center provides emergency response times among the fastest in the nation.

of sales and provides access control, cameras, security intrusion, and fire alarm. In 2010, EMC Security launched its Medical Alert System, which utilizes two-way pendants to put the elderly or disabled in touch with emergency response professionals at the press of a button. In 2012, the company introduced Secure Path Technology, which allows home security systems to be monitored by phone, wireless, or high-speed Internet.

The security company originated to serve only electric cooperative members but soon expanded its service to the public at large. Its sustained success has been attributed to the fact that EMC Security, like its owner-cooperatives, treats customers more like members, while striving for ultimate customer satisfaction.

On average, EMC Security added seven hundred new customers monthly in 2012. In partnership with another security company in Gainesville, Florida, EMC Security operates Universal Monitoring, a five-diamond, Underwriters Laboratories-certified central station that answers calls with response times among the fastest in the nation. While UL standards call for response to an alarm in two minutes or less, EMC Security's average response time is fifteen seconds.

In 2013, EMC Security provides security for forty thousand customers and ranks among the twenty largest residential security providers in the nation. About eighty employees work for the company, and representatives from its three owner-cooperatives serve on its board of directors.

Other Initiatives with Members in Mind

Along with adding and expanding services, Jackson EMC, under Pugh's leadership, increased exposure in its communities. The cooperative had been a team player for decades, its presence strong in local chambers of commerce, FFA and 4-H programs, and various efforts in which it practiced well the seventh of the Seven Cooperative Principles: concern for community.

In its mission to achieve across-the-board customer satisfaction, the cooperative worked toward increased community involvement from its employees, especially district managers and department heads who were called on to represent the co-op in the communities it served, particularly in leadership roles in local chambers of commerce and industrial development organizations.

"I wanted them to be highly visible, to be Jackson EMC in that district," said Pugh. "If we can promote, along with the chambers and community leaders, positive quality economic development and can create jobs and improve the quality of life for our members, then we're meeting our corporate obligations."

The improved exposure would lead to Jackson EMC being recognized as a major community player when competing for power customers. With a solid reputation, recognizable identity, and credibility as a power supplier, the cooperative was well equipped to compete.

While upper management was required to connect with local chambers of commerce and industrial development organizations, all employees were encouraged to be involved in civic, school, and charitable

Seven Cooperative Principles

Voluntary and open membership
Democratic member control
Members' economic participation
Autonomy and independence
Education, training and information
Cooperation among cooperatives
Concern for community

Luther Wilkes, a co-op employee for forty-four years, assisted with area youth activities during most of his career, coaching youth league baseball and working with FFA students for many years. In 1989, he was awarded the Honorary American Farmer Degree, the highest honorary award given by the National FFA. Wilkes was the first EMC employee in Georgia to receive this prestigious award.

Gainesville District Manager Bill Sanders, center, joined Eileen Lister, left, and Wanda Olivet of the Chattahoochee Baptist Association in December 1997 to survey the contributions to the association's Secret Santa Program in Hall County. Jackson EMC donated use of the Gainesville District's old auditorium on Dawsonville Highway as a collection point for Secret Santa donations. Lister called the auditorium the best place the organization ever had for storing donated items.

In early 1998, Lawrenceville District Superintendent Tom Cain, right, learned that the family of young Johnny Mitchell was in danger of having their power turned off. Jackson EMC employees took up a collection to keep the lights on. Lawrenceville District Manager Roger Willis contacted local builders who donated materials and labor to refurbish the Mitchells' house, and district employees donated their time to rewire, paint, and make repairs to the home. Cain continues to keep in contact with Mitchell.

Jackson EMC joined area schools to sponsor a Red Ribbon Drug-Free program with co-op employees of the Lawrenceville District office joining in the campaign. Accepting thanks from school representatives were, from left, Lawrenceville District Manager Roger Willis, Line Foreman Mike Cleghorn, and President/CEO Randall Pugh.

Co-op employees give of themselves in a myriad of ways, as exampled by Barbara Gooch, who in 2002 continued her twenty-six-year volunteerism at American Red Cross blood drives by working in the canteen, providing refreshments to blood donors like Benton Mobley.

Jackson EMC employees like Journeyman Lineman Jason McElwaney routinely serve as role models to youngsters who dream of one day climbing poles and stringing high wires like their line crew heroes.

organizations in order to create and maintain a stronger identity in the community. The cooperative's influence was spread throughout the counties where its lines were strung. Employees played active roles in civic organizations like Rotary, Lions, Jaycees, and Kiwanis and events like trade shows, home shows, and American Cancer Society Relay for Life, along with EMC-sponsored events like the FFA and 4-H beef show and FFA wiring contests. The co-op was a particularly strong player in Partners in Education organizations benefitting schools and students across its service area. Plus, Jackson EMC helped create several organizations, including a Habitat for Humanity chapter, Jackson County Human Resource Council, and the Jackson County Boys and Girls Club.

Most Jackson EMC employees—in some shape, form, or fashion—contributed to organizations and interacted with co-op members through volunteerism. While the co-op was not always the largest company in each of the communities it served, it often proved to be the most involved. Community involvement, through the years, became part of the Jackson EMC culture, instilled in the DNA of each employee.

With so many initiatives put in place to improve member relations, it was no wonder the co-op's customer satisfaction scores began to rise. Each time Jackson EMC participated in a survey, its scores improved and, in 2005, the cooperative achieved its second score of 90 in the American Consumer Satisfaction Index, a score far exceeding that year's electric industry average of 73. It was an extraordinary achievement matched by few electric cooperatives.

The challenge Jackson EMC faced, and met, was bringing automation and technology up to speed while dealing with phenomenal growth, all the time seeking to satisfy its residential and commercial members. As soon as a function of the cooperative was automated, computer software would be outdated within a few years. A three-year construction work plan would last barely over two years. All of that happened on top of the potential for deregulation, the foray into natural gas, and the establishment of EMC Security.

At Jackson EMC, it was foot on the throttle, all the time.

Line Crew Workers and Overall Safety

Jackson EMC linemen were among the busiest employees, ceaselessly working to build a constantly growing electric system. These in-the-field employees worked the job central to the cooperative's reason for being: to get the lights on and keep them on.

In the early days of the cooperative, management leaned toward hiring young men raised on farms because they tended to be jacks-of-all-trade, typically skilled in construction and mechanics. As farming declined and technology advanced, new employees entering line construction typically possessed more computer and technology skills than experience in manual labor. Ample training bridged the gap.

Prior to the early 1990s, linemen at Jackson EMC were hired and placed on the line the first day to learn their craft through on-the-job experience. Inevitably, the training varied from lineman to lineman as different crew leaders taught varying methods of line construction. Beginning in 1991, the cooperative incorporated the Tennessee Valley Public Power Association (TVPPA) training program, which added some course work but was not targeted solely to the lineman's work.

In 1996, Jackson EMC hired Bob Whatley, who had worked as a trainer at Oglethorpe Power Corporation. Whatley recognized a weakness in training at the co-op and began developing a Jackson EMC-specific training

Working from a Hi-Ranger bucket, Journeyman Lineman Chad Hemphill drills a pole, preparing it for wire.

The pole yard is stocked with one of the most important tools in the lineman's job, the poles from which power lines are strung across the co-op's ten-county service area.

Co-op linemen load up in company trucks to start their workday.

Safety equipment utilized by co-op linemen includes protective rubber gloves, hard hats, safety glasses, and fire retardant clothing as worn by lineman Jeff Chandler, in bucket, and Scott Hudson, on the ground.

Jackson EMC linemen start the day with tailgate briefings, in this case a hood briefing, where they go over the day's line construction plans. By 1989, more than 50 percent of lines were installed underground with infrared technology used to locate and repair problems before equipment failure causes a power outage. Linemen planning the day's work schedule here are, from left, Derrick Ansley, Joey Brogdon, Willie Hutchins, Steven Crowe, and Ithier Martinez.

program. In the process, he discovered Tampa Electric Company's (TECO) Power Pro Lineman training modules, which Jackson EMC purchased. Whatley spent several months shaping the program to fit the co-op's construction methods and progression schedule for linemen.

Now when linemen are hired, they initially take basic safety training before being placed on a crew; they continue to study modules directly related to their work and are tested on knowledge in each of these areas. Work competency is tested in multiple areas, with supervisor certification, and this competency is the means for progressing as a lineman. It takes seven years for a line worker to reach the status of journeyman lineman. A line crew employee starts out as a helper for six months before promoted to apprentice lineman, and it's another year-and-a-half before he's made lineman. Five more years of on-the-job training are required to become a journeyman lineman.

Just as Jackson EMC worked to enhance a culture of exceptional customer satisfaction, it adopted a culture of safety geared toward all employees, particularly linemen. Before any line job starts, a required tailgate briefing brings all crew workers together to discuss the day's job and potential hazards associated with it. Whether by increasing attention to OSHA requirements, putting preventive maintenance programs in place to ensure vehicle safety, or purchasing fire retardant clothing for line workers, the new emphasis focused on enhancing the working environment for outside employees.

Salaried and hourly employees worked closer as a team. All joined in the cooperative's safety initiatives with each employee taking part in safety training to become certified in cardiopulmonary resuscitation and to learn how to use automatic external defibrillators. Today, defibrillators are kept at each co-op office; one was used in recent years at the Jefferson District office to save the life of an employee. Every three years, Jackson EMC is accredited through the NRECA's Rural Electric Safety Accreditation Program, which measures the effectiveness of safety procedures to ensure preservation of life and prevention of injury.

In 1997, Jackson EMC included another component to lineman training by competing in the Georgia Lineman's Rodeo in Perry and the International Lineman's Rodeo in Kansas City, Missouri. Preparing for events like pole climb and hurt man rescue proved a fun and productive way to train. Over the years, the co-op's linemen have amassed more than one hundred trophies, including First Place Overall in Georgia in 2005 and Second Place Overall in Kansas City in 2004. Jackson EMC's linemen have on numerous occasions brought home the top prize in individual hurt man rescue competition, which involves a 165-pound manikin attached to the top of a utility pole. The competing lineman must climb the pole, safety off and tie a rescue rope around the manikin, and lower the "hurt man" to the ground.

In 1997, teams of Jackson EMC's best linemen started competing in the state and international lineman's rodeos, events that promote safety and efficiency in a fun, competitive way. Celebrating success at the state competition in May 1999 were, from left, front, Bill Sanders, David Dorsey, Donald Palmour, and Terry Whitworth. Second row: Randall Pugh, Terry Jones, Phil Strickland, Bruce Whitmire, and Jeff Vogt. Third row: Paul Eckstein, Tim Burns, Scott Mitchell, and Wayne Connell. Fourth row: Marty Jacobs, Steve Streetman, and Ben Ivie. In September 1999, the team of Jeff Vogt, Bruce Whitmire, and Wayne Connell took First Place Overall honors at the national rodeo while Phil Strickland, Tim Burns, and Terry Jones placed fifth in competition that involved teams from seventy other co-ops across the country.

Jackson EMC linemen proved themselves tops again in 2000 at the International Lineman's Rodeo in Kansas City, Missouri. Celebrating their success are, from left, kneeling, Ricky Hardy and Phil Strickland. Middle: Wayne Connell, Paul Eckstein, Scott Mitchell, and Terry Jones. Back: Bruce Whitmire and Greg Angel.

Competition at lineman's rodeos is intense and compelling as line workers from across the state compete in Georgia, followed by crews from across the country competing at the international event in Kansas City, Missouri.

With homes served by the cooperative in the background, Journeyman Linemen Paul Everett, left, and Jeff Baker work to keep the power on.

A different kind of competition, but even more satisfying, is getting lights back on when called to help in emergency situations outside Jackson EMC territory. Leaving their own families, sometimes for days on end, linemen have volunteered to go help others, knowing it's the right thing to do. Most will tell you, it's a matter of pride.

Part of what may entice linemen to the job is the thrill of risk. Added to that is the camaraderie of linemen, which is never more evident than when they volunteer to help others. Through the years, Jackson EMC line crews have assisted in restoring power after storm damage in Kentucky, Mississippi, Louisiana, Alabama, North Carolina, South Carolina, Tennessee, Maryland, and throughout Georgia. When people in need see Jackson EMC line trucks roll up, they start clapping and cheering.

In 1989, the co-op sent thirty-five linemen to assist in restoring power at Mount Pleasant and Moncks Corner in South Carolina after Hurricane Hugo devastated the coast there. Line crews worked more than a hundred hours their first week, but the men didn't want to come home because they had not been able to get lights turned on. The workers stayed three weeks and finally returned to Georgia, only after power was restored.

The entire Jackson EMC family got involved with assisting communities devastated after Hurricane Hugo in 1989.

Working to restore power at Mount Pleasant and Moncks Corner, Charlie Watson was among many Jackson EMC crew members who toiled one hundred hours in one week to help South Carolinians affected by Hurricane Hugo.

While co-op line crews worked to restore power in South Carolina after Hurricane Hugo in 1989, office staff back in northeast Georgia collected relief supplies to send to the affected communities. Assisting the effort included, from left, front: Tammy Kesler and Lynn Potts. Middle: Faye (Law) Aker, Christy (Carr) Hamilton, Claire Guined, and Brenda (Smith) Parnican. Back: Debbie (Bennett) Smith and Diane Wilson.

Among the seventy-five "Georgia Boys"—Jackson EMC linemen and crewmen who volunteered to travel to South Carolina to assist Hurricane Hugo victims—were these Gainesville crew members, from left, seated at top: linemen Aubry Elrod, Terry Jones, and Bruce Whitmire. Driving: journeyman lineman Marshall Veatch. Standing: linemen Kevin Cape and Chris Quillian and journeyman linemen Phil Strickland and Greg Hanes. Kneeling: journeyman lineman Ray Bryson, foreman Darrow Carruth, service representative Danny Strickland, and lineman Scott Mitchell.

Just as they'd done after Hurricane Hugo in 1989, Jackson EMC line crews travelled outside the state to assist North Carolina victims of Hurricane Fran in September 1996 after lines along the interstate were downed as far as the eye could see. A total of thirty-one co-op employees volunteered to assist in the out-of-state power restoration.

The drama of damage caused by gale-force winds was evident after Hurricane Fran downed lines, resulting in dozens of lineman called on to restore power, pole-to-pole, for miles alongside the interstate in North Carolina.

The camaraderie of EMC lineman is perhaps never more evident than when working storms, as in 1996 in the aftermath of Hurricane Fran. Employees who travelled to the North Carolina coast to assist included Terry Whitworth, Tim Burns, Chris Quillian, and Scott Mitchell from the Gainesville District; Bryan Smith, David Holloway, and Darrell Bond from Neese; Mike Cleghorn, Chuck King, Heath Burell, Russell Morton, Travis Lovin, Ted Holcomb, and Ricky Shubert from Gwinnett; John Stevens, Jeff Halley, Rickey Nixon, Charles Boyd, and Van Bullock from the Jefferson District; and Roger Dills, Tim Sweat, Terry Fulcher, Larry Banks, Keith Hardy, Keith Hall, Greg Mathis, John Whitmire, Scott Hudson, Dan Varner, John Stringer, and Willis Wilbanks from the corporate office.

Co-op linemen restore power after local wind and storm damage in 1998.

On another out-of-state power restoration mission, linemen worked to get electricity back on at a school in Kentucky that had been without power for a month, and then took money from their own pockets to make a donation to the school.

In 2005, twenty-five Jackson EMC linemen travelled to Mississippi to assist in power restoration following Hurricane Katrina. Most agreed that of the numerous storms they had worked through their years as Jackson EMC linemen, few could match the devastation that resulted from Katrina.

Top: Linemen held a ramped-up tailgate briefing before heading out to assist in power restoration after Hurricane Katrina wreaked havoc along the Gulf Coast in 2005. Those who travelled west to help included Kelly Slater, Judson Irvin, Larry Banks, Jeff Chandler, Van Bullock, Tim Sweat, Daniel Wofford, Shannon Love, Mark Hood, Jeff Halley, Chad Hemphill, Joey Thompson, David Carlton, Sterling Cross, John Stringer, Terry Fulcher, Byron Montgomery, Brian Berry, Dwight Byrd, Joey Brogdon, Dan Giles, Jacob Benton, Kevin Thompkins, Joey Poss, and Ricky Shubert.

Bottom: Leaning power poles and drooping lines were common sights throughout the Gulf Coast region after Hurricane Katrina stormed through in August 2005.

The co-op linemen don't have to leave the state to make a positive impact. In recent years, a line crew working near Oakwood noticed smoke coming from an attic of a house across the road, rescued people from the house, and helped put out the blaze. The sharp eye to detect trouble, and the bravery of heart to meet it head on, is shared by Jackson EMC linemen and leaders.

By the late 1990s, employee relations and communications had improved to the extent that employees petitioned the National Labor Relations Board and, in 1999, unanimously voted to decertify the union representation at the cooperative.

As president/CEO of the cooperative, Pugh chose to lead in a direction that called for change to meet change, for growing the co-op to meet the growth of its communities. He and the senior management believed that by providing excellent service, on the electric system itself and through exceptional customer service, Jackson EMC would excel, even though retail deregulation never came.

One of the board and management's greatest achievements during the period of monumental growth at Jackson EMC was leading the cooperative through significant change while avoiding organizational upheaval. They transitioned the cooperative from an old way of doing business to a new way, while avoiding potential problems amidst the constant distraction of explosive customer growth and industry deregulation.

Jackson EMC employees like Tracy Rogers work during annual meetings to ensure co-op members and their families, young and old, enjoy themselves at the biggest event of the year.

The barbecue chicken dinner tradition continued through the 1990s, with co-op employees distributing boxed dinners to members and their families at the 1993 annual meeting.

Families filled the tables at the 1995 annual meeting, held at the Jefferson District office where the annual events have been staged since 1980.

Chapter Fourteen
New Millennium, New Milestones

"Fibre optic is becoming like electricity. If you look at how electricity spread around the globe 100 years ago, that's what's happening now."

—Reed Hastings
Co-founder of Netflix

Nearing the turn of the century, Jackson EMC had grown to become the second largest cooperative in the state and the fourth largest in the nation in terms of meters connected; only Cobb EMC was larger in Georgia. In terms of sales, Jackson EMC bested Cobb with more kilowatt-hours sold; while Cobb had seven thousand more members, Jackson EMC sold more power, primarily due to its total electric saturation and quantity of commercial and industrial loads.

Jackson EMC's growth in an area multiplying in cultural diversity necessitated adding seven bilingual customer service representatives to the staff to serve non-English speaking members. The five most requested languages were Spanish, Korean, Bosnian, Russian, and Vietnamese. The cultural shift was most evident in Gwinnett County, where the Hispanic and Asian population had grown significantly.

While numerous technological advances had been incorporated to service the diverse and ever-expanding membership, two innovations that improved efficiency most were voice mail and e-mail, both introduced in the 1990s. Before, if a fellow employee needed to contact a customer service representative, he or she called on the phone or got in a car. Co-op staff wrote paper memos and depended on the US Mail

While the cooperative updated operations to better meet customer expectations by adding new ways members could pay their bill, customer service representatives Cindy Whitehouse, left, and Tracy Morris, at the payment remittance processing machine, made sure that customers who prefer mailing payments have their accounts updated accurately.

Residential Marketing Director Amy Bryan leads a customer contact employee workshop teaching the ins and outs of the new Right Choice TuneUp and HomePlus Loan initiatives.

Opposite page: Corporate staff moved into a new headquarters building on the Jefferson campus in 2006, giving the Jefferson District full use of the 1980 facility that district staff and corporate employees had shared for twenty-six years.

before eventually hiring a courier to travel to every office each day. A quantum leap in productivity was realized when word processing, coupled with e-mail, was introduced, providing personnel the ability to communicate with a multitude of people at the same time. To communicate with its members en masse, Jackson EMC rolled out its first Internet website in late 1997.

As the new millennium approached, worldwide worries over the coming new year reached Jackson EMC. Concerns were that computer systems would break down at midnight when clocks turned from 1999 to the year 2000 because systems that read years in two digits rather than four would read 1-1-00 as January 1, 1900. In the years leading up to the new century, alarmists sparked fears that the entire electric system could collapse when the clock turned twelve on New Year's Day 2000. Businesses were warned the reading error could cause major glitches, if not downright havoc, at the onset of the new millennium, so they upgraded their computer systems to address the problem.

Upgraded accounting and financial systems went live in October 1999 and proved Y2K compliant. Several dozen Jackson EMC employees spent New Year's Eve at work at the Jefferson headquarters, on hand at midnight in case there was a blip, or worse, in the system. At Jackson EMC, and throughout most of America and the rest of the world, the day proved uneventful except for celebrations.

Educational Initiatives

In August 2001, Jackson EMC joined a dozen other Georgia electric cooperatives to form Green Power EMC, a cooperative that would contract for electricity generated by renewable resources and offer members of participating co-ops the option to fill some of their power needs with "green" resources. The bulk of green power available through the new cooperative was derived from reclaimed methane gas from landfills. Green Power EMC's solar education initiative brought the Sun Power for Schools program to Jackson EMC, which teamed up

Below: Jackson EMC's inclusion in Green Power EMC brought with it a dedication to developing and promoting renewable resources for power generation, including solar power. Sun Power for Schools is a Green Power initiative Jackson EMC sponsors in local schools.

Various solar energy-related youth programs offered by Jackson EMC include the Junior Solar Sprint Race, conducted at Braselton's Road Atlanta in 2012. With multiple area schools taking part in the competition, Jackson EMC's is the largest solar sprint race in the state and an exciting way to teach students about alternative energy sources.

with Mill Creek High School in Gwinnett County to install the area's first grid-tied photovoltaic system designed to harness energy from the sun; students use computers to monitor online data retrieved from the system. Sun Power for Schools was the first statewide academic program to teach the benefits of solar energy.

Jackson EMC's support for education expanded even more in 2005 with passage of a state law granting Georgia's electric cooperatives permission to make charitable contributions of margin refunds unclaimed by former members. Previously, after a given period of time, unclaimed funds were returned to the state to use at its discretion. The new law enabled cooperatives to use the funds to improve their communities through charitable donations, education, or economic development. Jackson EMC presented its first gift of unclaimed margin funds in February 2006 by donating $20,000 towards development of an early education center at Gwinnett Technical College. "Jackson EMC is a great giver to the community," said Mary Beth Byerly, Gwinnett Tech's executive director of institutional advancement. "We are thrilled to be the recipient of such a generous donation."

Since the earliest years of the cooperative, its employees have worked with local school students to teach about electric safety, a tradition it continued into the new millennium. Here, Senior Residential Marketing Representative Claire Guined leads a Power Town demonstration at Banks County Elementary School.

Jackson EMC employees like Ganella Bolden, department/district secretary at the Jefferson District office, take time from their busy schedules to tutor area school students, including these at Benton Elementary in Nicholson. Benton Elementary is one of numerous schools Jackson EMC works with through the Partners in Education program

Other gifts of unclaimed margins have included a $35,000 donation to Lanier Technical College for its Industrial Systems Technology Program, which supports manufacturers in Jackson, Banks, and Barrow Counties by providing certificate and diploma programs in industrial mechanics. A $30,000 donation was made to Athens Technical College toward construction of a new life sciences facility to address the growing shortage in healthcare professionals.

In 2005, Jackson EMC was presented NRECA's National Community Service "Building for the Future" Award for its Electric Vehicle Program, which was deemed the best youth program in the nation sponsored by an EMC. The program started almost a decade earlier when students from Jackson

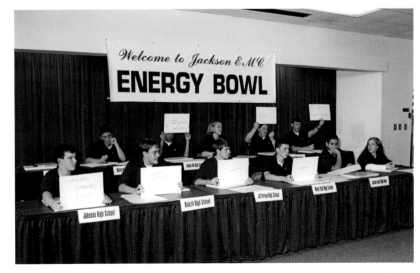

The Jackson EMC Energy Bowl served as a fun and exciting way to teach students about electricity as demonstrated at this 2000–01 meet.

Left: Jackson EMC's Electric Vehicle Program kicked off locally in 1997 and now is utilized in middle and high schools across the nation. Right: Commercial/Industrial Engineer Alan Shedd, center, was instrumental in starting the program and coordinated competitions among schools.

County Comprehensive High School asked the co-op to help them learn more about alternative transportation technology and environmental issues through construction of an electric go-kart. With funding from the co-op and technical assistance from employees, the students built Georgia's first high school student-constructed electric vehicle in late 1997. Recognizing the educational impact on local students, Jackson EMC worked with businesses and educators throughout the state to expand the program that utilizes electric vehicles to teach science, technology, and environmental concepts. By 2005, more than thirty middle and high schools in the state and forty across the nation had included the Electric Vehicle Program in their curriculums.

Chi Wania Woods is one of many co-op employees at the centralized call center who cheerfully tend to needs of members when they phone in for service or information.

More Expansion of Technology and Facilities

By August 2002, Jackson EMC was the second largest cooperative in the United States, and that year's annual meeting focused on its growth. "Over the past several years, we've been adding eight to ten thousand new meters every year," Pugh told members. "To put that in perspective, the average-sized EMC in the United States has a total of about eight thousand meters." Growing at the rate of an average-sized co-op each year, Jackson EMC served almost 170,000 members.

A centralized call center was established at the Jefferson District in 2002, with all calls to Jackson EMC received there, making customer service more efficient and user-friendly. In early 2004, per members' request, the co-op revised its bill format to simplify monthly power bills; the new statements included concise account summaries on front and, on back, details on how to pay bills by credit card or online.

At the same time the new bills were introduced, the cooperative's new customer information system debuted, giving members the option to view and pay bills electronically as well as reviewing account information online. The co-op board and management had determined the homegrown customer information system that served the cooperative well for almost two decades required extensive upgrades or replacing. Since upgrades would cost as much as a new

system, and a new system would accomplish more, the co-op chose to go with a new system. It took two years to evaluate, select, and implement the Cayenta customer information system, which went live in February 2004. Whereas some companies install similar systems that never operate at capacity, even after spending millions of dollars and months of manpower, Jackson EMC's new system worked from the start and has been upgraded twice since, proving its ability to advance as technology advances.

The co-op linemen and engineering technicians, who might never have imagined their manual job would call for computers, were equipped with laptops in their line trucks. The portable computers took the place of thick map books and handwritten work orders and, at first, raised a few eyebrows among linemen who had never used a computer. Some balked at the notion, but eventually they worked through the anxieties of entering the computer age and, by the end of 2003, all line trucks were equipped with laptops.

As technology progressed, automation was introduced to simplify outage restoration. Whereas linemen previously had to walk or ride all the lines to manually detect faults after outages occurred, an automated phone system coupled with an outage management system (OMS) were deployed in January 2007 to help identify problems by computer, which reduced the area linemen had to walk or ride. The state-of-the-art OMS provides cooperative-wide, real-time information, which is gathered from the SCADA monitoring system, geographic information system, customer information system, input from employees in the field, and customer reports. The immediate access to this vital information enables the co-op to efficiently map outages and track the causes for them, often leading to a specific piece of problem equipment.

The outage management system marked a significant evolution from tables piled high with stacks of paper outage reports, most handwritten by an operator on the phone and placed in stacks according to which community was out of power. Today, by simply looking at a computer, staff can detect where power is out and, with automated vehicle location, can determine which truck is closest to the outage and should be deployed for repairs.

Jackson EMC entered into the new century with state-of-the art technologies that enhance operations throughout the cooperative's four districts. Employees underwent extensive training on the new Cayenta customer information system (CIS) during a system conversion completed in 2004. Training consultant Brince Neidlinger, left, instructs customer service representatives, from right, Marianne Daughety, Yonnah Stovall, Joy Knight, and Mary Ann Shope, with assistance from Cayenta trainer, Nicole Wendland.

In recent years, the cooperative developed a disaster recovery center to replicate its systems as a measure of security, upgraded its phone system, implemented an automatic geographic information system with a comprehensive database of the electric network, constructed a fiber-optic loop around the system to provide high-speed broadband communications, added a microwave network, and integrated all these systems. Interfacing between systems is a challenge. Data must flow back and forth among the various systems, including the mapping system with Global Information Systems that keeps up with the physical lines; the accounting system that maintains work orders, payroll, and accounts payable; the customer information system, which involves meter readings, billing system data, and customer account records; the outage management system that tracks outages; and the newbie, the automated metering infrastructure (AMI) system, which, among other things, reads meters from a remote computer.

In 2006, construction of a new corporate headquarters was completed on the Jefferson campus. The four district managers would report to the vice president of customer and district services whereas before they had reported to Pugh, who was spending increased time on power supply issues and serving on the boards of Oglethorpe Power Corporation and Georgia System Operations Corporation.

THIS BUILDING DEDICATED TO RURAL ELECTRIC SERVICE AND
IN HONOR OF RANDALL PUGH
FOR HIS MANY YEARS OF SERVICE TO THE RURAL ELECTRIC INDUSTRY

JACKSON ELECTRIC MEMBERSHIP CORPORATION
2006
DIRECTORS

Bill Carpenter, Chairman, Jackson County	Ray Jones, Hall County
Otis Jones, Vice Chairman, Gwinnett County	John Mitchell, Banks County
Chuck Steele, Sec.-Treas., Barrow County	Haywood O'Kelley, Lumpkin County
Rodney Chandler, Madison County	Paul Burroughs, Director Emeritus
Charles Gorham, Jackson County	Thomas Wilson, Director Emeritus
Balfour Hunnicutt, Clarke County	Upshaw Bentley, Jr., Attorney

Randall Pugh, President/CEO
Millard Inc. Architects

Jim Crawford, Vice President Customer and District Services	Greg Keith, Vice President Finance and Accounting
Bill Ormsby, Manager Corporate Administration	Jim Smith, Vice President Engineering and Operations
Roy Stowe, Vice President Marketing and Member Relations	

Above: Members of the Jackson EMC Board of Directors and their family and friends celebrated the grand opening of new corporate offices at a 2006 dedication ceremony, from left: Balfour Hunnicutt, Otis Jones, Chuck Steele, Charles Gorham, board attorney Upshaw Bentley, Bill Carpenter, Randall Pugh with his son and wife, Brad and Pat, Rodney Chandler, and John Mitchell.

Lee Chapman, Jackson EMC director of commercial/industrial marketing, left, and Joe Dorough, director of system engineering, right, discussed capabilities of the new state-of-the-art data center during an open house guided tour that introduced community leaders to the new corporate headquarters.

Opened in 2000, the QuikTrip distribution center in Pendergrass was one of several Jackson EMC commercial/industrial customers to locate in the Jefferson District, where most underground service was installed by the co-op in the late 1990s.

By 2005, the Jefferson District had taken the baton from the Gwinnett District as the fastest-growing area in Jackson EMC's service territory. Among the businesses to locate there was Mayfield Dairies. The co-op wooed the customer choice load in 1996 with a creative pitch showing Jackson EMC employees toasting with Mayfield milk, from left, standing: Scott Martin, commercial/industrial marketing representative; Joel Davis, line construction foreman; Paula Hill, Lee Chapman, and Randy Dellinger, commercial/industrial marketing representatives; Jeff Pratt, commercial/industrial marketing director; and Dwayne Ansley, engineering/operations district coordinator. Seated: Roy Stowe, division manager, marketing, and member services.

Phenomenal Growth, Eventual Slowdown

At the peak of the colossal growth that consumed the cooperative for the bulk of two decades, Jackson EMC employed more than 450 full-time staff members and utilized 260 contract employees. One of the co-op's biggest challenges was being consistent in how it served communities that greatly varied. Of the ten counties the co-op serves, all have their own nuances within their county governments, so regulations differ from county to county. The co-op serves a few members in Oglethorpe County and Franklin County, both rural communities still farming based. At the other end of the spectrum, Gwinnett, Hall, and Clarke Counties bulge with suburban and urban populations.

In the middle is Jackson County, which by the mid-2000s was the fastest growing county in Jackson EMC territory. Jefferson District office employees had worked with county officials and community leaders to absorb the overflow of growth from Gwinnett County into Jackson, Banks, and Barrow Counties. A turning point in the district had involved the ability of industrial development leaders to attract developers who were willing to

Poultry houses continued to round out the variety of commercial and industrial businesses served by Jackson EMC in the new century.

invest in large tracts of land to create private industrial parks. Those developers saw competence in the area's leadership and the growth potential with I-85. When the community put all its infrastructure pieces together—including water, sewer, gas, electricity, and roads—the stage was set for colossal development. The challenge was how to fund the infrastructure improvements. In 2004, Jackson County, through its Industrial Development Authority, financed bonds to fund a series of roads, water, and sewer projects; another series was issued four years later.

While the co-op's district offices worked with local development authorities, the corporate office worked with the Georgia Department of Industry and Trade and the Governor's Development Council to enhance economic potential throughout northeast Georgia.

Jackson EMC reached a significant milestone in 2007 when it connected its 200,000th meter. Since first extending lines in 1939, it had taken the cooperative fifty-four years to reach 100,000 meters, an achievement accomplished in 1993. In just fourteen more years, membership doubled. From 1997 to 2007, the customer base had grown a staggering 66 percent; in 2006 alone, the co-op ran 536 miles of energized wire, upgraded forty-two miles of existing wire, and added four new substations.

From the mid-1980s to 2008, the incredible growth in its communities necessitated new hires, new equipment and buildings, and new loans to cover the cost of doing business at Jackson EMC. For two decades, the cooperative did all it could to keep up, but all it could do often seemed wanting. The co-op couldn't buy equipment fast enough—couldn't do anything fast enough, employees recall.

A slowdown was on the horizon. The waves that had splashed and crashed into Jackson EMC territory for two decades were about to subside.

Opposite page: Eventually, the unprecedented growth that had consumed Jackson EMC territory for twenty-plus years shifted to a slower pace like that which had been routine for decades in the rural countryside of northeast Georgia, where farming continued to be a way of life for rural families. No matter where co-op members lived, keeping their power on continued to be the first priority for Jackson EMC linemen.

Chapter Fifteen
Recession, Regroup, and Recharge

"In going on with these Experiments, how many pretty systems do we build, which we soon find ourselves oblig'd to destroy! If there is no other Use discover'd of Electricity, this, however, is something considerable, that it may help to make a vain Man humble."

—Benjamin Franklin
American statesman and inventor

Employees at the Jefferson District had noticed a slight slowdown in new construction in their communities, but they started to sense that things were beginning to deteriorate in early 2008 when a developer asked if the co-op would suspend billing on lights at his new subdivision. Soon another asked, and another, and before long numerous developers were having trouble paying their light bill.

It was like someone turned off the spigot.

Jackson EMC felt the impact of the recession. By 2010, almost seventy subdivisions in the Jefferson District resembled ghost towns, and the sight was common in the cooperative's other districts as well. Roads, sewer, water, underground lines, lights, pad mounts—infrastructure that had been put in place—lay defunct. Subdivisions that had been in the making had all the essential components in place, except for houses and people. Chains forbade entrance into overgrown lots, planned as upscale neighborhoods but never built. In some of the subdivisions, early dwellers who purchased prime property to build first found themselves alone in a wilderness of scraggly trees and underbrush with sidewalks leading to nowhere. Numerous developers, stung by an economic crisis, had simply walked away.

During the Great Recession, when many Jackson EMC members had to tighten their fiscal belts, the cooperative's ongoing energy efficiency and cost-saving initiatives, from promoting compact fluorescent light bulbs (left) to auditing the home's complete energy envelope (right), helped them save energy and money.

Opposite page: Jackson EMC groups and individuals routinely received accolades for electric cooperative achievements, community volunteerism, and other successes. Employees at the Gwinnett District celebrated being named Best of Gwinnett by *Gwinnett Magazine* readers in 2008.

Jackson EMC members Chris and Julie Sexton of Gainesville peruse the Right Choice Home Energy Audit Kit to discover easy ways to conserve energy and reduce their power bill.

What some have termed the Great Recession began in December 2007 following a downturn in the US housing market that led to a massive reduction in new home purchases and building along with a parallel increase in mortgage foreclosures. The result was major financial losses for banks and lenders, and their customers. The longest economic downturn since the Great Depression, the recession lasted eighteen months, through June 2009, according to the National Bureau of Economic Research.

Few at Jackson EMC in 2009 felt like the recession had ended. Its impact was evident from the industrial parks in Gwinnett County to the farms in Madison County as both commercial and residential growth stood at a standstill. While Jackson EMC over the previous decade had added several thousand new members annually, the co-op in 2009 for the first time in its history experienced a net loss of accounts. Homes were foreclosed on, apartments vacated, and businesses closed. Factories cut back on their hours or shut their doors for good.

Jackson EMC was not immune. The co-op's largest customer at the time, Louisiana Pacific, closed not long after the economic crisis stunted the construction industry. In the Gainesville District, which in previous years had averaged adding 2,500 new members annually, the average fell to two hundred new members added each year.

With construction embattled, homes foreclosed, and businesses cutting back on hours, the co-op sold less electricity. At the same time, operating costs did not decrease and the cost of power generation rose. To combat the bad economy, Jackson EMC instituted a hiring freeze and cut expenses in every department. Employee travel was restricted; for the first time in his thirty-year career as manager of an electric cooperative, Pugh would not attend the upcoming annual meeting of the National Rural Electric Cooperative Association.

Throughout the nation, companies shuttered their doors or let employees go in hopes of staying open. At Jackson EMC, not a single employee was laid off due to the recession. This good fortune did not come by happenstance; it was a plan put in motion years earlier when

Jackson EMC employees kept close contact with their commercial/industrial customers during the economic downtime, offering their assistance in shaving off energy-related expenses where possible. Shown with Commercial/Industrial Marketing Director Lee Chapman, center, are, from left, Marketing Representatives David Lee, Joe Hicks, Todd Evans, and Brittany Caison.

the cooperative hired contract crews to keep up with the monumental growth. When the growth slowed, the safety net was in place: as contractors were let go, crew by crew, employees remained, their jobs secure. As positions came open due to retirement, most were not replaced immediately, if ever.

In the absence of new industry coming in, Jackson EMC multiplied efforts to maintain its relevance in the economic and development arena. Recognizing the crunch its business customers were experiencing, the cooperative offered its expertise, significantly increasing the number of commercial energy audits it conducted and assisting several large commercial and industrial members in retrofitting their lighting to help save on power bills. Always a community partner, Jackson EMC worked even more with chambers of commerce, economic development agencies, state offices, and technical colleges to attract new industries and jobs and keep existing business open.

In the meantime, the cooperative continued to research ways to save money in the midst of a recession. In 2008, the board of directors approved implementation of Advanced Metering Infrastructure (AMI), a program that would replace meter reading with handheld devices, the method of meter reading deployed since 1985. The new method would cost a significant amount upfront but deliver simplicity in meter reading, enable members to better manage their energy use, and provide substantial savings for years to come.

The Advanced Metering Infrastructure involved retiring old meters throughout the system and replacing them with "smart meters" to enable the co-op to read meters remotely, through readings transmitted over a radio network. Transportation and manpower savings would result when meter readers no longer were necessary to drive to members' homes and businesses each month. The AMI system not only would monitor monthly power usage but automatically alert the co-op when a member's power was out, pinpoint and display the locations that were out, and even alert the cooperative when a member's power was restored. The AMI technology would provide useful information for engineering and line loading

Senior Metering Tech Ray Walton prepared for implementation of an Advanced Metering Infrastructure system that began in late 2008 with old meters replaced by "smart" meters that can be read remotely at office computers.

analysis, including exactly how much wattage was demanded and what voltage was at any meter. In addition, members would soon be able to go online to review their hourly energy usage, information that would enable them to monitor and control their energy use.

The massive undertaking to replace the 200,000-plus meters on Jackson EMC's system began in 2009 with an average of six thousand meters installed each month until the three-year, $25 million project was completed in March 2012, a significant accomplishment and one of the largest capital upgrades in the cooperative's history. Integrated technologies help Jackson EMC meet one of its greatest challenges—keeping up with the massive volume of data about the electric system, its poles and power lines, and historical data about the system and its member accounts.

Establishing New Electric Service

While the line crew does the hard labor of line construction, building the power system calls for concentrated efforts leading up to, and following, the actual placement of poles and stringing of electric lines. Benny Bagwell, district coordinator of engineering and operations, described the internal operations that accompany the external chore of establishing electric service to a new member:

Say you have a custom home on somebody's acreage. They apply for service, meet with a customer service rep, the application goes in, and engineering and operations folks meet with the member to see where his house is going to sit and find out where the mechanical room and electrical rooms are. Then we design the line and a computer creates a location record for that member. We key in assemblies that explode out a material list and that's all shipped to the warehouse. The job goes into work order tracking and is assigned to a foreman who assigns it to a crew, and the crew goes by the warehouse, picks up the material, and constructs the job. When they come back, they verify the material with the warehouse and all of that is keyed in as built. The completed work order goes into accounting and they verify the amount of wire, poles, and other material used versus what was called for under the assembly. Then it's sent to mapping to finalize the drawing units, and that completes our maps, which update the outage management system.

Awarded for Customer Satisfaction

Unknown to Jackson EMC, while the co-op was researching the AMI system in 2008, J.D. Power and Associates was researching the cooperative, including it in their annual study of electric utility residential customer satisfaction. When the study was complete, Jackson EMC ranked highest in customer satisfaction among mid-size utilities in the South, earning it the 2008 J.D. Power and Associates Award for Customer Satisfaction. In fact, Jackson EMC's customer satisfaction ranking topped *all* utilities in the nation.

"When I look at this award, I'm reminded of the four hundred plus reasons why we received this honor—our employees," said Pugh. Jackson EMC won the coveted honor again in 2010 and 2011,

A continuing focus on customer satisfaction led Jackson EMC to earn the J.D. Power and Associates national award for highest customer satisfaction among mid-sized utilities in the South. Customer Service Representative Monica Jackson was one of Jackson EMC's four-hundred-plus employees who made winning the award possible.

missing it in 2009 by only one point. In 2012, J.D. Power and Associates named Jackson EMC a Customer Service Champion, placing it alongside Apple, Amazon.com, and Southwest Airlines to earn that distinction. Jackson EMC is recognized not just locally but throughout the nation as a leader in customer service excellence.

"We do not focus on customer satisfaction because we receive these awards," said Pugh. "We receive the recognition because we give great customer satisfaction." After Jackson EMC started winning the J.D. Power awards, the co-op staff was often asked by utility industry peers, "What's your secret?" Their response: "Treat other people the way you want to be treated."

In conducting its studies, J.D. Power and Associates examines an array of issues important to electric customers, from power quality and reliability to billing and payment. By the time the first J.D. Power award was presented in 2008, Jackson EMC for a quarter of a century had built on its cooperative values of financial pragmatism and community commitment by consistently looking for new ways to better serve its members. The cooperative's senior staff and board of directors, along with its outside and office employees, concluded that the key to customer satisfaction was more than meeting one need; it was learning what the needs were and striving to meet the various needs of a diversified service territory.

While areas within the co-op territory were rural and urban, blue collar and white collar, and represented two dozen nationalities by the mid-2000s, all Jackson EMC members agreed on this: they wanted reliable, affordable electricity and ease in obtaining it. The Residential Electric Customer Satisfaction Study Model utilized by J.D. Power and Associates in its annual study

Jackson EMC won its first J.D. Power and Associates award in 2008 and continued to receive honors from the esteemed agency in the years that followed.

Customer satisfaction became the buzz phrase at Jackson EMC where a culture of customer service started with one-on-one interaction with co-op members. Here, Gainesville District Customer Service Representative Yonnah Stovall provides exceptional service to an appreciative customer.

Employee meetings at Jackson EMC are routinely held with customer satisfaction the ultimate goal. Meeting here are, from left, Jim Smith, vice president of engineering/operations; Jim Crawford, vice president of customer/district service; Greg Keith, vice president of finance/accounting; Lori McCutcheon, engineer; and Dwayne Ansley, director of operations services.

of utilities ranked power quality and reliability as the most important criteria sought by the nation's electric customers with prices as a close second. Criteria most relevant to consumers, in order, include:

Power quality and reliability, 27 percent   Corporate citizenship, 13 percent

Price, 22 percent   Communications, 13 percent

Billing and payment, 19 percent   Customer service, 6 percent

Intuitively, Jackson EMC throughout most of its history focused on these six relevant items, ever working to maintain and enhance the system to ensure a quality product and reliable electric service—to keep the lights on, in other words. Simultaneously, as a business born in the decade of the Great Depression, keeping costs down in order to charge minimal prices to consumers was always of utmost importance to the board of directors and remains a point of pride at Jackson EMC, where electric rates are among the lowest of all utilities in Georgia.

These two items alone—power reliability and price—make up almost 50 percent of what's most important to the electric consumer, according to J.D. Power and Associates. Jackson EMC ranks high in the remaining four categories as well: billing and payment, which is made easy for members with multiple methods of paying power bills; corporate citizenship, a priority for the cooperative for decades; communications, where a variety of means are utilized to share information with and educate members; and customer service, the personal ties that bind all the rest together as sincere and caring employees strive to make the product purchased and the services rendered as excellent as humanly possible.

Residential marketing representatives like Tiffeny Tolder continued to make a difference in the lives of co-op members by making home visits to perform energy audits aimed at saving customers money on their power bills.

Paying their power bills at drive-up windows provides ease and convenience to co-op customers.

When Randall Pugh came to Jackson EMC in 1984, the cooperative served 54,000 meters. By 2013, the co-op served more than 210,000 meters. In those twenty-nine years, Jackson EMC essentially rebuilt its distribution system and significantly increased its infrastructure while maintaining one of Georgia's lowest electric retail rates. The cooperative's balance sheet has remained strong with a high equity level. But nothing has pleased Pugh more than the co-op's constant devotion to its members.

"What I'm the proudest of in terms of accomplishments would be the level of customer service we have achieved, and I give all the credit for that to the employees who embrace customer service and practice it every day," he said. "And another thing, and quite honestly I'm even surprised myself, is that we handled the growth."

With the right people empowered to do the right thing—its employees mandated to provide exceptional customer service—Jackson EMC experienced progress amidst daunting growth. In the economic downturn, it continued to meet that challenge and sought to help others ride the financial storms as well.

Operation Round Up®

One of Jackson EMC's most far-reaching initiatives, Operation Round Up commenced in 2005 when co-op members were given the opportunity to assist nonprofit organizations

The Jackson EMC Foundation uses Operation Round Up® funds to support nonprofit agencies that meet a wide variety of needs in communities served by the electric cooperative. The Madison County Habitat for Humanity is one of numerous organizations to benefit from funds contributed by Jackson EMC members via Operation Roundup.

and individuals within their communities by rounding up their power bill to the nearest dollar. The extra change would go into a fund managed by the Jackson EMC Foundation, a volunteer board formed to assess applications for grants and appropriately distribute funds to groups and individuals in need.

Palmetto Electric Cooperative in Hampton, South Carolina, originated Operation Round Up in 1989 and since then, cooperatives throughout the nation have adopted the program. At Jackson EMC, an extensive communications campaign rolled out the new initiative, with members barraged with information via the newsletter, bill stuffers, and through every imaginable way the co-op could think to fully explain its intentions, how it would implement the new program, and how members could opt out if they did not want to participate. Cooperatives could expect about 75 percent of their membership to participate in the program, Palmetto Electric representatives reported. At Jackson EMC, participation has averaged 90 percent since the program's inception, a participation level unrivaled among EMCs offering Operation Round Up.

The Jackson EMC Foundation was formed in 2005 and led by a volunteer board of directors that included charter members, from left, front, Gwen Hill, Amber Casper, Beauty Baldwin, Joyce Britt, and Gus Lobo. Back: Robert Hooper, John Mitchell, Shade Storey, and Sherry Rogers. Also serving as charter directors were Rev. Mandy Brady and Bill Hardman. Others who have served as Jackson EMC Foundation directors include George Evans, Johnny Fowler, Anna Gines, Andy Byers, Jim Puckett, Steve Blair, Dick Perpall, Lisa Maloof, and Christy Moore.

One recipient of Operation RoundUp funds is For Your Glory, a Hall County organization that provides wigs, pressure bandages, and other mastectomy supplies to breast cancer patients whose insurance does not cover those items.

The Jackson EMC Foundation Board of Directors is an autonomous group structured similarly to the Jackson EMC Board, with nine directors representing all communities served by the cooperative. The first round of grants was awarded in October 2005. By mid-2013, the Jackson EMC Foundation had distributed more than $7.8 million in grants, including 768 awarded to area nonprofit organizations and 270 to individuals. The funds have supported a multitude of initiatives, including programs that help the disabled, send at-risk kids to summer camp, or mentor youth. Funds have purchased medical equipment and services for clinics serving the uninsured or underinsured. Individuals have received life-changing medical equipment and dentures, and funds have been used to replace leaking roofs and heat pumps, build wheelchair ramps, and make car repairs.

In the past eight years, there is no way to measure the significant impact these gifts have made on the quality of life in the counties served by Jackson EMC, which could not have fathomed the volume of money Operation Round Up would raise or the bearing it would have on northeast Georgia communities. The generosity of Jackson EMC members made it all possible. It is their foundation, and their success. And it has built upon and enhanced the cooperative's reputation as a strong community partner.

Meeting Power Needs

In 2013, Jackson EMC owns approximately 12 percent of Oglethorpe Power Corporation's generation, which contributes about 40 percent of its power needs. Currently, the bulk of the remaining power is supplied through Constellation Energy Group, an unregulated division of Baltimore Gas and Electric, which owns the contract the cooperative negotiated in 2001 to secure fixed rates for electricity through 2015. The cooperative has committed to additional generation from OPC and, after 2015, expects to receive around 93 percent of its power needs through Oglethorpe and the remainder from the wholesale marketplace.

In 2008, Gwinnett District journeyman linemen Joey Thompson and Jason Carey joined the NRECA International Program to help build electric infrastructure in Guatemala. The trip to Central America was sponsored by NRECA and brought linemen from several Georgia EMCs together to set poles, string wire, and help train linemen in Guatemalan villages. Since 1962, NRECA has established rural electrification programs in Latin America, Africa, and Asia, providing seventy-five million people in more than forty developing countries with safe, reliable, and affordable electricity.

Negotiated long before the economic crisis, the Constellation contract has been partly responsible for the co-op's steady rates. Due to the current economy, energy resources, environmental regulations, and politics, retail rates are almost certain to rise in the future. To meet power needs, Jackson EMC and its partners at OPC in recent years committed to building additional generating facilities and are participating in expansion at Vogtle Nuclear Power Plant.

While it's less expensive to build a natural gas plant, the risks associated with the potential volatility of natural gas prices make coal a more consistent and cost-effective solution, but arduous environmental regulations placed on coal power generation plants make building them a moot effort.

"Nuclear is crucial because it's the only option we have other than natural gas," said Pugh. "The federal government is making it impossible for anybody to build new coal-firing generation, even with the emission controls we have now. We have reduced emissions at existing coal-fired plants in this state significantly. At Plant Wansley and Plant Scherer, we have invested more money in environmental infrastructure to meet the environmental regulations than we invested in the plant originally."

Fortunately, most lawmakers support expanding nuclear power, but it won't be cheap. The energy challenge in the coming decade can be summed up in one provocative question, according to Pugh: How do we meet the

Jeff Chandler, in bucket, and Jacob Benton worked to construct the new East Hall substation, which was completed in 2006 before the Great Recession slowed growth in Jackson EMC territory.

Just as Jackson EMC equips its linemen with a toolbelt filled with essential gear, the cooperative equips its consumer-members with energy-saving ideas and cost-saving measures.

environmental regulations and provide enough electric energy for this country to run our industries and power our homes and businesses at a price we can afford without destroying the economy and chasing jobs offshore?

Jackson EMC and electric industry peers have a solution—clean coal technology—and it's backed by the science community and the majority of the Georgia congressional delegation in Washington, DC.

If extreme measures are not taken soon, consumers could see dramatic increases in their power bill within the next ten years. But it could be too late then if most coal plants have been replaced.

"We continue to wage the enduring battle with government forces that would implement new regulations and new standards without regard to their impact on our members' electric bill or their wallets," said Pugh. "We have a long history of supporting the environment, renewable energy, and energy efficiency—but in a manner that provides not only good stewardship of the land but also of our economy."

Coming Back

While growth has been stagnant over the past few years, the staff at Jackson EMC knows the pendulum will swing back again. In the meantime, a break from the hectic pace demanded by frenzied growth has provided welcomed opportunities.

Given a breather, Jackson EMC is planning, staffing, and working to get ahead. The pause has allowed the cooperative to build its own fiber optics network and complete line capacity upgrades. The co-op already had converted most of its system from twelve kilovolts to twenty-five kilovolts, enabling twice the capacity without changing conductor sizes; now, everything new is built to twenty-five kilovolt specifications. Electronic controls and distribution automation are being added to enable system operations outside the substations. Advances in electronics are adding capabilities.

During the rigorous years of perpetual growth, system maintenance took a back seat while the workforce concentrated on building new lines. Since the slowdown, the co-op has redoubled its system maintenance programs.

Over the past three years, while replacing old meters with new smart meters, workers discovered and tended to a variety of problems, including conductors and insulators that had been shot, poles splitting, and even an opossum living in a padmount transformer. A dedicated line inspection program involves scrutiny of the cooperative's 13,000-plus miles of power line and includes repairs as necessary to transformers, meter bases, switching cabinets, and other components. A pole inspection team inspects each pole on the system and treats it or replaces it when necessary. Right-of-way maintenance is handled by twenty-seven contract crews supervised by four co-op crew leaders. The right of way is cleared fifteen feet on either side of the power line with mowing and trimming, followed by herbicide applications to keep brush at bay while leaving low-growing grasses intact. In recent years, due to its active right-of-way maintenance program, storm-related outages have decreased significantly.

Determining when to make the next system improvements can be tricky, just as challenging as it was when growth was heavy. The co-op board and management weigh all options, and the entire staff works together to position Jackson EMC to be in a good place when growth picks up again.

In 2013, signs point to an improving economy within the cooperative's territory, particularly on the commercial side. Jackson EMC also is preparing to serve the Toyota Industries Compressor Parts America (TICA) facility in Jackson County, served by the new Valentine Farms substation. When its expansion is complete, TICA's 624,000-square-foot facility, together with the adjacent existing TD Automotive Compressor Georgia (TACG) plant, will represent the largest load ever served by the cooperative, a load expected to be as high as 28.5 megavolt amperes (MVA) by 2016.

In 2013, growth in Jackson EMC territory is picking up, as evidenced by construction of the new Toyota Industries Compressor Parts America (TICA) plant in Jackson County. A Jackson EMC line crew assisted in getting the new plant up and running by installing a pad mount air switch in front of the facility. Switches are used on underground systems to provide tap points and disconnect points for underground cable.

Agricultural businesses and area farms continued to be important co-op members served by Jackson EMC employees, including Nick Anderson, field service representative.

Jackson EMC's conservative management and use of technology helped hold down costs and stave off increased rates to members in a bad economy. Here, System Control Coordinator Kelly Porter monitors the electric distribution system using the outage management system (OMS) and SCADA.

Also in 2013, the cooperative began serving the new 95,000-square-foot BITZER US commercial air conditioning and refrigeration manufacturing plant in Hall County and the 522,000-square-foot Kubota Industrial Equipment compact tractor manufacturing facility in Jackson County. Mitsubishi has announced expansion plans in Suwanee, and a new Carter's Clothing plant in Braselton is on the drawing board and slated to add six hundred jobs. In Hall County, new industries setting up shop include ZF Wind, a wind turbine transmission manufacturer, and King's Hawaiian Bread, on tap to add two hundred jobs as a manufacturing distributor.

In all, more than 1,000 new commercial/industrial members have been added since onset of the Great Recession.

On the residential side, three retirement communities in the Gainesville District promise to put people in new homes. New single-family home construction is returning to Gwinnett and Hall Counties, albeit slowly, and new apartment developments are going up in Gwinnett and Barrow Counties. In fiscal year 2013, almost 2,400 new residential meters were added.

While the cooperative experienced a net loss of meters in 2009, there were small gains in 2010 and 2011. At the close of the 2012 fiscal year, Jackson EMC had added 1,500 meters, but the board of directors and staff continued with a cautious approach in managing the co-op during uncertain economic times. Caution did not equate to inaction, though, as the cooperative worked diligently to complete installation of its new Automated Metering Infrastructure, outage management system, and fiber optic system.

The Jackson EMC website was redesigned in 2012 with input from members playing heavily into the new design. The refurbished site functions as a self-serve tool for members.

Jackson EMC is an extremely strong company financially. It has done a good job of positioning itself with a wholesale power supply. It is able to charge among the lowest rates of any electric utilities in the state and still maintain a strong financial position. It has a solid equity level and an extremely good cash flow, with an adequate source of loan funds available at an attractive price. Expenses were minimized during a tough period over the last five years, and those efforts have paid off.

In December 2012, Jackson EMC mailed $5 million in margin refunds, bringing the total amount returned to members since the co-op formed to a whopping $90 million.

The cooperative now employs more computers than people. Jackson EMC rolled out its revamped website in mid-2012 following an eighteen-month redesign process that began with member input into what they desired from their cooperative's Internet presence. The redesigned site provides improved service, including an around-the-clock,

In 2013, co-op members enjoy multiple ways to access their account and pay their bills, including online capabilities.

self-service option for starting and discontinuing service, reporting power and streetlight outages, and obtaining services and rebates. The site offers members the opportunity to create an online account profile where they can check their usage, manage their accounts, and sign up for services like paperless billing. The co-op promoted

Jackson EMC President/CEO Randall Pugh, center, greeted guests at annual meeting.

paperless billing in 2012 with 4,054 members signing up for the new service, which better protects members' identity and provides them easy access to billing records. These paperless billing signups are estimated to save the cooperative $22,560 in billing costs annually.

Another service offered through the improved website is the Filter Change Program. This service provides properly sized HVAC filters through the mail at a reasonable cost along with email reminders when it's time to change the HVAC system's filter. Continuing its long-standing tradition of offering information and services for members to more wisely use energy resources, the co-op also introduced the HomePlus Loan program via the website to make energy efficient improvements and appliance replacements easier to afford.

Since the website redesign, visitor page views have increased by 59 percent with more than 1.7 million page views in 2012.

In the meantime, work began on a full mobile website, marked in early 2013 by the introduction of a mobile outage reporting form, an app that makes it possible to report an outage, quick and easy, from a smart phone or tablet. The mobile form is simply the first step in Jackson EMC's initiative to develop a full mobile website with contents and functionality based on what members have indicated they want and need to simplify communications with the cooperative.

Ever attempting to meet member needs, the cooperative today offers multiple methods for paying bills including bank draft, US Mail, or paying with cash, check, or credit card at the drive-up window or inside one of the district offices. Members may pay by credit card, debit card, bank ATM card, or electronic check by phone or through the co-op's website at jacksonemc.com.

Improved customer service is also the impetus for constructing a new facility to serve the Neese District, where the co-op outgrew its circa-1958 office at Hull several years ago. Building a new office complex had been planned earlier but was put on the backburner after the recession hit. Construction is set to begin in 2013

at the intersection of GA Highway 29 and Spratlin Mill Road, about two-and-a-half miles from the current office in Madison County. The new facility will increase the co-op's ability to serve members throughout the district quickly and more efficiently while ensuring the safety of employees going to and from work assignments and members visiting the office.

Designed by Millard Architects, Inc., the new complex will include a 14,324-square-foot administrative building, drive-thru canopy with three drive-thru lanes, warehouse/truck storage area, transformer/pole yard and fleet parking area. As a community service, the new administrative building will include a 3,064-square-foot auditorium that can accommodate 160 with seats set in rows or 120 with tables set for meals. The auditorium will be available to civic and non-profit organizations by reservation on a first-come, first-served basis.

The year-long construction project is scheduled to begin in late summer 2013.

The new Neese District office at GA Highway 29 and Spratlin Mill Road in Hull will replace the current Madison County office and increase the co-op's ability to serve Neese members quickly and more efficiently.

Chapter Sixteen
Looking Forward

"People came together in a grassroots effort to form Jackson EMC and created a better way of life for themselves and their neighbors. They generated not only electric power but a power of purpose, if you will, that ultimately brought progress to the region. This power of purpose propels us into the future as we, like them, continue to work toward the common good."

—Randall Pugh
President/CEO of Jackson EMC

Throughout its history, Jackson EMC has strived to be progressive while managing costs. It has upheld cooperative values while employing progressive corporate strategies. It has always risen to the challenge to embrace change and do what's best for its members. One key to Jackson EMC's success has been its strong board whose directors are committed to making decisions in the best interest of the cooperative and its members. New board members undergo a lengthy orientation and participate in NRECA's credentialed director program. Jackson EMC utilizes a strategic, deliberate, and thoughtful process it developed in the late 1980s to select new members to the board of directors.

"We developed a process that helped the nominating committee identify candidates for the board," recalled Pugh, noting that a comprehensive set of criteria was established, including formal evaluations and intensive background screening. A keen commitment to community service, reputation, and the ability to evaluate financial statements are among the criteria.

Board Chairman Otis Jones greets co-op members at a recent annual meeting.

Opposite page: As the future unfolds, Jackson EMC linemen maintain the current electric system and build new lines and substations. Linemen at work are, from left, Jeff Chandler, Jacob Benton, and Scott Hudson.

Sara Bell, left, employed with Jackson EMC for forty-eight years and secretary to the president/CEO for the past twenty-five years, continues to assist President Randall Pugh, second from left, in business and board matters. In January 2013, Georgia Governor Nathan Deal named Pugh to the Georgia Department of Economic Development, continuing a long tradition of Jackson EMC employees serving on prominent state boards.

The Jackson EMC Board of Directors, cooperative counsel, and president/ CEO in 2012 included, from left, Directors Ray Jones and Chuck Steele; Attorney Upshaw Bentley; Directors Alton Thornton, Charles Gorham, John Mitchell, Lynn Price, Rodney Chandler, Otis Jones, and Bill Carpenter; and President/CEO Randall Pugh. Gorham retired from the board in April 2013 after twenty-two years of service. Shade Storey (inset) was appointed as new director.

"We needed well-qualified directors with the formal education and business experience necessary to make the important decisions facing the cooperative and move this organization forward in a different social, political, regulatory, and financial environment," said Pugh. "The formal process ensures the nominating committee looks closely at each candidate and evaluates them individually against this set of criteria. In every case, the most qualified rose to the top."

Current Board Chairman Otis Jones, who had been general manager of Intelligent Systems Corporation, joined the board in 1990 as the first director chosen using the new selection process. Since then, all but two of the board members have been selected using this method. Bill Carpenter and Ray Jones, who joined the board before the new criteria was established, are well-respected directors whose long tenure with the EMC has coincided with its growth and success.

Others on the current board, and the year they joined, include: Chuck Steele, 1998, retired from IBM Corporation; John Mitchell, 2006, retired Banks County director of the University of Georgia Cooperative Extension Service; Lynn Price, 2007, certified public accountant, former co-owner of AAA Tank Testers, and former Arthur Anderson accountant; Rodney Chandler, 2008, certified public accountant and managing partner of Smith Adcock & Company; Alton Thornton, 2011, retired from Ag Georgia Farm Credit, Agricultural Credit Association (ACA), and the Farm Credit Organizations; and Shade Storey, 2013, division senior vice president of Northeast Georgia Bank and former chairman of the Jackson EMC Foundation Board of Directors. The group of nine makes for what Pugh describes as "a very qualified, diverse, strong board."

Historically, the Jackson EMC board has been conservative, as is common in rural electric leadership, but when times have called for fresh ways of thinking and innovative ways to manage new challenges, directors have risen to the occasion.

"None of the board members have a selfish interest," said Pugh. "They are conservative, but they are progressive-minded and understand what we have had to do to grow this co-op and keep it financially sound, to give good customer service and be competitive."

The same can be said of the Jackson EMC senior management staff in 2013, which includes:

Randall Pugh, President/CEO

Jim Crawford, Vice President of Customer/District Services

Greg S. Keith, Vice President of Finance/Accounting

Jim Smith, Vice President of Engineering/Operations

Roy Stowe, Vice President of Marketing/Member Relations

Bill Ormsby, Manager of Corporate Administration

Randy Dellinger, District Manager/Gwinnett

Scott Martin, District Manager/Jefferson

Jean Mullis, District Manager/Neese

Bill Sanders, District Manager/Gainesville

Just as it has done for the past three-quarters of a century, Jackson EMC will strive to innovate, to build its electric system with emphasis on reliability, and keep its costs low.

Whether they have the thread in them before they're hired or whether it's cultivated once they start working here, co-op employees share a penchant for doing whatever it takes to serve the customer. It's a culture of service with the ultimate goal of customer satisfaction that runs deep in Jackson EMC employees, and it is readily apparent to others.

When he considers the history of Jackson County, *Jackson Herald* editor Mike Buffington believes that having Jackson EMC headquartered in Jefferson has been a strength for the community. "Over the decades, the EMC's

Side-by-side photographs of local chicken house interiors provide a quick snapshot of farming advancements made possible with electricity. At left, the Danielsville chicken house of Judge James in 1957 featured light bulbs hanging from the rafters, albeit electric brooders had been utilized to raise the chicks and were removed when the fowl grew larger. At right, a modern chicken house utilizes electricity from one end to the other to provide lighting, warmth, and ease in operations.

Employees like Senior Residential Marketing Representative Ann Pierce, right, greet annual meeting guests with information about the co-op and energy-saving tools.

Attendance at annual meetings in recent years has averaged about four thousand.

presence has made a huge difference," said Buffington. "They've been a leading voice through the Chamber of Commerce, through the Industrial Development Authority, and through the county government in industrial development. They provide the community with leadership."

He credits Jackson EMC with working alongside county officials and others involved in economic development to posture a conservative philosophy that has served the community well. With its background in engineering and finance, Jackson EMC helped cultivate local leadership within its communities, leadership often stronger than in similar-sized locales across the state. "They've had so many people, at so many levels, do so many different things," said Buffington. "They have contributed for seventy-five years, with roots seventy-five years deep. It's been a huge positive impact on this community."

Leaders in other communities served by Jackson EMC attest to the same.

When given the opportunity, Jackson EMC positioned itself as the power provider of choice, reaching out to obtain new customers in an effort to keep rates affordable for those already on its lines and for those to come in the future. And while the business of building and maintaining an electric system could have consumed all its time and efforts, especially in the 80s and 90s when population explosion in its southernmost territory stretched thin its resources and workforce, Jackson EMC continued to respond to the concerns, be it large or small, of its communities and the needs of members living within them.

From holding steer shows and academic bowls in support of youth education to raising funds through American Cancer Society Relay for Life for families affected by cancer to enlisting its members to help fund Operation Round Up endeavors, the EMC's board and staff have not shied away from what they consider an obligation to their members, indeed, a mandate as prescribed in the last of the seven principles of a cooperative: concern for community.

For employees at Jackson EMC, the multi-colored sky of a Georgia dusk paints the perfect backdrop for an equally beautiful sight—the electric system that brings comfort and convenience to members of the rural electric cooperative.

In 2013, Jackson EMC and its partners at Oglethorpe Power Corporation and Georgia Power are committed to building additional generating facilities at Vogtle Nuclear Power Plant in Waynesboro, Georgia, near Augusta. A new plant design and construction method are being utilized to construct two new reactors, and a new system of nuclear regulation will accompany the Vogtle addition, which marks the first nuclear construction started in the United States in the past three decades. Construction on the original plant began in the 1970s with the first reactor opened in 1987 and the second, in 1989.

Certainly, providing leadership and community support has been a hallmark for Jackson EMC. Yet in the meantime, its employees and directors have not forgotten the co-op's original mission: to keep the lights on.

As Frances Staton observed in 1988, the growth throughout northeast Georgia that brought an astonishing increase in membership to Jackson EMC was, in large part, sparked by the cooperative itself decades earlier when it brought possibility and opportunity in the form of electricity buzzing across rural power lines. Owning its role in creating an atmosphere seeded for growth, Jackson EMC continued through the decades to nurture what it had planted and, in 2013, continues to move forward.

"As a cooperative, Jackson EMC will always have one foot in the past and one in the future" said Pugh. "And we must always do it with an eye on the future. We spend many of our working hours exploring what's new and better in every area of our business. At Jackson EMC, the past, present and future will coexist."

Thanks to its people—and the marvels of electric power—Jackson EMC will continue as a cornerstone for progress in northeast Georgia and, among its industry peers, as an example of business acumen and customer service.

As it has for the past seventy-five years, Jackson EMC will continue to provide electric power and community leadership in northeast Georgia for years to come.

Bibliography

2010 US Census. US Census Bureau: http://www.census.gov/2010census.

Bellis, Mary. "History of Electricity, Thomas Edison: Improved Stock Ticker, Lamps and Dynamos," About.com Guide, New York Times Company, 2012. New York, NY: www.about.com.

Boland, Frank Kells. "The First Anesthetic: The Story of Crawford Long," Athens: University of Georgia Press, Athens, GA, 1950.

BrainyQuote: http://www.brainyquote.com.

Brown, D. Clayton. "Electricity for Rural America: The Fight for the REA," Greenwood Press, Westport, Conn., London, England, 1980.

Carlyle, Thomas. "The Carlyle Anthology," University of California Libraries, 1876.

Cato, Robert A. "The Years of Lyndon Johnson: The Path to Power," Alfred A. Knopf, Inc., 1981.

Edwards, Tryon. "A Dictionary of Thoughts," 1908.

Faraday, Michael. "Notes for a Friday Discourse at the Royal Institution," 1858.

Cohen, I. Bernard. "Benjamin Franklin's Experiments," Letter to Peter Collinson, 1941.

Gibson, Robert. "Big League Co-op: Jackson EMC out-hustles a big power company for Japanese industry," *Rural Electrification Magazine*, May 1988.

Heilbron, J. L. "Electricity in the 17th and 18th Centuries: A Study of Early Modern Physics." 1979. http://todayinsci.com.

Jackson EMC Collection. Richard B. Russell Library for Political Research and Studies, University of Georgia Libraries, Athens, GA, 2005.

(The) Jackson Herald, Jefferson, GA: www.jacksonheraldtoday.com.

Jemco News. Jackson Electric Membership Corporation, Jefferson, Georgia: 1952–2013.

Kay, Terry. *The Year the Lights Came On*, Houghton Mifflin Company, Boston, Massachusetts, 1976.

Lasdun, James. "The Wonder of Chekhov," *The Guardian*, 2010.

Long, C. W. "An account of the first use of Sulphuric Ether by Inhalation as an Anaesthetic in Surgical Operations," *Southern Medical and Surgical Journal*, 1849.

McQuade, Hank. "Light Up Our Land, Georgia Electric Membership Corporation: The First 50 Years," Georgia Electric Membership Corporation, Atlanta, GA, 1990.

Money Magazine/CNN: http://money.cnn.com/2008/12/01/news/economy/recession/index.htm.

National Rural Electric Cooperative Association (NRECA) Website, 2005–2012. Arlington, Virginia: http://www.nreca.coop.

(The) New Georgia Encyclopedia: http://www.georgiaencyclopedia.org.

Pence, Richard A. "The Next Greatest Thing," National Rural Electric Cooperative Association, Washington, D.C., 1984.

Roosevelt, Franklin D. "Address of the President," Barnesville, GA, 1938.

Walsh, Kenneth T. "The First 100 Days: Franklin Roosevelt Pioneered the 100-Day Concept," *US News & World Report*, February 12, 2009.

Wells, Herbert George. "A Modern Utopia," 1904.

Wikipedia, The Free Encyclopedia: http://en.wikipedia.org.

Word Press: http://ss8h9.wordpress.com/coast/brunswick-and-savannah-shipyard.

Index

About the Author

Jackie Kennedy is a freelance writer whose twenty-seven-year career evolved from covering crime, government, health, and education at the *LaGrange* (Georgia) *Daily News* to working as a self-employed writer/consultant. Her articles have appeared in numerous regional, state, and national publications, including *Georgia Magazine, Georgia Backroads, Alabama Living,* and *US News & World Report.* She helped launch and served as senior editor for *ON Magazine,* a city magazine serving Plano and Collin County, Texas.

Kennedy has won writing honors from the Georgia Press Association, Georgia Associated Press, Magazine Association of the Southeast, and the National Rural Electric Cooperative Association. She has produced award-winning marketing materials for various corporations and received an ADDY award for Copywriter of the Year from the Advertising Federation of Columbus, Georgia. She has interviewed and photographed presidents and performers, comedians and criminals, and is always on the search for a good story.

Her previous books commemorating the seventy-fifth anniversary of American electric cooperatives include *Diverse Power: From Light Bulbs to Laptops, Building the Electric Co-op* and *Upson EMC: Small Co-op, Big Impact.* This is her third book in as many years.